PIONEER

RANCH

LIFE

IN

ORANGE

PIONEER RANCH LIFE

IN

ORANGE

A VICTORIAN WOMAN
IN SOUTHERN CALIFORNIA

MARY TEEGARDEN CLARK

EDITED WITH PREFACE &
INTRODUCTION BY PAUL F. CLARK

Charleston   London

THE
History
PRESS

Published by The History Press
Charleston, SC 29403
www.historypress.net

Unless otherwise noted, all photos and illustrations are from the editor's collection.

Back cover, center: Mary Teegarden Clark in 1916 with four of her eleven California grandchildren.

First published 2013

Manufactured in the United States

ISBN 978.1.62619.074.0

Library of Congress CIP data applied for.

To the Children of Yale Grove

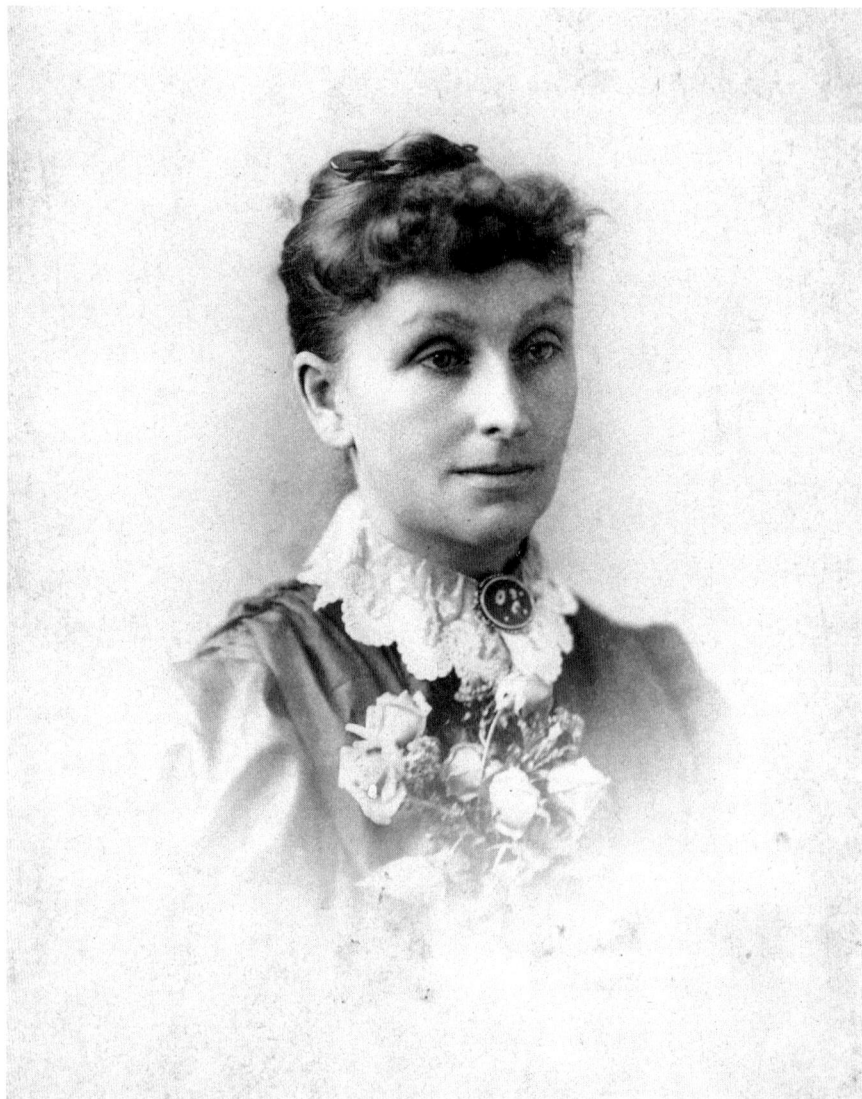

Mary Teegarden Clark.

CONTENTS

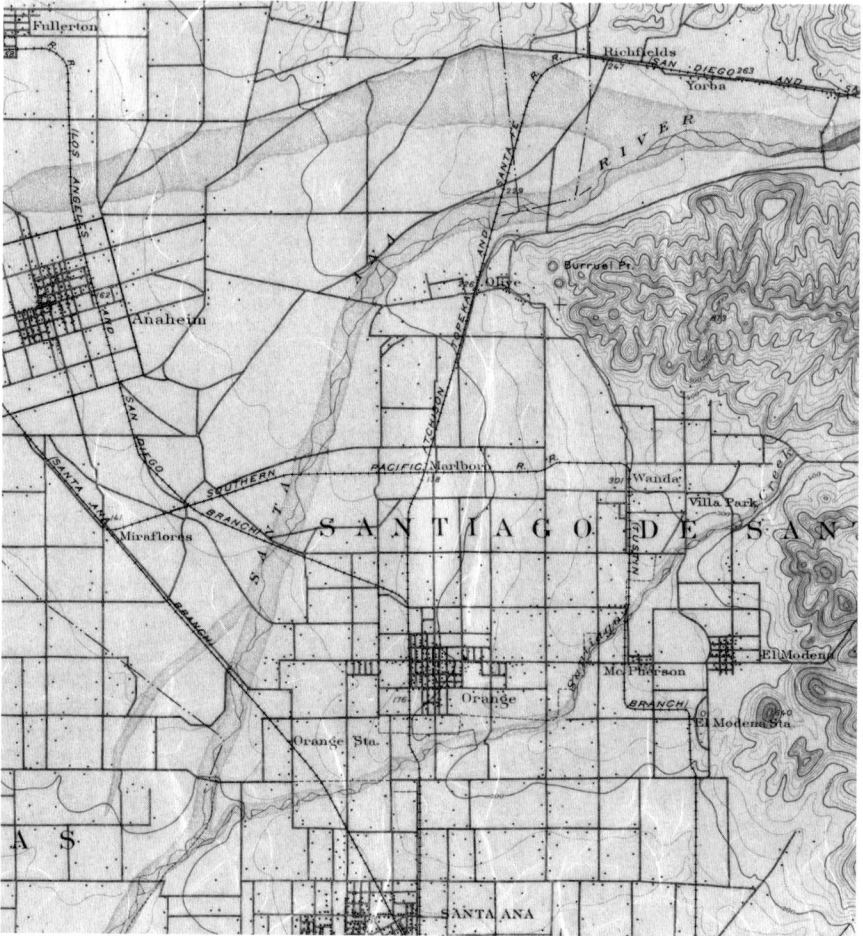

A portion of an 1896 USGS Anaheim topographic sheet showing Orange and surroundings.

EDITOR'S PREFACE

Sometime more years ago than I care to admit, I spent most of a night reading a typed manuscript preserved in an old-fashioned leather document holder inscribed "Story of California Life by Mary T. Clark." As a then–college student majoring in history, I confess some experience in pulling all-nighters. But this was special. My father, George H. Clark, who had protected this document for many years, pulled it down from a shelf in our home in Orange, California. The typed *Pioneer Ranch Life* manuscript by Mary Teegarden Clark rang true to me as history personally lived from 1875 to 1887. Previously, I knew vaguely of Mary Clark from my childhood. I remember being told that she was my great-grandmother and being shown a memorial book collection to her in the Orange Public Library. Relatives back east in Indiana had provided for this civic tribute. I also recall being told that she kept a journal from pioneer times, which as a child I assumed described her covered wagon travels. That night, I discovered her most important work—the core of this book—a first-hand account of life in Southern California during the pioneer days.

I quickly realized the value that my great-grandmother's story held, given its spirited and detailed descriptions of California life long before freeways, surfboards and refrigerators. I discussed the manuscript with various local historians and college professors. All agreed on its wider importance. Some encouraged a rush into publication. I sought an estimate from a printer. I received advice in various ways. I knew more was needed to unfold this narrative written down so long ago. Questions about the original document existed. This was a typescript. What happened to any earlier handwritten documents? The front page of this typescript contained a handwritten statement, "names of characters are fictions." What did this mean? And could persons in the text be re-identified? Could events be verified? A historical document needed notations and a well-written introduction—demanding more research. The practical considerations of publication costs and time required for marketing, a much greater factor in the 1970s, forestalled any "rushing" to publication, particularly considering I was then a busy college student with only part-time employment. Over the ensuing years, I kept an eye out, researching microfilmed newspapers, interviewing family members and visiting, as time and place allowed, libraries and archives around the United States. Blessed with good fortune and retirement from full-time employment in 2009, I picked up this project again.

My search over the years failed to uncover any evidence of a handwritten version of *Pioneer Ranch Life*. A reference in Mary Clark's 1922 obituary speaks of her keeping "old note books," suggesting she did possess a handwritten account, but none appear to have survived. Her completion of the memoir by 1906 is demonstrated at the end of Chapter 16, "The Flight of the Duchess." Comments made by several relatives confirmed that the typescript derived in the 1920s was the product of Mary Kate Clark (also known as Kate Clark), daughter of Mary. Kate either typed up the document herself or had a professional typist complete the job. She added the last chapter, "The Fulfillment," in which she identified herself with the initials "K.C." and dated it 1924. Kate obtained the original notebooks while she lived with her mother as a caregiver in La Porte, Indiana. An unfortunate consensus exists that she discarded the written notebooks once typing was finished. By 1926, she left Indiana and returned permanently to California. She lived in Orange, but records show that she also lodged in Hollywood awhile and sought to promote the typescript as a movie screenplay. While Kate engaged in the typing process, she renamed many of the persons in the original document. This was probably intended for privacy, given the consequences of public exposure that a successful motion picture would bring to then-living family members. To my knowledge, no film ever materialized. After failing to catch the eye of Hollywood, the typescript, fictional names and all, sat aside and entered into family legend. Kate spent the remainder of her life in Orange and is fondly remembered within the family as "Aunt Kate." After her death, her estate passed to her nephews and nieces, and my father came into possession of the original typescript, while additional copies found limited distribution among other Clark family members.

All this leaves a certain amount of uncertainty about the typescript's originality. How much was Mary Clark's work, and how much could have been Kate Clark's? Fortunately, Mary did produce at least one other document independently that parallels *Pioneer Ranch Life*. While visiting California during the winter of 1916–17, she read a paper to the Orange Woman's Club. A local newspaper, the *Orange Star*, printed her essay. Later, in 1938, the *Orange Daily News* reprinted this earlier *Orange Star* text, making some slight revisions and updating it with pre-script and post-script commentary related to the Clarks then living in Orange. The January 1917 version of this paper is reprinted (see Appendix A) and provides the most direct evidence of the original *Pioneer Ranch Life* manuscript. The paper both supports and supplements Mary's *Pioneer Ranch Life* story, giving both greater credibility. Of note, some details mentioned in the Woman's Club paper appear in *Pioneer Ranch Life*, while other episodes are dropped. While Kate Clark may have made unknown revisions, the *Orange Star* article ensures the credible usefulness of *Pioneer Ranch Life* as Mary Clark's words.

To further deepen this story of pioneer life, I added another text written by her and created in much the same way as the Orange Woman's Club paper. Mary Clark read a chronicle of her father, Abraham Teegarden, to the La Porte County Historical Society in Indiana in 1907. This work afterward appeared in the local newspaper the La Porte *Daily Herald* (see Appendix B), and clippings found their way to the historical society's archive. This biography of Abraham Teegarden enhances this publication and underscores Mary's pioneer heritage.

Mary Clark's Southern California memoirs have not been previously published. However, over the years, some versions, variations or perhaps "take-offs" have materialized. Unpublished copies of *Pioneer Ranch Life* previously found limited distribution among Clark family members from Orange. For example, my cousin Richard Clark maintained for a time in the late 1990s a "Yale Grove" website. The website included a copy of *Pioneer Ranch Life* acquired by his father, Oliver Joseph Clark. One or two copies also came into the hands of others outside the family, including some local historians. One of the earliest uses of Mary's work shows up in the *Santa Ana Register*, November 22, 1939, with an article entitled "Clarks Watch Orange Grow." The reporter, Marah Adams, reviewed the earlier *Orange Daily News* article and obtained letters that Mary had written to Indiana relatives. The article contains quotations from these letters, which unfortunately no longer exist in any other form. Another example of prior use appeared in the November 12, 1948 issue of the *Register*. The newspaper reported a radio play performed by Orange High School students that utilized portions of Mary's memoirs, retelling her uncomfortable hotel stay and her melodramatic period of homesickness. This radio adaptation used actual family names. Bertha Barron's "California Christmas," published in 1967, exists among a compilation of short stories in *Rawhide and Orange Blossoms* (Pioneer Press, 1967). "California Christmas" employs remarkably similar storylines to ones used by Mary Clark and includes such characters as heroine "Mary Gordon" and her husband, a Harvard man, "Al," and contains a Chinese house servant named "Ah Fong." Despite this—or perhaps because of all this—these past treatments express the continuing human interest in Mary's original writings.

Using the 1917 Woman's Club paper as evidence of Mary Clark's willingness to recognize persons in her narrative, I reversed the fictitious names, identifying actual persons herein. Any need for privacy seems long gone, and the natural curiosity of the modern reader demands the identity of the persons recalled so vividly in these pages. Fortunately, aided by ample genealogical and archival documentation, as well as the good preservation of newspaper clippings, photographs and other ephemera by Clark family members, I have been surprisingly successful in finding the identity of many—or at least offering the reader an intelligent guess. Some remain elusive. Mary perhaps intended some to remain so, either from faded memory or other reasons. Where persons could be identified, they are. Where persons remain obscure, no note will be found. A few key individuals, repeated in the text, are provided thumbnail biographies in the Introduction; further details of this process will be discussed there. Some genealogical information is provided for better individual clarification. This reproduction of the original typescript remains faithful to Mary's words.

Where information used in my notations is derived from a common or encyclopedic source, Internet or otherwise, I cite no specific source. I claim no special botanical or scientific knowledge, but given the frequent mention of plant names, similar sources were used with the intent to better guide the reader. For original sources used for introducing and annotating these memoirs, I visited a range of locations across the United States, including the National Archives in Washington, D.C. and at Riverside, California; the La Porte County Historical Society and Museum, La Porte, Indiana; the Lilly Library, Wabash College, Crawfordsville, Indiana; the Southington Public Library, Southington, Connecticut; and the Yosemite National Park Museum and Research Library. I also visited the following California institutions: the California State Archives and the California State Library at

Sacramento; the Orange Public Library and History Center; the Anaheim Public Library; the Santa Ana Public Library; the Sherman Library in Corona del Mar; the Pollak Library, California State University, Fullerton; and the private collections and recollections of friends and family.

Many persons have assisted over the years in providing advice, information sources and photographs, and I can name only a few: Dr. Harv Galic of Stanford University; Dr. William Hendricks and Jill Thrasher of the Sherman Library; the staff at the La Porte County Historical Society, including but not limited to Fern Eddy Schultz; the staff at the Lilly Library, Wabash College, including but not limited to Beth Swift; and various individuals, including Phil Brigandi, Ronald Gregory, Joanne Coontz, Leslie Mouriquand, Linda Smith, Rosamond Makar, Richard Clark, Marjorie Petrie, Christine Clark, Phil Clark, the late Don Meadows, the late Suzanne Struck, the late Barbara McKee Clark, the late Marjory Clark-Barker and her late daughter Margery Barker. This listing should not be considered exhaustive, and I apologize to anyone not included who should be listed. All errors in my editorial writing are mine, but I extend to all those who assisted me a hearty thanks.

Many of the photographs that accompany this publication are family heirlooms. Unless otherwise noted by the captions, all photographs or other illustrations are from my personal collection. One set of photographs, however, deserves specific discussion. These were original photographs owned by Mary Clark that came into my possession by way of my father. These were taken by famed early California photographer Carleton Watkins (1829–1916), perhaps best known for his work at Yosemite. Watkins completed a photographic collection of Mary's ranch, the "Yale Grove," in Orange during the summer of 1880. Watkins's "New Series" and other identifying labels appear clearly. Watkins was a logical photographer for the job. Albert Clark, Mary's husband, had previously associated with him on the Clarence King expedition to Mount Shasta in 1870. The Orange photos contain handwriting, likely Mary's, on the reverse, identifying persons shown and the time frame. A notice in the June 19, 1880 *Los Angeles Evening Express* provides corroboration: "Mr. C.E. Watkins, the landscape photographer, is engaged in taking views of the most interesting portions of Los Angeles County for exhibition in the East by means of a magic lantern." Whether or not the Yale Grove figured in any "magic lantern" presentations, Albert used the photographs for promotional purposes, displaying them at regional agricultural expositions.

My concluding thoughts must start with Mary Clark's final words written in 1906: "We have stayed on [in Indiana] not one year or two but nearly twenty, and the life at 'Yale Grove' has become only a precious heritage of memory." I recall a much later Yale Grove of my childhood, coming as part of a subsequent "Baby Boom" generation. An active orange ranch, soon to decline, operated there in the 1950s. Within the ranch, an orchard surrounded a house with resident grandparents and uncles, who happily allowed my cousins and me to play on the floor of the old home with toys they kept for us while a fireplace crackled with warm flames and they talked of adult matters. The onrush of urbanization removed that place from existence in 1976, so my own recollections now constitute another precious heritage of memory. I hope this publication will act as a kind of substitute for the now long-gone Yale Grove. I hope it allows this heritage to be continued for new generations and to a wider audience, a legacy that my great-grandmother deserves.

PAUL F. CLARK
December 2012

INTRODUCTION

The pioneer endures as one of America's supreme icons. The pioneer traveled across and adapted to the demands of a great continent, breaking new ground and opening new places for others to follow. And today, the icon gives rise to many diverse perceptions. One very common perception, encouraged by Hollywood, mass media and popular literature, tells of the sturdy individual arriving on horse or covered wagon, overcoming a hostile environment and advancing the codes of civilization in a new landscape. While sometimes true, a more complex reality intrudes. The pioneer story interweaves many groups of people who transformed vast areas, produced great wealth and power and, too often, encountered dark and violent episodes. History works hard to grasp a pioneer story that extends from the grubby to the magnificent.

Mary Teegarden Clark (1846–1922) used the phrase *Pioneer Ranch Life* in the title of her memoirs. She very clearly identified her life in Southern California from 1875 to 1887 in the pioneer way. She lived it. The pioneer meant something to her. The pioneer was tangible to her. Yet her pioneering differed from the common Hollywood image. For example, she arrived in Southern California by boat and train, not covered wagon. Great drama of the silver screen variety probably did not test her. What did test Mary roused within her the will to survive, adapt and even thrive within demanding, fascinating and sometimes heartbreaking pioneer realities.

Southern California seemed a largely vacant landscape to outsiders in 1875, even though long inhabited by various Native American peoples and occupied by Latinos for over a century. From Mary Clark's perspective, she saw it as an empty unrefined place but full of simple beauty and promise. U.S. Census records for Los Angeles County, which at that time included what is today Orange County,[1] totaled about 15,000 residents in 1870. This had risen to a little over 33,000 in 1880. These small numbers nonetheless reflect the beginnings of a transformation. The Los Angeles *Daily Herald* observed these changing times, as the editor in 1880 looked back on the growth of Los Angeles County and said, "Seven years ago, the country below Anaheim scarcely boasted of any settlement whatever until San Juan Capistrano was reached. Where Westminster, Orange, Santa Ana and the heavy Gospel Swamp settlements now stand, there was then absolutely nothing in the shape of habitations to be seen."[2] Contrast this to the regional population count of nearly 540,000 in 1910—just after Mary completed her memoir in 1906—and one can see why she considered herself a pioneer.[3]

Into this largely vacant land came Mary Clark, a woman settling with her family in Orange, California,[4] a place selected by her husband as a refuge for health and in hopes of profit. While Mary's memoirs speak of many persons and events, they above all reveal a woman determined to express her life as she saw it. In these pages there exists a typical Victorian lady's sense of duty for her family mixed with richly detailed stories of

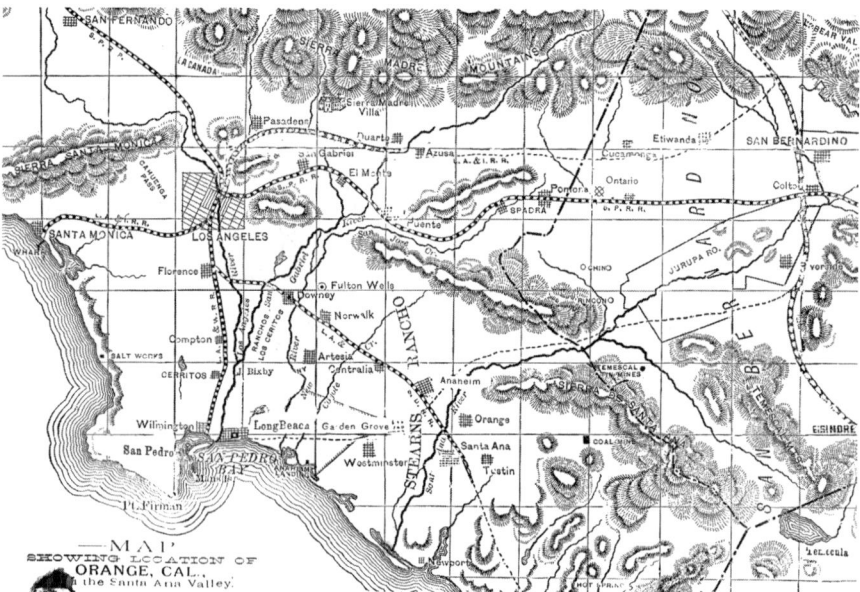

An 1886 map of the Los Angeles region of Southern California. Note that Los Angeles County includes the future Orange County at this time.

daily life, right down to evening meal menus. She celebrates the loyalty she and her husband achieved as a team of helpmates. He acted as the provider and community leader and she the manager of the domestic household and children. Later, after his untimely death, she willingly assumed the reins of ranch boss and provider.

Mary Clark's narratives contain larger implications. Fundamental change confronted Southern California and the state though the 1870s and 1880s. The semi-frontier landscape began to alter, with new settlers bringing new growth and new ideas. No longer an open and isolated countryside, this period saw railroads entering from the outside bringing fresh means of economic connection, natural watercourses engineered into vital irrigation facilities, the lifestyle of sheep and cattle grazing supplanted and land subdivided into wheat, citrus and other farmlands. All of this demanded more sophisticated means to promote the products of this newfound society. On a more negative side, this era saw development of a social hierarchy between increasingly well-organized land-owning ranchers and the often ethnically divergent farm laborers working in the fields harvesting and packing the produce of the land. The agricultural industrial system later dominating Southern California began to take form during this period; the land and society was being shaped for many decades into the next century. While other remembrances exist, Mary contributes her own perspective as a woman witnessing this turbulent time.[5]

Fortune smiled on January 19, 1846, in La Porte, Indiana,[6] when Mary Treat Teegarden came into the world, born the elder of two daughters of Dr. Abraham Teegarden (1813–1883). Dr. Teegarden and the La Porte community had just lived through their own pioneering era. A man of scholarly and enterprising inclinations, Abraham was among the first doctors in La Porte, coming there with a college

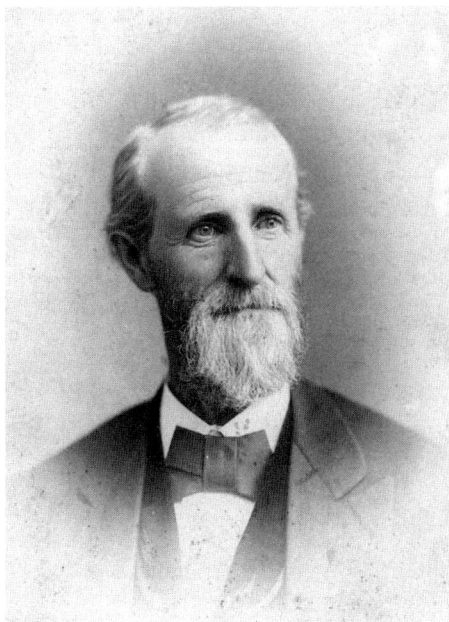

Abraham Teegarden.

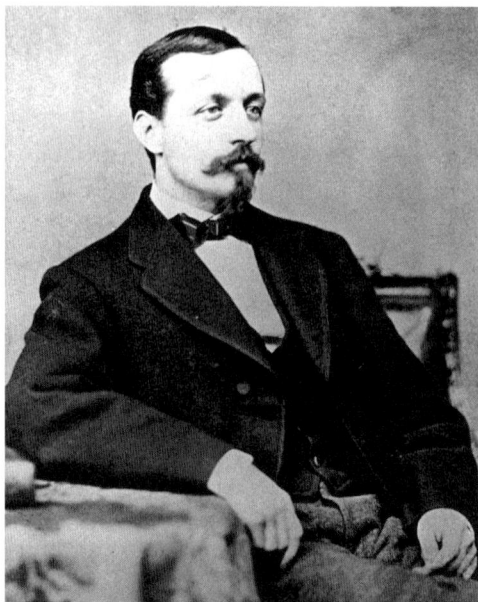

Albert Barnes Clark.

medical education in the 1830s. He fostered learning in both his family and his community. As a result, Mary came to possess a reputation for education and culture, reflecting the formal schooling her father bankrolled through her childhood and young adulthood—a time when American life preordained female education toward household skills, rarely progressing beyond basic literacy.[7]

Fortune also smiled in 1872 when marriage paired Mary with a man of leadership and imagination, Albert Barnes Clark (1842–1883). Albert provided a well-to-do income for her and their first child, Elsie, through a court reporter business in Chicago. However, his ill health changed their lives and brought them to Southern California in 1875. Together, Albert and Mary built a citrus ranch and raised a family with undying commitment and devotion. Albert wrote about their deep relationship. "Mary, my heart is forever longing for you to be my companion," he penned during an excursion separating them in 1882. He continued:

> *You are the only one that gives me any satisfaction or delight. How true I know it—there is no lady in the world so good and so admirable as your little self. I do not believe the Lord ever made another your equal, and when I am home again, I wish greatly to show you what a good place you hold in my heart.*

His sickness and death in April 1883 tragically ended their partnership. Mary never remarried.[8]

Mary Clark did not greatly advertise her ability to write, confining herself to notebooks and letters. It came to be said about her in 1904 that she was "so unobtrusive with her talents that this fact is known and appreciated by comparatively few in the community where she resides."[9] When she completed her California personal history in 1906 and later spoke to community groups, her dedication to the written word expressed itself in unmistakable terms.[10] The reader will notice she often retained the name "Richland," the first name used for Orange. Orange replaced Richland by 1873, but Mary loved the older name, which brought for her more poetic connotations. Her portrayal of everyday living from a woman's perspective is strong, detailed and revealing. One example notes:

> *There was seldom a day in the whole year except May Day when farm work was entirely suspended, as, when it was too wet to plow, it was time to clean harnesses or make fruit creates and boxes, and when irrigation was not in progress, cultivation was going on. As for the housewife, she did the cooking, washing, ironing and baking of about fifteen loaves a week, single handed, unless her husband had time to aid her.*

Mary delighted in the simple, outdoor living experienced in her adopted state, and she could describe nature with great joy:

> *Now the winter rains set in, and the whole country blossomed as a rose. Everywhere about us, the vacant acres were carpeted with nemophila, or "baby blue-eyes," a most charming little flower, while blushing spring beauties lifted their graceful heads, and plumy Indian pinks, lemon-drops, poppies of every hue, and lupines of rare beauty seemed to spring forth, as by magic, after the warm rains.*

Yet this intellectual exuberance was not the only Mary Clark. Reflecting a more divergent side, a youthful Mary was remembered as "a beautiful, impetuous girl,"[11] perhaps a belle of La Porte County. Above all, she exhibited a resilient personality, particularly later in life, as she faced and overcame many setbacks and disappointments. She displayed her sense of duty by standing by her husband, and following her husband's early death, taking the reins of family leadership. Raising her children, managing her business, writing her memoirs and visiting her grandchildren, Mary continued to remain fully engaged in life—both physically and intellectually—right up to her death.

The most important person in Mary Clark's background is Abraham Teegarden, her father, a pioneer in his own right and a subject of one her narratives in this book (see Appendix B). Abraham descended from colonial

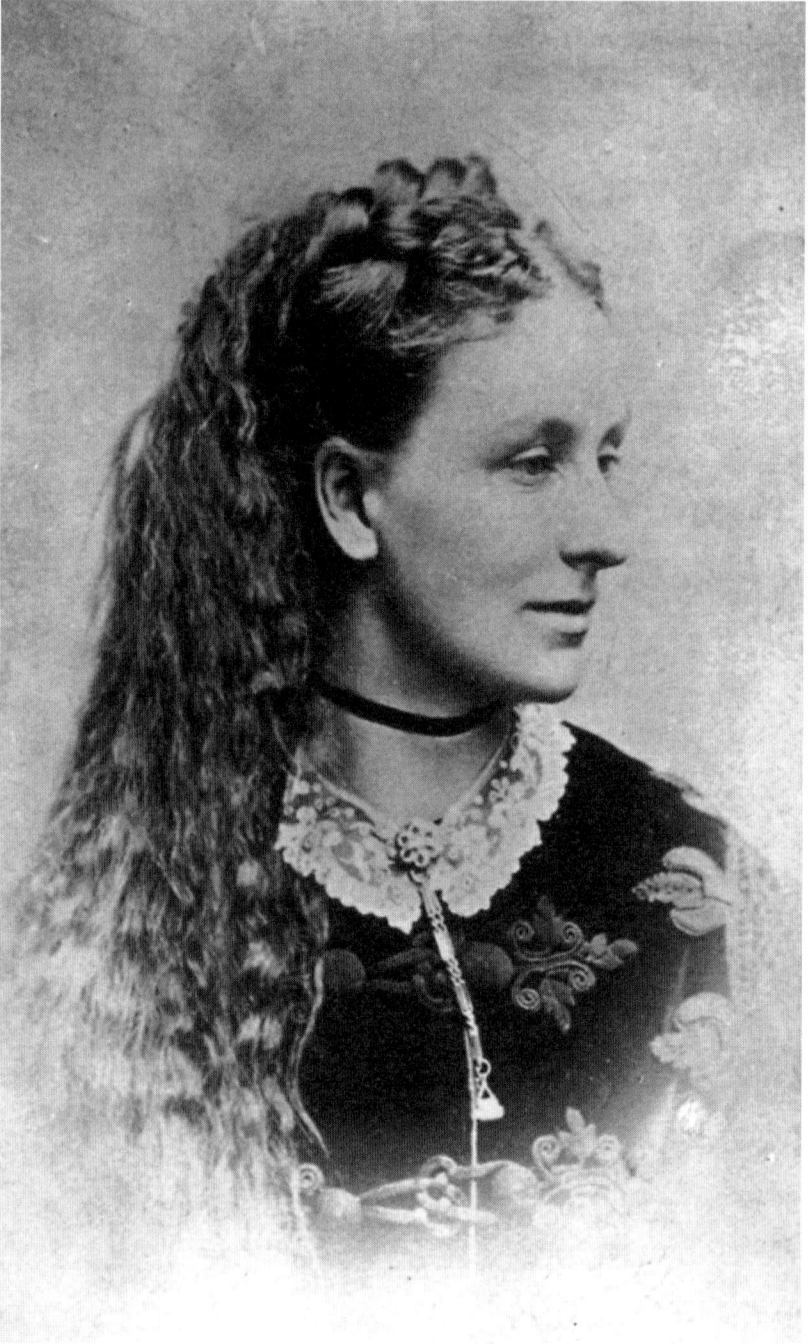

Mary Teegarden Clark as a young woman.

German immigrants,[12] being born in Ohio in 1813, the eleventh of fifteen children reared by William Teegarden and Susannah Rafelty Teegarden. Like a number of his siblings, Abraham stood over six feet tall, and like many of his brothers, he abandoned farm work in his youth and became a doctor. He studied under one of his brothers and attended several Ohio college institutions that taught the Eclectic[13] school of medicine.

In 1837, Abraham traveled west by horseback from Ohio with a saddlebag full of books, medications and some cash. He settled in La Porte and there married Lura Treat (1814–1868) in 1840. Lura was born to Samuel Treat (1787–1849) and Elcy Tracy Treat (1787–1880).[14] The Teegardens raised a family of two daughters: Mary, and a second daughter, Myra Bell Teegarden (1853–1928). Abraham placed their home within a grove of pine and chestnut trees. As time progressed, his practice expanded, and he also branched into teaching. This required home remodeling, as recalled by Mary Clark, to include "accommodations for students who were eager to profit by his instructions. The attic was devoted to skeletons and dissecting rooms, and as a child, I had very gruesome ideas of this forbidden spot."[15]

Besides being a physician and mentor, Abraham achieved success as a businessman, politician and community leader. In 1852, he opened a four-story brick hotel called the Teegarden House, taking advantage of new railroad connections through La Porte. Abraham is believed to have prohibited the sale of liquors at his hostelry.[16] His active political life saw service in the Indiana state legislature, including two terms as a state senator. He is said to have assisted the Union armies as a physician during the Civil War. Misfortune visited Abraham in January 1868 with the death of his wife, Lura. He remained thereafter a widower. He partially retired in 1870 but continued to oversee his affairs, which included farms in northern Indiana and Colorado.

Within Dr. Teegarden's household, Mary experienced a cultivated childhood. When she was about eight years old, her father sent her to private girls' schools. She graduated from a young ladies' academy known as the Union Seminary, operated by Mary McKee Holmes at La Porte. The Holmes school emphasized the learning of both English and German, with pupils expected to speak and write in each language. She then attended Vassar College at Poughkeepsie, New York, during the academic year of 1867–68. Unfortunately, her mother's death created a need for her at home, and Mary's Vassar experience was cut short.[17]

Abraham traveled to California in 1874 along the new transcontinental railroad. He recorded the trip in a handwritten diary that included

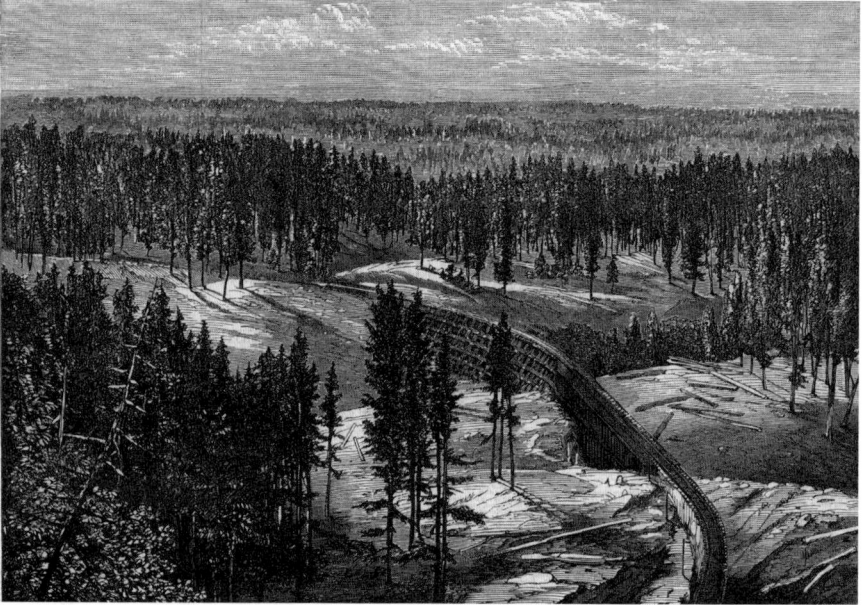

Transcontinental railroad bridge in the Sierra Nevada. *Taken from* Illustrated London News, *January 11, 1868.*

observations during a springtime visit to Los Angeles. Here he traversed the local landscape visiting orange groves and old mission sites. He wrote glowingly, "Much of the valley near and on the south of the city is under cultivation, orange, lemon, figs and almonds. On the south of the city, for 15 or 20 miles, a majestic beautiful country slopes towards the Pacific. Nearly every acre of this vast plain can be successfully irrigated from water taken from the Los Angeles River." Upon his return, he no doubt shared what he saw with Mary and Albert.[18]

Abraham was a very strong Swedenborgian, or New Church[19] member, to the end of his life and imparted this faith to his daughter Mary. He often served his La Porte neighbors by presiding over funerals and weddings. After suffering an accident while making repairs at his hotel, he died in October 1883. He is buried at La Porte's Pine Lake Cemetery.[20]

The next most important person in Mary Clark's life will be addressed at some length, given that he was the primary character in her Southern California memoir. Albert Barnes Clark became Mary's husband on November 21, 1872, and she settled with him in the Chicago suburb of Evanston, Illinois. Their first child, Elsie, arrived in January 1874. Evanston held several characteristics that probably influenced its selection for the

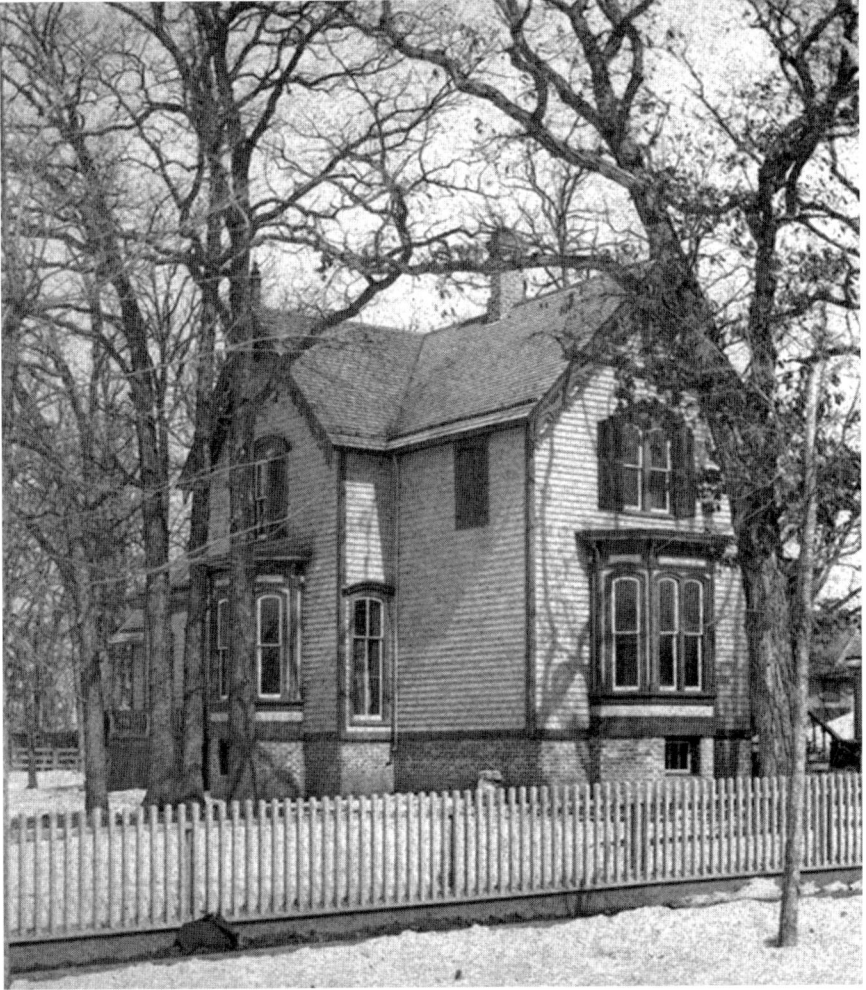

The Clark home in Evanston, Illinois, March 1875.

first Clark home. Evanston is located about ten miles north of downtown Chicago and was near Albert's work. But more intriguingly, the community prohibited alcoholic beverage sales and was the home of Northwestern University, a progressive institution that admitted women in 1869.

Like Mary, Albert lived his early life in La Porte, having been born there in 1842. His father, Amzi Clark (1798–1871), was one of La Porte's early merchants, arriving there in 1834. Amzi originally came from Connecticut and traced his ancestral roots to the founding of New Haven in 1639. Albert's mother was Candace Roberts Bailey (1810–1848).

Amzi and Candace raised a family of three boys and one daughter, Albert being the youngest. He was only five years old when Candace died of bronchial consumption. Amzi remarried the following year to a local teacher, Harriet Crosby Clark (1814–1902), and they had two additional children.[21]

Albert attended Wabash College in Crawfordsville, Indiana, starting as a sixteen-year-old prep-school student in 1858 and continuing on through his sophomore year in 1862. He then transferred to Yale College (now Yale University) at the start of his junior year. He joined in student debate and boating activities at Yale and was a member of several fraternities, including the famed Skull and Bones society. Probably popular in his social life at Yale, he achieved only average academic grades but received a degree nonetheless. He graduated in July 1864.[22]

After Yale, with the Civil War still raging, Albert accepted a naval commission as "Acting Assistant Paymaster" assigned to the USS *Pampero* from December 1864 to July 1865. Part of the West Gulf Blockading Squadron, the *Pampero* mounted six guns and contained a crew of up to fifty-five, composed mainly of "contrabands"—freed black slaves. The ship performed, while rotating among the mouths of the Mississippi River, a solitary and likely uneventful duty. Major naval conflict had long passed New Orleans. During this time, however, the Louisiana environment bestowed on Albert an unwelcome gift.

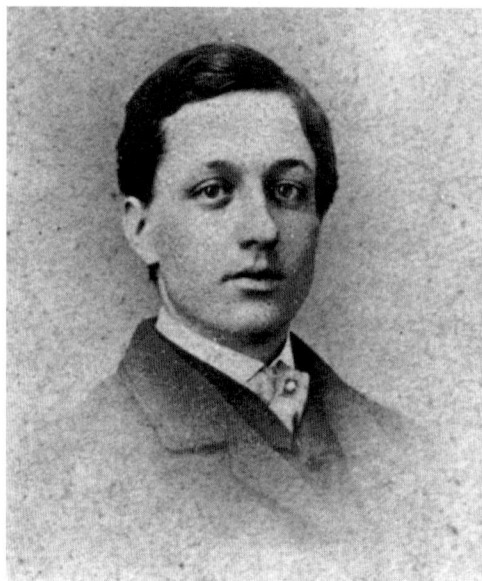

Albert Barnes Clark as a young man at Wabash College, 1862.

Medical documentation reveals a life-threatening affliction called *Remittens* fever caused "in the line of duty, being the result of exposure to malaria." His treatment ran from July through September 1865, leading to discharge from the naval hospital in October 1865. He was sent north on doctor's orders. While surviving, the effects of malaria probably troubled Albert for the rest of his life. Veterans of the Civil War commonly retained lingering service illness. His seeking a warm, dry climate in California probably grew out of this wartime experience.[23]

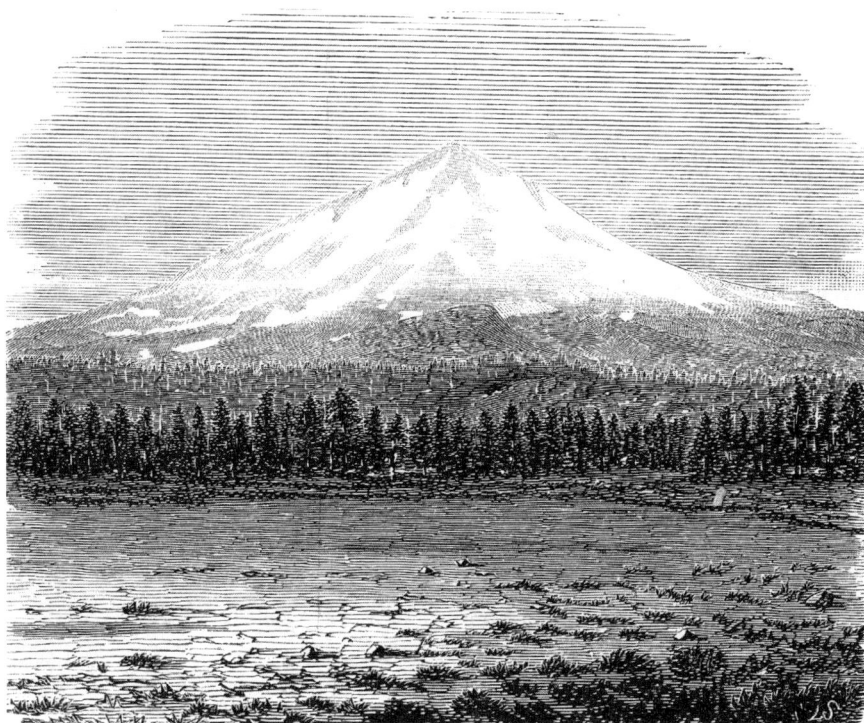

Drawing of Mount Shasta, California, from a Carlton Watkins 1870 photograph. Albert Clark climbed Mount Shasta that same year.

Following the war, Albert drifted from a Connecticut insurance business to reading law in Ohio to working for the federal Bureau of Education in Washington, D.C., to serving as a business assistant for J. Young Scammon, a prominent Chicago banker and lawyer. The highlight of this bachelor time came during the summers of 1870 and 1871, when an opportunity arose to serve as a "barometrical aid and general assistant" with the U.S. Geological Exploration of the Fortieth Parallel, under the direction of Clarence King. He discovered that this outdoor work provided robust health—enough to climb Mount Shasta (as detailed in King's book *Mountaineering in the Sierra Nevada*) and spend a summer in the Rocky Mountains, where he achieved the summit of Longs Peak. Seeing the West for the first time, Albert took note of Colorado irrigation projects, traveled several times to California and wrote for the *Chicago Evening Journal* describing his adventures while trekking in Colorado and Wyoming.[24]

Leaving the geological survey, Albert spent a time staffing the U.S. Senate Committee on Enrolled Bills. He returned to La Porte to take Mary as his bride in 1872, and thereafter until 1875, he built up a Chicago court reporter business. His half-sister, Rose Clark, recalled that this venture was successful but required long, strenuous hours, often into the night. Along with the cold climate and the consequences of his wartime disease, his health began to fail.[25]

The idea of moving to California increasingly grew in Albert's mind. In March 1875, Albert left to scout out Los Angeles for himself. Early June found him registered at an Anaheim hotel. Given his quick return a few months later, this journey delivered confirmation of what he sought. Southern California, given Albert's health issues, presented a logical location. Mary had relatives in the San Francisco Bay and Marysville areas. Little doubt Albert sought their advice, but he looked to the southland. As both Mary and Albert were from Evanston, interest in a temperance community would have been high among their criteria. Orange was strongly temperance minded in composition, and at the time of Albert's scouting visit, the hamlet was going through a conspicuous anti-saloon agitation.[26]

Albert and Mary's trip from Illinois to California finds colorful expression in *Pioneer Ranch Life*. They arrived in Southern California by late September, traveled to Orange and immediately began a search for a home. While Mary's account dramatically tells of her initial misgivings, they eventually acquired twenty acres on October 22, 1875. Noteworthy without explanation, the deed listed Mary as the sole landowner—no mention of her husband. Perhaps financial support from Mary's father, along with Albert's health issues, recommended that the land be placed in her name to avoid future complications. At any rate, with this purchase, they staked their entry into Orange and began to raise a family. Three more children were born in California: Marjory, Mary Kate and Donald.[27]

Planning for their Southern California ranch had begun prior to leaving Illinois, with orders for nursery stock placed and even a home designed (the design bears a general likeness to what eventually evolved at the Orange property).

Once it had been purchased, Albert lost no time improving his land, which he dubbed the Yale Grove in honor of his alma mater. (The site, now

Opposite, top: The first drawing of the Clark ranch house at Yale Grove by John William Munday, prepared the night prior to their departure for California, 1875.

Opposite, bottom: The Clark ranch house at Yale Grove looking southwest. Carlton Watkins photograph, 1880.

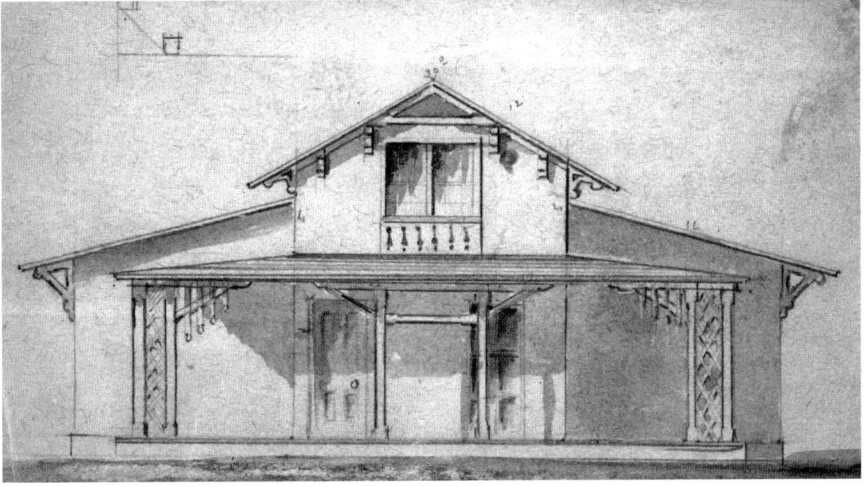

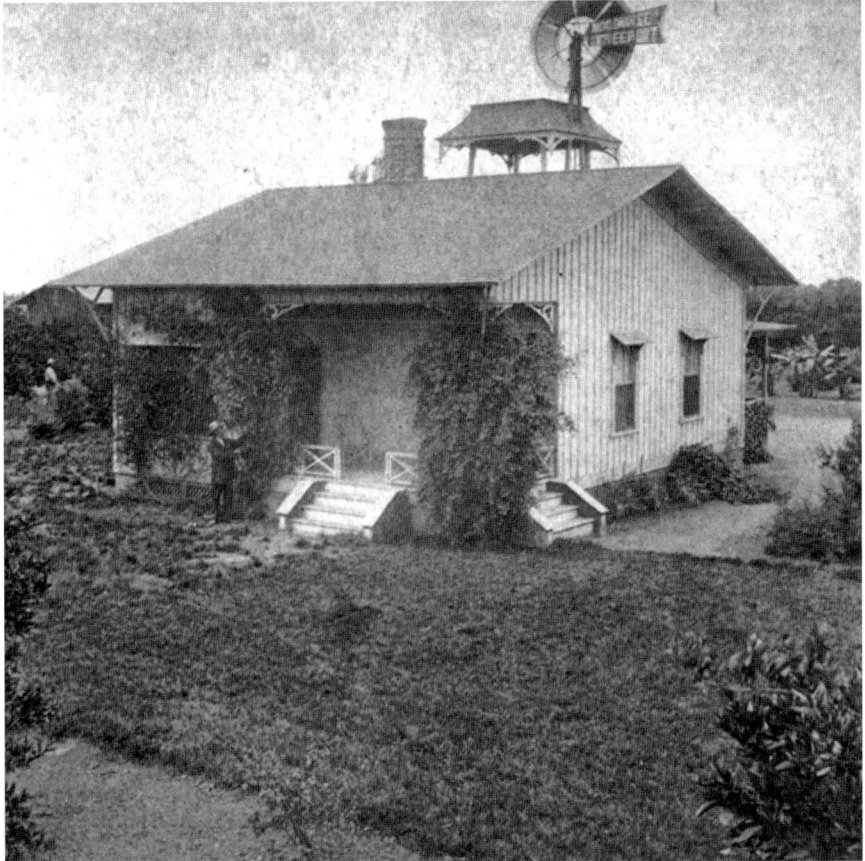

urbanized, was at the northeasterly corner of Batavia Street and Palmyra Avenue.) These efforts were noticed in early November 1875, as the *Anaheim Gazette* reported, "Mr. Clark, of Chicago, is building a fine residence." The home was set back two hundred feet from Palmyra Avenue and reached by a broad circular driveway. Accessory buildings included a barn, packing shed and windmill tower. Mary vividly tells of the boring of a well in early 1876 for on-site water and the setting out of the orchard, with her home soon being surrounded by ornamental trees, vegetable gardens and flowers.[28]

Even with on-site wells providing a water resource, the community needed a secure flow of irrigation water from the Santa Ana River, north of Orange. The problematic state of the water system drove Albert to join the movement to organize the Santa Ana Valley Irrigation Company (SAVI). Prompted by a heat wave and drought in 1877, the SAVI incorporated by August as a mutual water company. Albert was listed as among the founding directors and prepared the initial sale of stock. "The subscription books," recalled Mary, "were opened August 21, 1877, and stock to the amount of $10,000 was at once taken." The first stockholders meeting, on September 6, saw the adoption of the SAVI bylaws, and Albert was soon thereafter elected its first president. The work to finance and build new irrigation infrastructure consumed Albert from then on through January 1879, which marked the achievement of the final assessment securing the SAVI future. He estimated the total cost at $55,000. "Many thanks are due Mr. Clark and his associate directors," celebrated a local reporter for the *Gazette*, "for their untiring energy and sacrifice in pushing this work against all sorts of disadvantages and discouragements. It has required statesmanship, financial skill, persistency, forbearance and a thousand other good qualities," adding, "to Mr. A.B. Clark's clear insight and quiet persistency much belongs."[29]

The organization and development of the SAVI constituted the high point of Albert's short life in Orange. After this effort, between 1879 and 1883, he remained engaged in an array of community activities, including running unsuccessfully for state senator from Los Angeles County during the summer of 1879. He had stepped down as SAVI president in June 1879 to make his political try, and afterward, he served a second term on the SAVI board from November 1879 to June 1880. He accepted appointment as Orange's postmaster from June 1881 to March 1882 and held a brief directorship with the Southern California Horticultural Society in 1881. He dabbled still in politics, attending the short-lived "State Division Conference," which quixotically debated the idea of statehood for Southern California, in Los Angeles during September 1881.[30]

As the squire of Yale Grove, where his real heart probably lay, Albert also devoted time to making property improvements. His efforts appeared in the *Anaheim Gazette* in September 1879: "Mr. A.B. Clark has just erected the finest combination of windmill tank and observatory that I have yet seen in the country. It is a substantial ornament to his place and the town."[31] Best of all, Mary and Albert finally began to see some financial achievement, as the Yale Grove became a source of revenue, with trees bearing fruit commercially.

Now Albert saw the need to promote this harvest. Showing his fruit at local and regional agricultural fairs offered him one marketing tactic. Yale Grove oranges received notice locally in January 1880 in the *Gazette's*

Top: A political election notice headlining Albert Clark, Republican nominee for Los Angeles County State Senator. *From Los Angeles* Daily Commercial, *August 27, 1879.*

Right: The response to Albert Clark's traducers during the 1879 campaign. *From Los Angeles* Daily Commercial, *August 27, 1879.*

The meetings will be addressed by

HON. A. B. CLARK.
Candidate for State Senator.

HON. P. M. GREEN,
..AND..
JOHN J. MORION
Candidates for Assemblymen,

H. A. BARCLAY Esᴬ.
Candidate for District Attorney.

HON. A. G. COOK.
And other prominent speakers,

Vindication of Hon. A. B. Clark

ORANGE, Los Angeles Co., }
Aug. 21st, 1879. }

ED. COMMERCIAL.—The letter signed "Voter" in the issue of the Los Angeles Herald for Aug. 12th, 1879, was satisfactorily answered by "Voting Democrat" in your paper a day or two since. It was therein stated that a document was in circulation which would contain a brief statement of facts over the signatures of the Directors and ex-Directors and stockholders generally, fully exonerating Mr. A. B. Clark from any suspicion of malfeasance while connected with the Santa Ana Valley Ir-

INTRODUCTION

"Orange Items," which remarked that Albert's crop was among "the largest, finest and richest fruit." He went on to mount a prize-winning display, as reported in the *Los Angeles Evening Express*, at the 1881 Southern California Horticultural Society's Citrus Fair. His Yale Grove soon became recognized as a prime example of citrus horticulture. The orchard grew to eventually contain up to 1,700 orange trees by 1886, of which 3.5 acres were devoted to the Washington navel variety. In August 1881, the *Riverside Press and Horticulturist* reported:

> *The Yale Orchard at Orange, the property of Hon. A.B. Clark, is a very fine property. The trees have been set six years and are the largest of the age we have ever seen. Most of his trees are of the Wilson's Best variety, which Mr. Clark considers, barring the Riverside Navel, the best orange grown in California. He will have about 2,000 boxes of fruit this year, as against 500 boxes last year.*[32]

Combined with showing his fruit, Albert sought improved shipping methods for his oranges bound to markets in San Francisco and Chicago. The technique of packaging oranges in tissue-paper wrappings is first attributed to him, according to the *History of Los Angeles County*. Albert enclosed each orange, as the *Pacific Rural Press* reported in February 1880, with paper printed with "Yale Orchard Oranges" along with his guarantee prior to boxing them for transport. The innovation proved profitable and was hailed as a "new departure" in citrus promotion. Mary recalls these wrappers in Chapter 10, "The Marketing of a Crop," when she writes that only perfect specimens were "reserved for the fancy wrappers which were a guarantee of their excellence." Sometimes dubbed "Yale Wrappers," their use attracted keen newspaper interest and, after some skepticism, soon became a prime citrus industry marketing tool.[33]

As revenue increased from Yale Grove, so too did the depredations of insect pests. Forced at one point to burn down a bug-infected tree in his grove, Albert combated the pests with a formula containing heated whale oil and soap, spraying it directly on the trees. He confidently offered, once he perfected his treatment, first, one dollar, and then ten dollars for anyone finding a red or black scale bug in the Yale Grove. It appears that no one collected. He seemed to be busily promoting this solution right up to late September 1882.[34]

But warnings of trouble to come can be sensed when Mary Clark recalls in Chapter 13, "Changes," that "the tired ranchman" joined an excursion to Alaska in August 1882. Perhaps some of his old geologic exploration days

INTRODUCTION

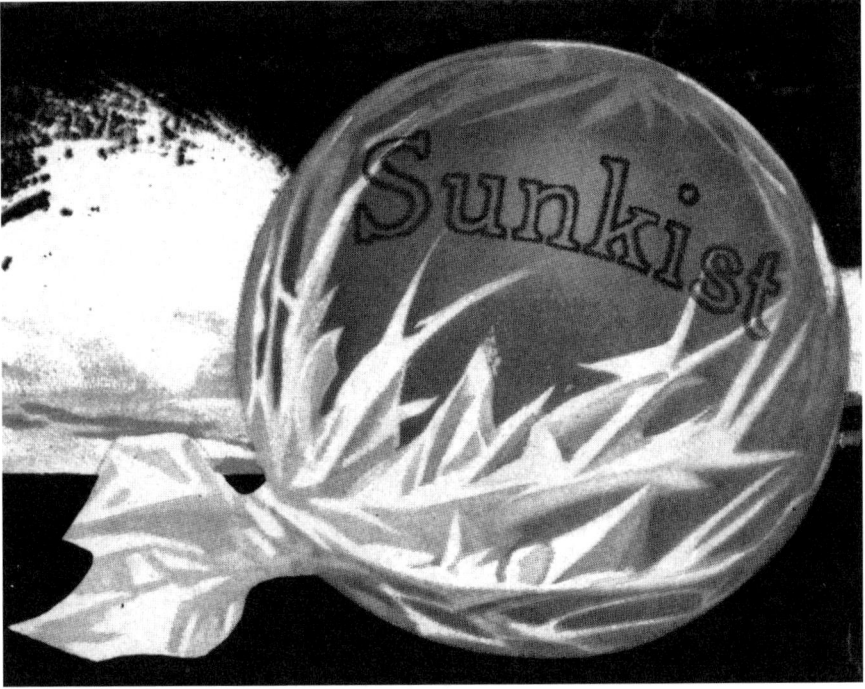

Example of tissue paper–wrapped fruit—an invention of Mary Clark's husband, Albert—taken from a twentieth-century orange crate label. *Courtesy of Anaheim Public Library.*

beckoned to him, as this Alaskan tour was one of the earliest organized sightseeing ventures to that territory. Albert returned to Southern California in early September. He then received notice in several newspaper articles (the last appeared shortly after the first of October) that identified him as well and fully engaged in ranch business.[35]

Sometime in October 1882, typhoid fever struck Albert and other members of his family. He survived but never fully recovered. Mary received tender letters of encouragement during this difficult time, expressing sympathy and wishes for Albert's recovery. The *Los Angeles Times* monitored his illness, printing, "Mr. A.B. Clark of Orange is yet in a critical condition" in early November. Ever responding to his family's need, Abraham Teegarden came west to Orange to offer his medical assistance. After he returned to La Porte, he learned from Mary in February 1883 that, with aid, "Albert was able to walk about the house and yard."[36]

In this precarious state, Albert and Mary decided to go to Oakland, hoping to better his health. Albert's condition instead deteriorated. Suffering from a lung disease that continued to grow worse, he quickly returned to Orange. His death on April 24, 1883, was announced by the *Los Angeles Times*:

> *Mr. Albert Clark, a prominent fruit grower of Orange, died at his residence in that place…while the state of his health for some time past has been such as to preclude the possibility of his recovery, the news of his decease will be received with surprise and regret by his friends throughout Southern California.*

The *Riverside Press and Horticulturalist* echoed the *Times*, noting that "his death will be learned with deep regret by a large circle of friends." Albert was buried a few days later in a well-attended funeral at the Yale Grove. His body was shortly thereafter returned to La Porte, where he now rests at Pine Lake Cemetery.[37]

Very shortly after Albert's death, Mary Clark confronted the decision as to what she would do. Some quickly grasped that she held valuable property, and she faced inquiries about whether or not to sell the Yale Grove. Help

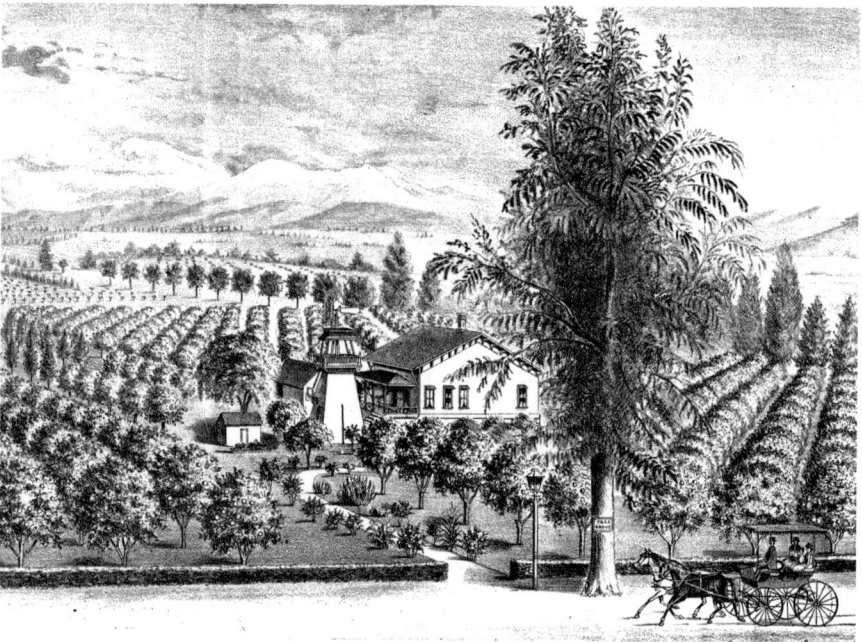

A drawing of Yale Grove taken from *Orange, Cal., Illustrated and Described* (1886). This is the view looking north from Palmyra Avenue. Notice the large Eucalyptus Blue Gum tree, planted in 1873, in the foreground.

surrounded her in the form of relatives and friends, and by May 1, her father returned.[38] Stiffened, her answer to the question of what she would do next can best be sensed by a statement appearing in the *Los Angeles Times* in May 1883, which noted that "an offer of $20,000 was refused a few days ago" for the Yale Grove.[39] Praising Albert, this pithy news release worked to dash any thinking of pursuing Mary with easy offers—reading between the lines. She likely gained a period of peace and quiet. While some may have thought it easier to leave Orange and return to La Porte, she did not do so. This is more remarkable given her father's unexpected death later that year. Mary's refusal to sell signified her decision to remain and become the manager of Yale Grove.

Mary Clark retells her life over the next four years as part of these memoirs. Many relatives and friends offered assistance and companionship. Her story proves her resiliency in the face of great upheaval and sadness. She bravely went on with life. Mary tells of many family episodes after her mourning period ended, including trips to Yosemite, San Juan Capistrano and the San Francisco area. Beyond these reminiscences, she is known to be connected with other events receiving little or no notice in this work. Newspaper stories and other documents indicate that Mary did not remain secluded on the Yale Grove. She enjoyed great respect throughout the Orange locale and ventured into the public eye on occasion.

One such venture involved two Los Angeles "Floral Festival" exhibitions. Given Mary's love of flowers, this is not surprising. The *Pacific Rural Press* observed during the 1885 festival a display of "very fine Mediterranean Sweets and Washington Navels from Mrs. Clark's Yale Grove, in Orange." Mary acted as a matron for the Orange exhibit during the 1886 festival, as reported by the Los Angeles *Daily Herald*, "The floral temple from Orange, in charge of Miss Minnie Joslin, assisted by Misses Lida Condit and Minnie Bryan, and Mrs. A.B. Clark, is down near the platform. It was lovely. All sorts of musical instruments are there wrought out of flowers." The booth even included cages of singing birds. Unfortunately, no mention of these events appears in Mary's memoir, but her involvement seems natural.[40]

Real estate matters kept a keen place in Mary Clark's mind during these years. Given the surrounding real estate "hot house" bubbling around her, most minds in Southern California were equally fixated. Through much of the 1880s, new railroad connections and easy credit encouraged extravagant land promotions during the "Boom of the Eighties." Mary's most well-known contribution to "all this parade" appeared with the 1886 publication of *Orange Illustrated and Described*. This pamphlet came about as an advertising

Yale Grove.

A MONG the many lovely homes of Orange is that of Mrs Mary T. Clark. It consists of forty acres, and adjoins the town site on the southwest. The buildings are neat and tasty, and are situated about midway of the tract east and west, and about 200 feet from the road. A view of this fine place is given in this work, showing the buildings and water tank, from the top of which an extensive view is obtained of the valley. The entrance to the grounds is by a broad, circular drive, with a walk up the center, lined with nearly every variety of orna-

The opening paragraph of the Yale Grove chapter within *Orange, Cal., Illustrated and Described* (1886).

pitch for Orange and surrounding communities. The booklet spoke glowingly of Mary's land in a chapter titled "Yale Grove" and offered a sketch of the ranch, carefully noting a plan to subdivide and create "thereon several pretty cottages for rent or sale."[41]

One of the era's most colorful land promoters was Charles Z. Culver, also known as C.Z. Culver. He reached Orange by 1881 and soon came to manage a diverse number of overplayed ventures, leading later local historians to call him the "prince of speculators" and Orange's "consummate Boomer."[42] His tentacles extended through Southern California and even came to ensnare Mary Clark, as Culver convinced her to participate in a mortgage guarantee for one of his properties. This eventually exposed her to a court proceeding after Culver's downfall when creditors sought to recover assets. Being listed in the newspapers as a guarantor of a failed mortgage no doubt displeased Mary but likely caused her limited financial loss. Culver's insolvency and other legal entanglements drove him to bolt to Baja California in late 1888, where he presumably lived for the rest of his life.[43]

Mary Clark supported alcoholic beverage temperance ideas that mirrored a concern widespread throughout America at this time. Glimpses of this can be seen occasionally in *Pioneer Ranch Life*, such as when she comments disdainfully about the prescription of "whisky instead of milk" for typhoid fever. Many in Orange shared her opinions. When the town incorporated in 1888, among the first municipal ordinances passed included a prohibition of saloons and alcoholic beverage sales. A family tradition suggests that she actively took up this cause while in Orange and spent significant sums from her inheritance in a legal battle against Orange drinking houses. Contemporary records provide no evidence that she pursued such litigation. Whatever activism she pursued, she avoided living in communities in which alcohol was widely sold, instead selecting anti-saloon communities such as Evanston and Orange. All said, she did not make temperance a central part of her personal legacy writing.[44]

Mary Clark ended her time in Orange in late June 1887 when she was forty-one years old. Taking her children, she returned to La Porte and re-established her permanent residence there, visiting Orange occasionally. The *Orange News* notes one trip in November 1895 during which she, along with her son Donald, stayed for a time at the Yale Grove. She journeyed again to Orange in 1909 with Donald and assisted him as he settled permanently on a portion of the property. While in La Porte, she lived in a now sadly vanished home in a residential part of the town.[45]

Once returned to La Porte, Mary Clark focused on her business affairs and the education of her children. Both she and her sister Myra inherited the Teegarden House. They oversaw that asset, which probably constituted a major share of the family income until it was sold in 1911. Mary must have been writing during this time in her notebooks. One of the first fruits of her compositions was the 1907 Abraham Teegarden paper published in the La Porte *Daily Herald*. The winter of 1916–17 saw one of her last trips to Orange. While enjoying her grandchildren, she took time to present an abbreviated version of *Pioneer Ranch Life*, which thereafter saw publication in

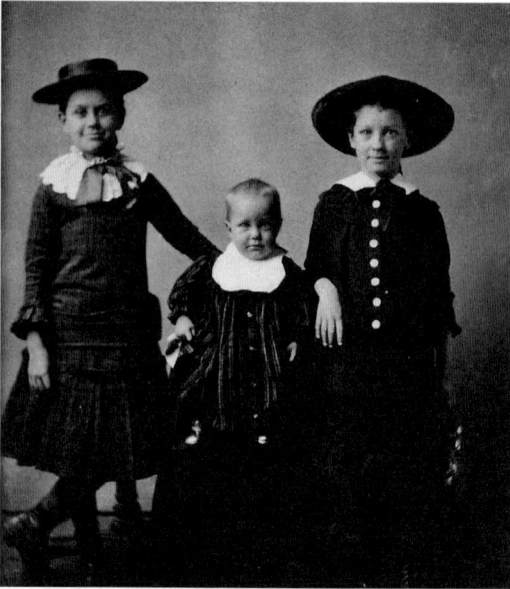

Elsie, Donald and Marjory Clark, circa 1884.

the *Orange Star*. Seventy-six-year-old Mary Teegarden Clark died in La Porte on October 30, 1922, of a heart affliction caused by influenza. A minister of the Swedenborgian church conducted her funeral, which concluded by laying her to rest beside her husband, Albert, in Pine Lake Cemetery.[46]

Besides Mary Clark's father, Abraham, and her husband, Albert, other persons surface throughout this memoir. As previously stated in the Preface, some individuals could not be identified. In that case, no notation will be found. Otherwise, following a rule that if a person was mentioned only once or twice, that person will be provided an inserted name and/or note within the text to help the reader identify them and their relation to Mary's overall story. Others mentioned more often constitute key personalities. Rather than provide lengthy notes in the text, thumbnail biographies follow for the most important persons.

Elsie Treat Clark (1874–1932), the first of Mary Clark's children, was born in January 1874 in Evanston, Illinois, and lived twelve years throughout her childhood in Orange. She left Orange with her mother and other siblings in the summer of 1887 and thereafter spent her teenage years in La Porte. Elsie reportedly attended a school of elocution in London in 1895 and lived in New York in 1897. By 1900, she had returned to La Porte and married Wilson B. Parker, a La Porte architect. Her marriage to Parker eventually ended in divorce, and in 1917, she remarried to Herman R. Hunt. No children came from either of these unions. She continued teaching dramatic arts in later life. She died in Cheyenne, Wyoming, and is buried at Pine Lake Cemetery.[47]

Marjory Clark (1876–1974), sometimes called Margaret, was born in Orange in August 1876 and lived there for eleven years. Thereafter, she

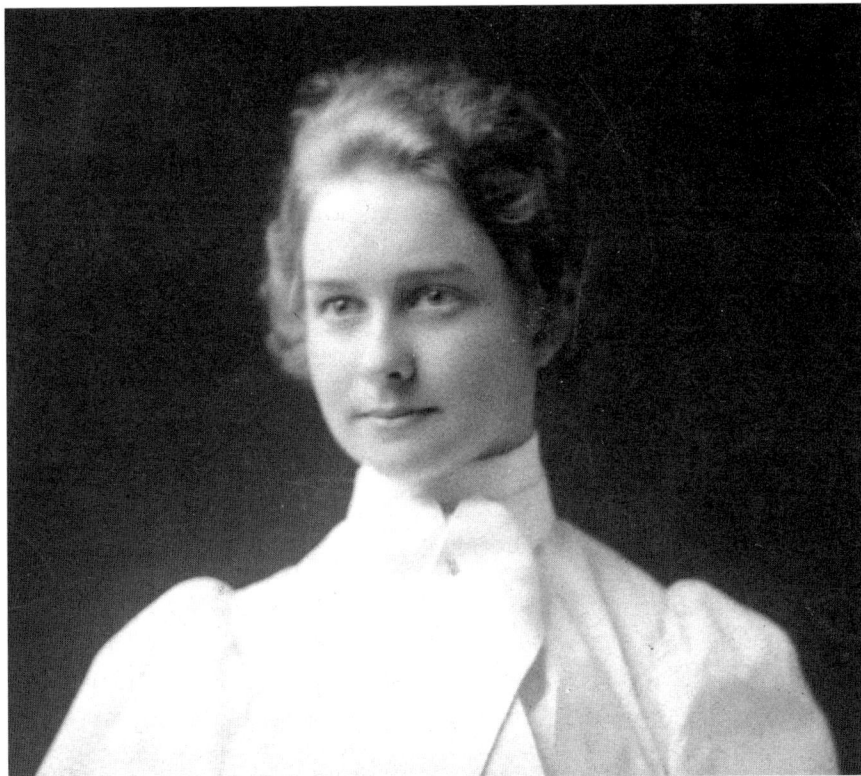

Mary Kate Clark, "Aunt Kate," circa 1897.

resided in La Porte and lived her later life in Michigan City, Indiana, not far from La Porte. She attended Abbott Academy at Andover, Massachusetts, graduating in 1895. She married Norton Wallace Barker (1875–1953) in 1896. While their marriage eventually ended in divorce, they had two children, mentioned in Mary Clark's memoir. Marjory never remarried. After her passing, she was buried at Pine Lake Cemetery. Today, her Michigan City home stands within a protected forested area. Marjory responded in May 1974 to the editor's request for early Orange information. Her letter arrived just a few months prior to her death. Some of her brief memory snippets are included hereafter in endnotes.[48]

Mary Kate Clark (1879–1960) resided in Orange eight years after her birth there in July 1879. She later attended Abbot Academy, like her sister Marjory, but did not graduate and went on to the Chicago Art Institute. She lived in La Porte until after her mother's death in 1922 and thereafter coordinated the typescript of *Pioneer Ranch Life*. She left La Porte and returned to Orange in 1926. There she lived in an apartment bungalow through at least 1929 and was employed as a stenographer and a nurse. Kate maintained at least part-time lodging in Hollywood during and perhaps before 1932. However, in 1932, she rented a house in Orange on East Palmyra Avenue. She later purchased another home on West Culver Avenue near her brother and his family. Kate never married. She lived her last years in an Orange residential care facility, dying there in 1960. She was buried at Pine Lake Cemetery.[49]

Donald Clark (1882–1957) lived in Orange less than five years after being born there in December 1882. He largely grew up in La Porte. Attending Philips Exeter Academy in New Hampshire, he thereafter entered Yale University, graduating in 1905. He settled in Seattle, Washington, for about four years but eventually left Seattle and came to Orange with his mother in 1909, intending at first to assist her in selling the Yale Grove. He changed his mind and decided to acquire for himself the easterly ten acres of the original twenty-acre site. He retained the old name while establishing a "new" Yale Grove. He cleared the older orange trees and planted trees of the Valencia orange variety, finding time to write his old Yale classmates, "I moved to Orange in October 1909 and settled on my father's old place, 'Yale Grove.' Still single but have hopes."

These hopes were fulfilled in 1912 when Donald Clark married Celia Mable Nunn (1881–1974) at the Palmyra Hotel, purchased in 1906 by Celia's father. Thereafter, the Palmyra Hotel, notorious in Mary Clark's remembrance of the boom of the 1880s, ironically continued a Clark family connection. Donald and Celia Clark raised a family of eleven children— nine boys and two girls. Donald prospered during World War I and was able to expand the original home to keep pace with the rising number of children. In the early 1920s, he moved the home slightly from its original location and added a second floor. The Depression hit him hard, and he struggled to keep the Yale Grove and the family together. With World War II, the demand for agricultural goods grew and financial stress eased. He and Celia proudly saw eight of their nine boys serve in the military during this conflict, all returning home. After World War II, Yale Grove achieved financial stability, and Donald could begin to retire. He maintained a high level of fitness at his age and could often be seen traveling on his bicycle. It was because of this activity that he died in November 1957 from injuries sustained by an automobile accident. He and his wife, Celia, rest at Fairhaven Memorial Park in Santa Ana, California. After his wife's death, sale of the property and subsequent urbanization saw the removal of Donald Clark's second Yale Grove in 1976.[50]

Frederick Augustus Clark (1840–1920), also known as F.A. Clark or Fred Clark (and hereafter referred to as Fred Clark), was affectionately called the "soldier uncle" by Mary Clark. Born in La Porte, he was an older brother of Albert. He started Wabash College as a prep-school student in 1856 but never graduated due to the Civil War. Enlisting in the Union army in April 1861, he eventually became a first lieutenant in the 29th Indiana Infantry Regiment. Here he performed topographic engineer duties and saw combat at the Battle of Chickamauga, Georgia, in 1863. He resigned his commission in April 1864 due to a "tubercular disease of the left lung."[51]

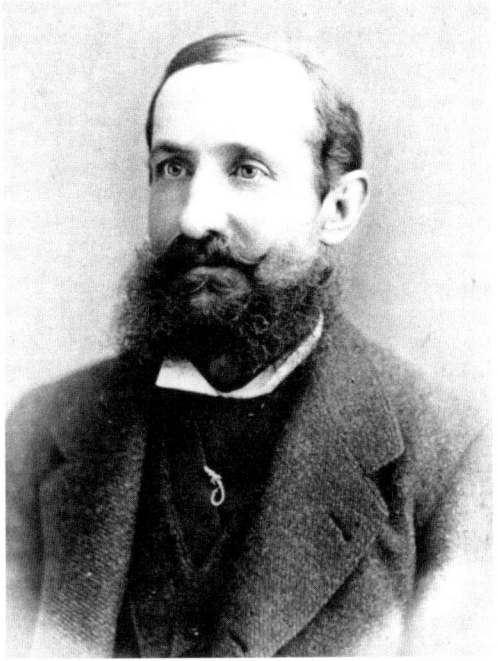

Frederick Augustus Clark, the "Soldier-Uncle," circa 1880. *Courtesy of La Porte County Historical Society.*

Despite this disability—or because of it in search of better health—he traveled to California. He found work in the Sierra Nevada foothills with the Mariposa Company, where he surfaces in October 1864 as part of Clarence King's survey party delineating the Yosemite park boundaries—activities that gave him special association with Yosemite when he joined Mary Clark and her daughters during their 1884 visit. He is mentioned several times by name in King's *Mountaineering in the Sierra Nevada* and in 1867 joined King's U.S. Geological Exploration of the Fortieth Parallel. He eventually did U.S. Geologic Survey topographical work in 1880 at Eureka, Nevada. That year, he married Sarah L. Dutcher in San Francisco. They lived in Oakland, where Fred worked as a Central Pacific Railroad terminal superintendent. Their marriage was short-lived, meeting with divorce in 1886. Fred remarried to Mary Adeline Clements, also known as Addie M. Clark, in 1888. Mary died in 1894, and Fred remained a widower thereafter, having one child, a stepdaughter named Pearl Clements Lewthwaite, by marriage to his second wife. After suffering financial setbacks, he accepted a clerical appointment

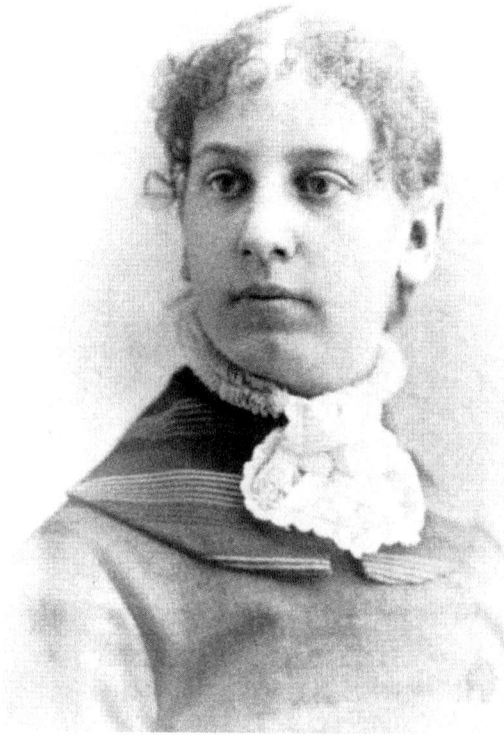

Unidentified photograph thought to be Harriet Candace "Rose" Clark, the "Artist Aunt." *Courtesy of La Porte County Historical Society.*

to the U.S. Army's West Point Academy in 1904. He lived his final years with his stepdaughter in New York City, passing away in 1920. He is buried alongside his second wife in the San Francisco National Cemetery at the Presidio.[52]

Harriet Candace Clark (1852–1942), called "Rose," figures in three of the later chapters of *Pioneer Ranch Life* as the "artist aunt." She was born in La Porte and was Albert Clark's half-sister, through his father's second wife, Harriet Crosby Clark. Rose graduated in 1872 from a progressive prep school known as Ferry Hall School in Chicago and later studied in New York City and Europe. Her specialty was portraits, flower arrangements and photography. She maintained studios in New York City and probably San Francisco. She went to Florence, Italy, in one of her foremost projects to help restore the Villa Curonia for Mabel Dodge Luhan, a wealthy arts patron. Her most important work was a portrait of a child entitled *Hester*, which is understood to hang at the Albright Art Gallery in Buffalo, New York. She taught art in later life but due to a fall was unable to do much work during her last years. She never married. Rose died in Buffalo, New York, in 1942 and rests at Pine Lake Cemetery.[53]

A final and frequently difficult issue deserves attention. As these memoirs now appear during this time of civil rights advancement, Mary Clark's remarks about ethnic and racial groups seem stereotyped and sometimes jarring. As a longtime meeting place of diverse populations, California often presents an unexpected jolt to newcomers—and even old-timers. In Mary's day, rural Indiana and even Chicago contained an overwhelming

INTRODUCTION

white European population, and as such, her previous diversity experience remained limited. She had to be familiar with the issues associated with the Civil War, including the African American–based slavery practiced in the antebellum South. In California, Mary confronted for the first time large numbers of Chinese and Latinos, coming into close association with some, particularly the farm help. Her reactions emerge from time to time sometimes couched with condescension. Mary commonly used the term "Spanish" to mean native Latino Californians, and "Mexican" to refer to farm help and others. She concluded that California's Latinos were a colorful but waning society lacking a work ethic. Her comments about the Chinese reflect similar attitudes, even viewing activities of her Chinese domestic, Ah Chong, as mildly ludicrous. Contrasted with the rant, "the Chinese must go," repeatedly proclaimed by many political orators and newspaper editors of her time, Mary's judgments are calm. The fact that she was a woman assured her own subordinate role. She had no voting rights. But regardless, she held an advantageous position of race and wealth, which gave her a privileged place in the social hierarchy. This was moderated by the close-to-the-earth pioneer situation she experienced. The Clarks worked alongside their farm and household employees with relatively little day-to-day difference in the degree of stress and strain, even though they clearly assumed the role of employer and landowners. This was a small farming operation, not reflecting the highly organized citrus industry that developed in California within the next few decades. The Chinese and Latinos employed at Yale Grove lived in close proximity to Mary, they were fed by Mary and Mary trusted them for security. Albert worked with them, doing similar manual work, as he was able. Rubbing shoulders lessened social differences but did not eliminate them. Without overlooking or downplaying her observations, it is fair to say that Mary wrote with values typical of an educated Victorian woman. Her personal history contributes to understanding California as the always-dynamic meeting place of numerous ethnic, racial and national groups.

The pioneer experience in Southern California after the Civil War, and particularly after the completion of the transcontinental railroad in 1869, did not reflect the covered-wagon spectacle depicted by Hollywood. Mary Clark's legacy writing reveals drama of a different type. Her words tell in great detail the daily life of those who arrived and built a new life in a comparatively vacant landscape. Her father and mother's experiences from early Indiana, as she heard them as a child in La Porte, served her well for her own pioneer life. While she saw her share of life's grubbiness, she wrote deeply about the undeveloped magnificence of the land around her.

Mary's words will serve future generations to find their own pioneer spirit to overcome adversity, appreciate the great changes affecting our lives and cherish the natural environment.

CHAPTER 1

THE JOURNEY

In the fall of 1875, my husband [Albert Barnes Clark], a young Chicago court reporter, our little girl Elsie [Elsie Treat Clark], and myself [Mary Teegarden Clark], bade adieu to our families and friends in Indiana, to seek an out-door life in Southern California. The journey of ten days was enlivened by pleasant companions, picturesque scenery, and frequent glimpses of gaily blanketed Indians and their children, who invariably gave the pennies bestowed upon them, to their fathers, to squander in fire-water.[54]

Among our treasured possessions for this trip was a small alcohol lamp, or so-called pocket cook stove, upon which we were then permitted to cook eggs, make tea or coffee or, best of all, to cook rice or macaroni for the baby. It was before the advent of dining cars, and with a little child, stops at the eating houses were difficult. This useful stove was the parting gift of Miss Sally Hobbs, a pioneer dressmaker of L. [La Porte] who had made all my best gowns, when I, as a grown child, loudly protested against the stiff whalebones and padding then in vogue but which I later regarded as marks of distinction. I remember one occasion, when in the absence of my careful Mother [Lura Treat Teegarden], I had inserted slender barrel hoops in my newly quilted petticoat to simulate the crinoline[55] then worn by ladies of quality. I had gone to show the splendid effect to Miss Sally, who was sewing in an upper chamber, when, standing awkwardly against the wall, the vaunted hoops flew over my head and gave me a stinging rebuke which I have never forgotten. Miss Sally is still enshrined in the memories of many of

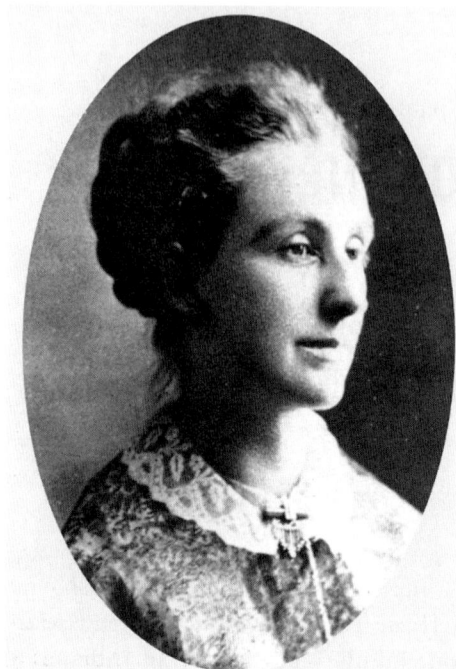

Mary Clark.

us, though she fell asleep by the wayside years ago and went to her well-deserved reward in the Better World.

But reminiscences must not crowd out the journey across the Continent, over fertile corn fields of Illinois, Iowa and Nebraska; the mountains and canyons of picturesque Colorado; Wyoming, full of interest to the mineralogist; Utah with its blot of Mormonism; and Nevada of the sage brush and alkali, crowded with mining prospectors, until, at length, the Golden Gate, in all its glory, burst upon our view. There stretched before us a vast ocean, whose boundaries were then more inaccessible than in this age of expansion, but flags of nearly every nation were even then flying in the harbor, from the familiar stars and stripes to the proud orange and red of Spain, the Union Jack, the Japanese standard, whose prowess has since become so great, and the pennants on the queer Chinese fishing junks. It was a sight never to be forgotten, and over all was the soft, cloudless sky, enveloped in the balmy, fragrant air, smiling down a welcome to the newcomers. Is it strange that once a Californian, one never proves recreant to his faith in the land, which enchants and holds one in its spell?[56]

Our first stop was with some cousins at the Occidental Hotel in San Francisco, where we were welcomed in true California fashion, and regaled with all the luxuries of the season. A drive to Cliff House was arranged for the first morning, where we breakfasted to the music of sea lions in their native haunts. Across the Bay, at Vallejo, a hospitable home [Starr Mansion] threw open its doors to us. Here I had my first glimpse of the graceful pepper and the acacia tree, the stately Australian eucalyptus and the golden orange, bearing ripe and green fruit and blossoms at the same time. In the flower garden, roses of every hue, pansies, heavenly-blue plumbago, violets and carnations ran riot in a mass of gorgeous color and delicious fragrance, while Japanese honeysuckles and a great variety of fuchsias clambered bravely up to the second-story windows. In this home, I first met "John Chinaman," who, in this case, was named "Ah Fong" and had on his right hand an extra finger, which added an element of mystery to this native of the Celestial Kingdom.[57]

It might be interesting to mention here that some years after this visit, the only daughter of these cousins, after extensive travels in foreign lands, married a Norwegian lawyer who now represents his country at the Egyptian Court, while his wife, a woman of rare accomplishments, graces society in winter in Alexandria and passes the summers in Norway, where her children enjoy all the pleasures of life among the fiords of that picturesque land.[58]

From Vallejo, we continued our journey southward by boat, touching at Santa Barbara, the home of artists and poets, one of the choicest spots in all California. Here we left the steamer and drove into the beautiful Montecito Valley, where for an hour or two, we sat under the vine and fig tree of our old friends, the B's [Bonds], whose garden was a revelation to us and whose Smyrna figs and cream food for the gods.[59]

On to Los Angeles—City of Angeles—by steamer via Wilmington, thence by rail to Anaheim, an early German colony, where we took a lumbering four-horse stagecoach five miles to Richland, now known as Orange.[60] We arrived at candle light and halted at the only hostelry—known as the "Hygean Home," kept by one Dr. Clapp, the whole place a travesty, for comfort there was none. The beds were rudely carved of redwood, without springs, and with straw ticks and calico curtains and valances.[61]

Devoured by curiosity, I arose early the next morning, from an uneasy sleep, to see what manner of country was to be our chosen home. And the first thing I saw was a diminutive owl perched on the windowsill, bowing and blinking at me with almost superhuman wisdom. As far as eye could reach, the

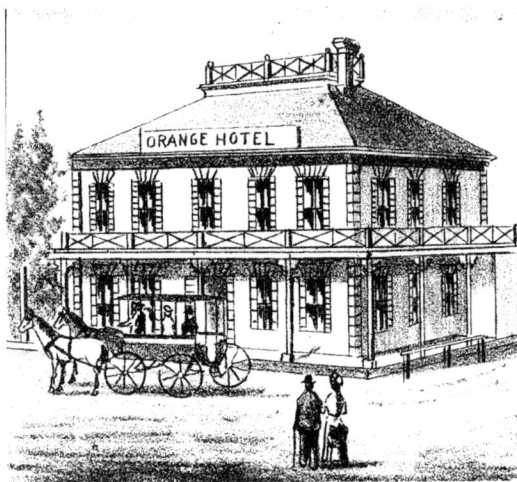

Drawing of the Orange Hotel, formerly the "Hygean Home" of abysmal memory by Mary Clark. *From Orange, Cal., Illustrated and Described (1886).*

boasted orange trees were mere whips between rows of corn. An unpalatable breakfast, served by a Chinaman, and the discovery that "ditch" water was the prevailing beverage gave me a mild fit of the blues.

As it had been heralded over the countryside, that we, the newcomers, wanted to buy a home, the settlers came to take us about to see their real estate. We drove in beach wagons through sheep ranches of immense extent, over arroyos and through canyons in search of a home. What a misnomer when only one house in the small settlement of a store and a blacksmith shop could boast of a real brick chimney and a rag carpet! The only way to get meat was to have the stage driver bring it from Anaheim, five miles away, and pay him a commission.[62]

Another feature of the country, which set in a few days after our arrival, was the Santa Ana wind, which came across the Mohave Desert, lasted three days and blew a perfect cloud of dust and heat—a mild edition of the African Simoon. The sunrises and sunsets were magnificent and the mountains grand, but we missed the twilight hour of home…as to fleas in the Hygean Hotel, they were legion, and we waged many hard battles to vanquish them, but without success. One dear lady from New York state somewhat allayed the pangs of my homesick heart by inviting me over to eat watermelon and home-grown raisins. And her kindness continued through all the years, as one by one, my little children picked clove pinks in her sweet garden, whose scent wafted me back to my father's garden of long ago.[63]

CHAPTER 2

THE FIRST CHRISTMAS

Aftter repeated efforts, since no ranch for sale but one had a house on it, and that one was set in a cactus patch and almost uninhabitable, the would-be farmer, seeing my fast increasing dismay and heart-ache, decided to go to the steamer landing,[64] twelve miles away, and remark our household goods for home, giving up his long cherished plans for an outdoor life in California. News of this latest move was at once sent to a devoted father [Abraham Teegarden], who began to prepare a ten-acre country place that he owned in Indiana for our occupancy. His message was, "If you must have country life, Lakeview is at your disposal as soon as the little house can be renovated." He went to work, painting and repairing and trimming up the orchard and vineyard. And if he thought his daughter lacking in the grit that she should have inherited from her Connecticut and Ohio forebears, he did not reproach her but showed once more his tender care.

It was Sunday, and I had been to say good-by to the dear old lady [Mrs. Beach] of the flower garden, my only friend in a new country. She had tried to encourage me to be brave and remain in the land that she had learned to love, despite its privations, but I was inexorable. Nothing appealed to me while the waves of homesickness surged over me. I sat on the hotel veranda, with Elsie on my lap, and all ready for the journey except to draw on my gloves. The stage drove up, with jolly Neal[65] [Henry Neill] on the box, looking a bit curiously at the "homesick lady from the East." The trunks were strapped on and every preparation made for departure, when all at once, with a great rush, I realized what a coward I was to turn my back on the

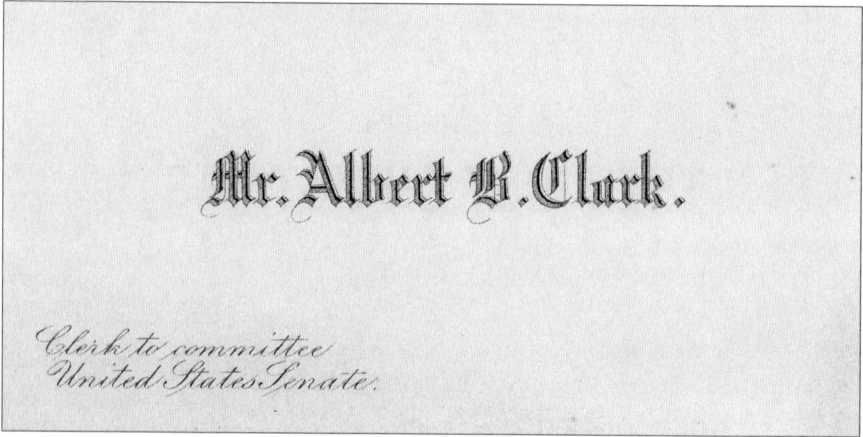

Card showing Albert Clark as a U.S. Senate clerk.

country which had been my husband's goal for years. If he—a college-bred man—was willing to give up a good business, with its advantages, for the sake of health and an outdoor life, why should I be a stumbling block instead of a help-mate? I braced up quickly, and the old Puritan in me flamed in my cheeks at the lack of courage I had displayed. When he had made all final arrangements and came to help me into the high seat, I refused to go.

> "Wonder of wonders! Will you really be content to stay? Are you sure that, woman-like, you will not change with the wind?"
> "No," I said, "give me one more chance, and I will show you what I can do."

The empty stage drove away, and the people about the hotel looked very incredulous as our trunks were carried in again. The next morning, the goods were remanded from the steamer landing, and I went out after breakfast to find a room in the cottage of an educated Irish woman who, through unfortunate investments, has lost all, save her home. We set up a few household goods here, as for instance, two beds and a couple of bureaus and chairs, and I was allowed the use of the kitchen stove. Under the bed was a loaded gun, a bath tub and a row of shoes; in one corner, two trunks and a table, while two clothesbaskets served as receptacles for groceries and other necessities. The china closet was in the lower part of the bureau, and in the upper drawers we kept table linen and silver. In another corner were ranged tea kettle, gridirons and frying pans, and on the shady side of the house was a dry goods box, where potatoes and the precious bottles of home-made yeast were kept. The only ice box was a small wire safe, open at both ends, and hanging in the breeze, to preserve the milk and meat, when I was so fortunate as to have any of the latter. It will be understood that cellars were not in vogue here, as the deeper one went under ground, the warmer it grew, one of the peculiar features of a semi-tropical country. Before it escapes me, let me whisper to the house-wives who may read this chronicle that I had real ice only once in thirteen years, and that was in a case of typhoid fever, when it was sent down by rail from Los Angeles.[66]

The settlement of Orange was only three years old, and while promising, there were many drawbacks for people whose lives had been spent in the cities and towns of older countries. A Methodist church had been built, which formed a strong bond to hold the settlers together, and it was an inspiring sight on Sunday mornings to see the simple-hearted people gathering around the altar, praising God in the good, old-fashioned way. I am most firmly convinced that this life of comparative hardship and sacrifice had uprooted all traces of selfishness. The generosity of neighbors in sending a pat of butter, a pound of honey or even a basket containing a shoulder of pork and a few quail was not at all uncommon. One day, a farmer came in, bringing his little daughter—a few

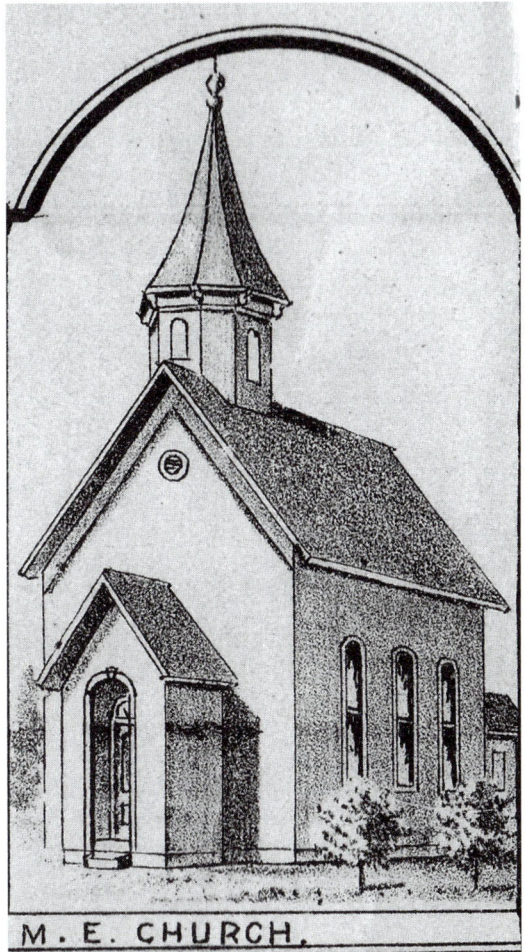

M.E. CHURCH.

Drawing of the Orange Methodist Church building. *From Orange, Cal., Illustrated and Described (1886).*

years older than Elsie. He told me that my father [Abraham Teegarden], in the early forties [1840s] in Northern Indiana, had been his family physician whose kindly services he could never forget, for in those days, doctors had to be nurses as well. And as Leroy Armstrong says in his novel *The Outlaws*, "There was unconscious pathos in the practice of those old doctors. Heaven rest them, for they earned it when the land was young." This neighbor unfolded a napkin from over his basket and took out a spare rib and two quarts of delicious strawberries, while the child presented Elsie a bunch of spicy pinks. Surely no life, save one lived close to God and Nature, can foster such sentiments as these.[67]

As horse thieves were about, the team which we had purchased was kept in a corral back of the hotel, and my husband swung his hammock and slept there—a loaded revolver under his pillow—while I stayed with the baby in our little room, which had taken on some homelike features, as familiar belongings were unpacked from our store.[68] Now began the search for a home, and twenty acres, in the heart of the settlement, was finally decided upon [deed dated October 22, 1875]. It was a mustard patch, and on Christmas Day in 1875, I sat on a flowery knoll of anemones and buttercups and saw my husband, with his strong horses—Bell and Rattler—clear it with a drag. The late afternoon shadows were falling about us. The baby was playing with what she called "spring beauty wildflowers," and the tall mustard stalks, whose seeds were scattered by the early Jesuit Fathers,[69] were everywhere laying in the path of the drag, when I suddenly remembered the Day. Quickly visions of richly-browned turkey; great mounds of cranberry jelly; and crisp, juicy mince pies, with my grandmother [Elcy Tracy Treat] presiding over it all, appeared to me. Then, in the next breath, I remembered our slender larder of bacon and potatoes, and the contrast was too great. I begged that the tired horses be given a rest, then harnessed up again to go—not exactly "twelve miles to a lemon," to quote Gail Hamilton,[70] but five miles to a mutton chop.

My request was smilingly granted. We made ourselves ready and were soon jogging along past vast orchards of almonds and orange, vineyards of Mission and Muscat grapes, and vegetable gardens of the patient Chinese. The earth's mantle of dingy brown was fast changing, by the marvelous touch of the Rain Goddess, into greens of most exquisite beauty. The near-by foothills were transcendent in their colorings, and the hitherto parched creek bed was warbling a song of plenty and peace; for the rain is indeed the gold of this favored land—so dependent upon irrigation for the success of its fruit, gardens and grain fields. At length,

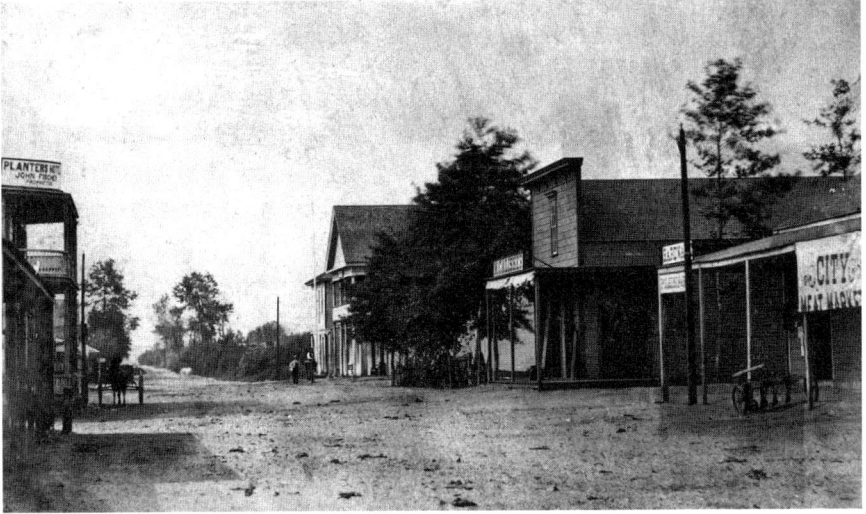

Anaheim street scene, 1875. Note the "City Meat Market" sign on right. Did the Clarks buy their Christmas mutton chops here? *Courtesy of Anaheim Public Library.*

our evening drive brought us to the haven of my desires, and in a very small but neatly kept shop on one of the quaint streets of Anaheim,[71] we found those mutton chops, which to this day stand unexcelled in my memory. Only think of it, ye people who dwell there now, with all the comforts and luxuries of an older country, at your doors, what a simple feast meant to us then, and on Christmas Day too!

We drove home through the fast falling darkness, for here we had not that magic twilight which envelops more northerly countries. The patient animals were tethered in their corral, for a barn had not yet been built, and the sleepy child was given her cup of milk and quickly undressed for the journey into dreamland. A fire of corncobs was lighted in the cook stove in the little room which served as both dining room and kitchen. The table was soon laid with a white cloth, a wheaten loaf and a pat of butter, while the juicy chops sizzled on the coals. I have never forgotten that meal or the content in our hearts, with the cricket on the hearth singing through it all. It was truly a feast, though not the typical Christmas cheer, and the old adage, "Hunger is the best sauce," was surely verified in this case. We did not attempt a tree for our little girl, but she had hung up her stocking in the good old-fashioned way, and as she had not yet learned to disbelieve in Santa Claus, he came down the chimney and left her a most gorgeous kite made of old London Graphics[72] with a wondrously long tail. The next day, she flew it nearly to the moon, and later, when her birthday was celebrated by a small party, the Christmas kite figured largely in the program.[73]

In order to arrange our business matters, it now became necessary for us to go by stage to Santa Barbara to the only national bank in the southern country at this time.[74] On the weird ride of over one hundred miles, stopping at small, rude stations in the deeply wooded country where corn bread, saleratus biscuits,[75] fried rabbit and muddy coffee were invariable served, we were accompanied by two San Francisco detectives on the look-out for Mexican horse thieves. Their muttered conversations in Spanish, as we drove all the dark night, through the still darker woods, their sudden exits from the stage at every stopping place, their revolvers, and general air of espionage gave a flavor of mystery to what would otherwise have been a tiresome journey.

The next move was the hauling of lumber to build a house, which had been planned the night before we left Chicago.[76] At this time, every man did his own teaming, and many a day have rosy Elsie and I perched on the wagon and made the twelve miles to Newport Landing, coming back on the load of lumber, every stick of which meant so much to us now—a dear home in a new country. Later, there were trips to the Willows[77] to bring the poles for firewood. Seventy-five poles made a load, and it took a dozen loads to last a year, at twelve dollars a dozen. The poles had to be sawed and split while green, and as it was done during the rainy season, when other work did not interfere, it was necessary to bake all the split wood in the oven before using. For kindling, we gathered dried leaves of eucalyptus, and for broiling, we saved up corncobs. An open fire, together with the cook stove, furnished all the heat we needed and added greatly to the cheer of our home.

About this time, there was an addition to our family—neither a calf nor a colt but a little Virginia girl who had lost her mother and who came to assist in the light work. She was only seven years old yet carried on her small shoulders much responsibility, for her parents had given her the illustrious name of Pocahontas, which I was obliged to curtail to Poca. She proved quite helpful for a short time, but when she became a care, I returned her to her father.

CHAPTER 3

HOMEMAKING

L ittle by little, the house went up—four good rooms—with wide porches in the front and rear, a brick chimney and a fire-place. The inside rooms were finished with unbleached muslin tacked over the boards, and years elapsed before we found time to put on all the wallpaper, but we appreciated it the more for having looked so long upon dark redwood wall. As fast as possible, the rooms were finished and our goods unpacked. And what joy it was to see once more familiar carpets, comfortable rocking chairs and the well-beloved books and pictures! Even the cook stove, which I had insisted upon bringing, looked at me gratefully and conjured up visions of delicious dinners in the past to be reproduced in the future. To say that our house was homelike does not half express it, for it was really beautiful to us in its simplicity, and we had already begun to realize the great possibilities of climate in the making of orchard and garden.

Now the winter rains set in, and the whole country blossomed as a rose. Everywhere about us, the vacant acres were carpeted with nemophila or "baby blue-eyes," a most charming little flower, while blushing spring beauties lifted their graceful heads and plumy Indian pinks, lemon-drops, poppies of every hue and lupines of rare beauty seemed to spring forth, as by magic, after the warm rains. The lady with the little child in the wicker carriage, piled full of blossoms, was a familiar sight in the country highway. We strolled miles without knowing it, in the pleasant winter sunshine, with the floral kingdom all around us—orioles, meadow larks and mocking birds

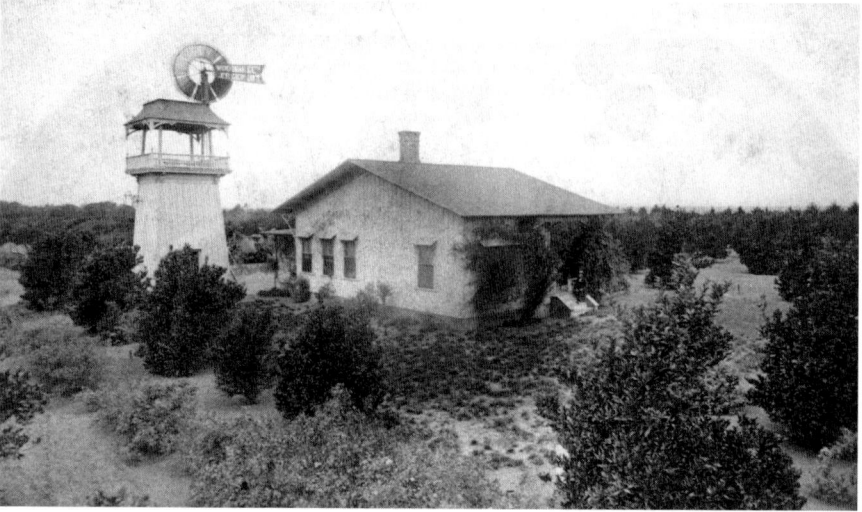

The Clark ranch house at Yale Grove looking northwest. Watkins photograph, 1880.

singing in the wayside hedges, and far away, the lofty peaks of San Antonio and Temescal wearing their snowy crowns.[78]

Now we began to find friends, for there were the Warrens from Pennsylvania, the Harrises from Indiana, as well as others from Michigan, Wisconsin and Illinois who had built homes and planted orchards and vineyards and were people of intelligence. Here, too, we met our first New Church people—an English family—with whom we always enjoyed much pleasant intercourse. Truly, the "Simple Life" so eloquently portrayed by Pastor Wagner was then at its zenith in favored Richland.[79] There were no castes or classes; all were alike in their hospitality and friendly regard. No one had an abundance, yet he was willing and ready to share with his new and less fortunate neighbor. Among the early settlers were many from the South, who had sought this favored land after the ravages of the Civil War had destroyed their homes. More kindly people I have never known than these who had lived through the times that tried men's souls, and women's too, yet were bravely building up the waste places and seeking happiness again. It would be base ingratitude, should I for a moment forget their freely offered help in time of great need.

In the course of time, we began to set out our orchard, planting first the northern fruits—peach, apricot, nectarine, pear, apple and a variety of plums—as well as a few English walnuts and bananas. We were loath to ignore the cherry, which while it blossoms does not fruit successfully in this

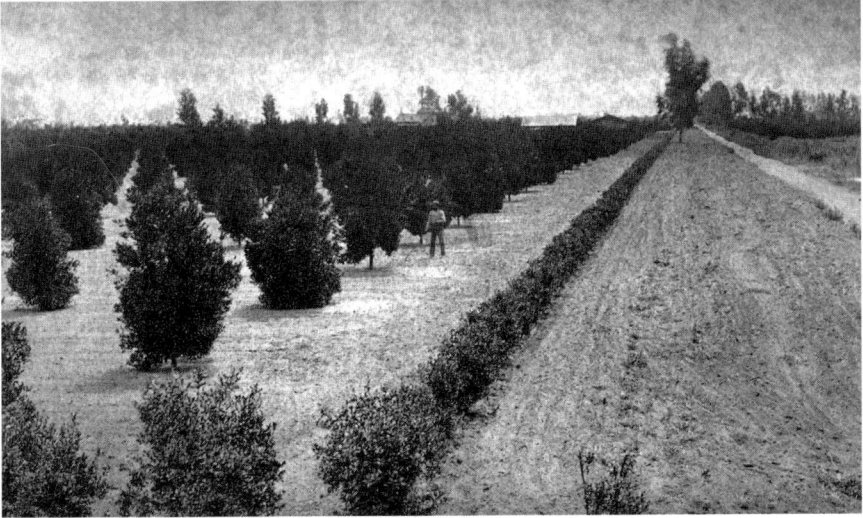

View of Yale Grove with lime-hedge border looking east along Palmyra Avenue. The person in the photograph is Diego Granillo, the resident farmhand. Watkins photograph, 1880.

section but attains its perfection in the far-famed Santa Clara Valley. Into furrows of soft, sandy loam, we scattered seeds of all the early vegetables. Delightfully long rows of marrow-fat peas and hills of early rose potatoes were planted—then a strawberry bed and rows of raspberry and blackberry bushes. An alfalfa patch was made, and early corn for fodder was put in, while a hedge of limes was planted on the border. The driveway, purposely irregular but broad and inviting, led up to the great porch in the rear, where we really lived most of the time, as here we worked and ate our meals and dreamed moonlight nights in the shadows cast by the roses and vines, with the ravishing mocking bird's song our only music. The path was purple with great clumps of heliotrope and rosy with real hydrangeas, tropical with palms and bamboos and fragrant with laurustinus and the choicest of roses. Fig trees were planted where their shade would be grateful, and the porches were twined with white banksia roses and jasmine, while violets and ferns grew in shady nooks. For the dear humming birds, we planted white and coral bouvardia and honeysuckle. And in the garden was a trellis of fifty tea roses which in after years was noted by every traveler as a "thing of beauty and a joy forever."[80]

CHAPTER 4

DEVELOPMENT OF WATER

As soon as possible, after the house and barn had been completed, the question of a well was agitated, since pure drinking water was a most important factor in our life. The water-works of the small town consisted of a tank in the center, with pipes in several directions, to supply the immediate neighborhood. Most of the farmers had crude cisterns which when they irrigated were filled with muddy water, for at this time, there was a system of bringing the river water from above in open ditches.[81] If they had intelligently boiled it before drinking, the ravages of typhoid might have been less. As it was, there were frequent cases of the fever, often fatal, with doctors in attendance who sometimes prescribed whisky instead of milk.

There was but one drive well in the vicinity, so when operations began at "Yale Orange Grove" (for the owner, with that lingering affection which every college-bred man feels for his alma mater, had thus named this orchard home), the whole countryside was interested. When the extensive well-boring apparatus, with men to operate it, for this was before the day of engines to do this work—in our valley at least—arrived on the scene, the heretofore quiet place took on the air of a small mining camp. Day after day, we were invaded by curious crowds—some sitting on the sawbuck or step-ladder, as most convenient, and others in groups all over the backyard. And as I stood at the pantry window, working over butter or mixing bread, such exclamations as these were wafted to my ears. "I reckon you all will strike ile [oil] if you keep on towards China." And the lank Southerner fixed his eye on a certain spot and aimed for it with great success, while old Mr.

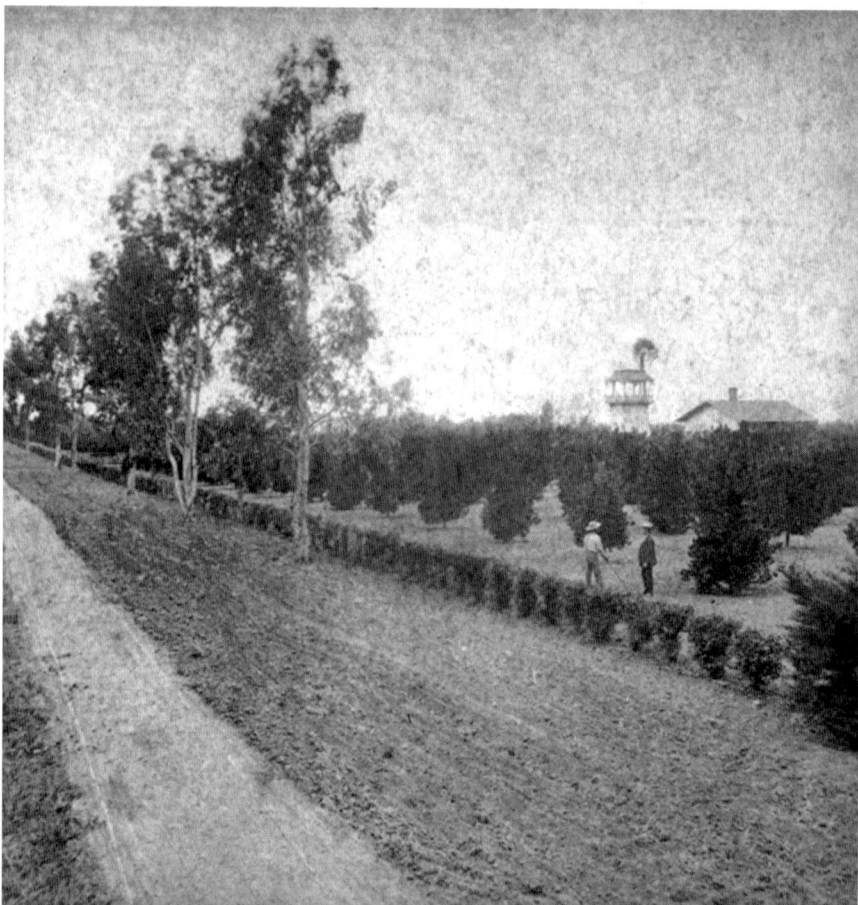

Yale Grove looking northwest along Palmyra Avenue with Granillo and ranch superintendent William H.H. Clayton. Watkins photograph, 1880.

Stickney, going on Yankee-like with his whittling, replied, "Wall! Onless I be all-fired mistaken, there's a good show here for artesian water." And so it went on, every fellow venturing an opinion, while the trimly built young ranchman, clad in knickerbockers, leggings and sombrero, in which attire he was often mistaken for an Englishman, made some droll reply, as he, with his assistants, drove harder the sledge hammers. The spectators sat and prophesied and chewed most industriously for hours at a stretch, often oblivious of meal time, while the slow work went on, for every now and then, tools would be lost entirely or broken in the attempt to bore through solid rock. The well was at length finished. It was one hundred feet deep, and the water was pure and soft. Some people came with barrels on wagons to cart our water away, and it was no easy task to convince them that our precious commodity, having cost nearly its weight in gold, could not be distributed except in emergencies. A windmill was erected and water piped to the house and adjacent garden.[82]

Next came the planting of the young orange trees which had been specially budded for us in an adjacent nursery. The varieties were Washington Navel, Mediterranean Sweet, St. Michael, Tangerine, Blood and a great many Seedlings—all on orange roots. At this time, the Seedling was in high favor, but it is now almost superseded by the Navel, whose main point of vantage is its lack of seeds. It would be interesting to trace back the history of this much-desired variety, which was originally sent out by the Agricultural Department at Washington and sparingly distributed in the form of buds among the nurserymen of Southern California. From this small beginning have come all the famous navel orchards of Riverside, Redlands, Pomona, Azusa, Duarte and many others.[83]

About this time, Japanese loquat and persimmons and the queer Chinese saucer peach were imported and planted in most of the orchards—more as curiosities than as a source of revenue. A camphor tree, from the Agricultural Department, became quite a curiosity, too, in our garden, and magnolias, as well as a variety of palms, were fast adding to the beauty of the scene.[84]

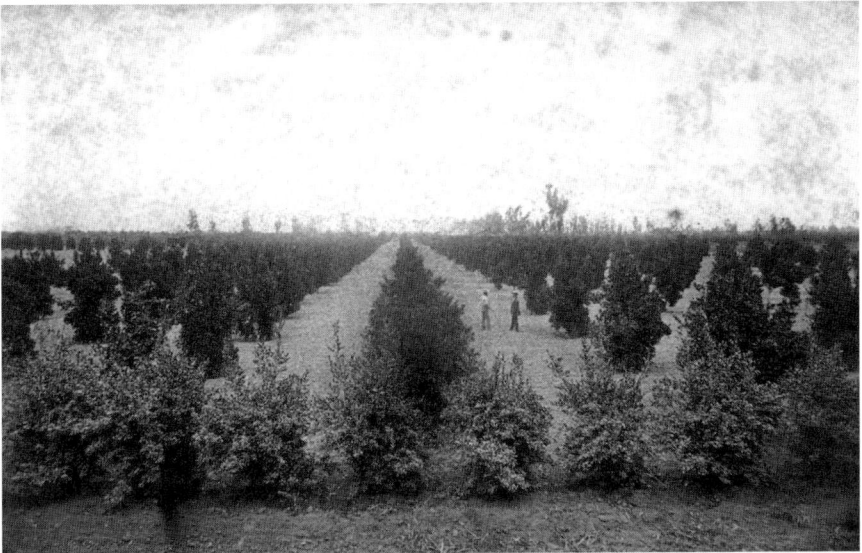

Yale Grove looking east from Batavia Street with lime hedge in foreground. Clayton is on the right, with Granillo in the orchard. Watkins photograph, 1880.

In order to irrigate, basins were made around every tree, and water was hauled in barrels and poured on plentifully so that the best results might afterward be obtained. In this way, by hard and constant labor, the young orchard was kept like a garden. The soil was continually stirred, either by irrigation and cultivation, or by deep plowing and harrowing. And as weeds grew all the year, the work of the fruit grower never ceased. As fast as one job was done, it was time to begin on another.

About this time, I was sent out with a barley sack to bag cats to kill gophers.[85] After making the rounds of an entire neighborhood, I returned with six lusty kittens and was, in consequence, received with open arms by the ardent orchardist. Now rabbits began to eat the young tender bark and shots of the trees, so tiny fences of lath, or layers of cloth, had to be put around the trunks. The next purchase was a Jersey cow—cost sixty dollars—giving sixteen quarts of milk a day. Then a kind neighbor presented us with a dog which ate a pound of raisins each day in his master's vineyard and was therefore no longer profitable to him.

When the first Independence Day came around [July 4, 1876], we were fired with patriotism and had a small display that night, all to ourselves. As little Elsie and I sat on the steps and clapped our hands as the rockets and Roman candles went off, we little reckoned what was in store for us. The next morning, when we looked for the baby carriage, we found only a skeleton, for it had been carelessly left out in the orchard, and a patriotic rocket had struck and burned it up, except the running gear.

I had received a very suggestive birthday present of a churn, and the first butter was so good that the baby ate it all off her bread at every opportunity. I will not omit to say that the bottom was churned out of more than one churn before I achieved success in butter making, and it was at first a matter of regret that I had not served an apprenticeship on a dairy farm before seeking California.[86] The question of working dresses soon became a problem, as this was before the day of ready-to-wear clothes and I was no seamstress myself. So I wrote home to my sister [Myra Bell Teegarden] to have a sewing-bee and make me some stout calico frocks, as plain as a Quaker. My own good dresses still reposed in the depths of a Saratoga trunk, not to reappear until later, when our orchard was in bearing.

CHAPTER 5

IRRIGATION

As I have before mentioned, there was in 1875 a system of irrigation which consisted of bringing the water from the head of the Santa Ana River in open ditches. But owing to seepage and evaporation, this method was very unsatisfactory. So, as the valley filled up with men of energy and intelligence, the burning question of a better water supply was agitated. In 1877, the Santa Ana Valley Irrigation Company was incorporated and the owner of "Yale Grove" chosen its first president. The first meeting of the new water board was held on our blue-grass plot, and I could but admire the grave earnestness of the few staunch men who had the welfare of our valley most deeply at heart.[87]

There were now many interruptions of farm work, owing to this new enterprise, so that meals often waited for hours, and it was no uncommon occurrence to have one after another come into the orchard, until finally the whole Board of Directors was there, to hold an informal meeting around my husband's plow. The subscription books were opened August 21, 1877, and stock to the amount of $10,000 was at once taken. This was not a movement savoring in the least of speculation but only the brave effort of honest men to secure better water facilities. Each season seemed drier than the preceding, and it was absolutely necessary that something be done. This was a time that tried men's souls, and those who put their shoulders to the wheel had many and great responsibilities. There were claims to be satisfied, all sorts of conciliations to be made and above all, capital to be secured to carry on the work. It required hard labor and steady brains, but the men of that day were

Santa Ana Valley Irrigation

COMPANY.

SUBSCRIBERS' MEETING.

NOTICE is hereby given to all Subscribers to the Capital Stock of the Santa Ana Valley Irrigation Company that there will be a meeting of the subscribers aforesaid at the School House in Orange, California, on

Thursday, September 6th, 1877,

At 10 o'clock A. M., for the purpose of adopting the By-Laws of said Company.
Called by order of

W. C. McCLAY,
Acting President of Board of Directors.
Orange, Los Angeles county, California,
August 23d, 1877. td

Official notice to SAVI stockholders of bylaws approval meeting. *From* Los Angeles Evening Express, *August 23, 1877.*

equal to the task. Their own farms were neglected and their services of time and money freely given rather than face the disaster which must come unless that water system was improved.[88]

The new canal was fifteen miles long, ten feet wide on the bottom and twenty-two feet on top and carried six thousand miners' inches of water. It followed, in the main, the path of the old Mexican canal, but it was necessary to tunnel through the hills at the head of the valley. And this tunnel, a quarter of a mile long, was a fine piece of workmanship, constructed through solid rock. The completed canal cost $55,000, and all disputed rights thereto were purchased. It was a heavy tax on those who had large acreage, but the majority were orchardists or vine-growers, owning from twenty to sixty acres; and it must be said that, one and all, they accepted the situation and supported the directors most nobly in the completion of the enterprise. It was good work—carefully planned and honestly executed by those in charge.[89]

It may be interesting to explain somewhat more fully regarding the management of the water system. The water directorate, elected annually by the stockholders at their first meeting, appointed a superintendent of canals and a number of zanjeros, of whom one was the head and under the superintendent directed the others. In the Santa Ana Valley Irrigation Company, they met at the water office every day at ten o'clock and conferred with each other—and the clerk and superintendent and any stockholders—and copied each for his own territory the orders for water which had come in. They were charged with the duty of measuring the water that went to each orchardist and of seeing that no one got more than his allotted share. I can see the little water office standing in the heart of the settlement—a beacon light to all who wished to invest in property there. For it meant that

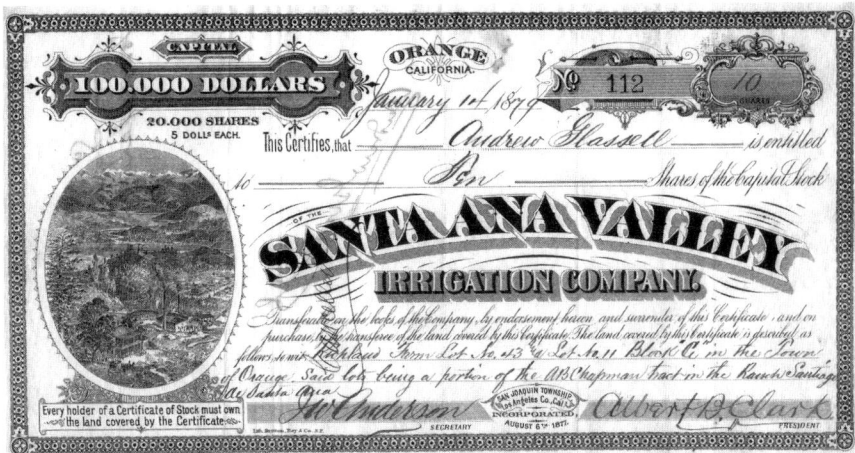

1879 SAVI stock certificate signed by President Albert B. Clark and company secretary J.W. Anderson. *Courtesy of Sherman Library.*

the canals were full of water when needed and that the rain and snow on the distant mountains would swell the river so that it could flow into their very door yards and keep their orchards, vineyards and alfalfa fields green and flourishing. It meant everything to that locality, which I have chosen to call by its early and, to me, pleasing name of "Richland."[90]

In describing the process of irrigation, my memory may be somewhat at fault, as eighteen years have elapsed since I abdicated my position as orange grower. However, be it understood that there was one main canal with smaller ones converging from it, and when the water was in the Chicago ditch, on our north line, it behooved us to be ready to take it in turn. Sometimes it took nearly a week to get ready for the irrigation. Your main ditch must be cleaned out and ready for use, with the big tapoons to shut off the water when necessary. Then furrows must be plowed in all the tree rows where the precious stream was to flow. At first, we used the basin system of enclosing each tree and flooding it, but later, the furrow system was universally adopted. When your turn came, the zanjero, whose duty it was to turn in your water and to see that the gates were all right, came tearing in on his broncho, and two stout Mexicans in huge rubber boots, armed with shovels, were in readiness to handle the water. Even the children sallied forth with small shovels to irrigate their playhouse garden, while the stream ran joyfully over the precious grass plot and the flowers near the house. It was full of little birds, hopping and bathing. In fact, all nature was brimming over with life, for in a dry and thirsty land, there is no treasure—

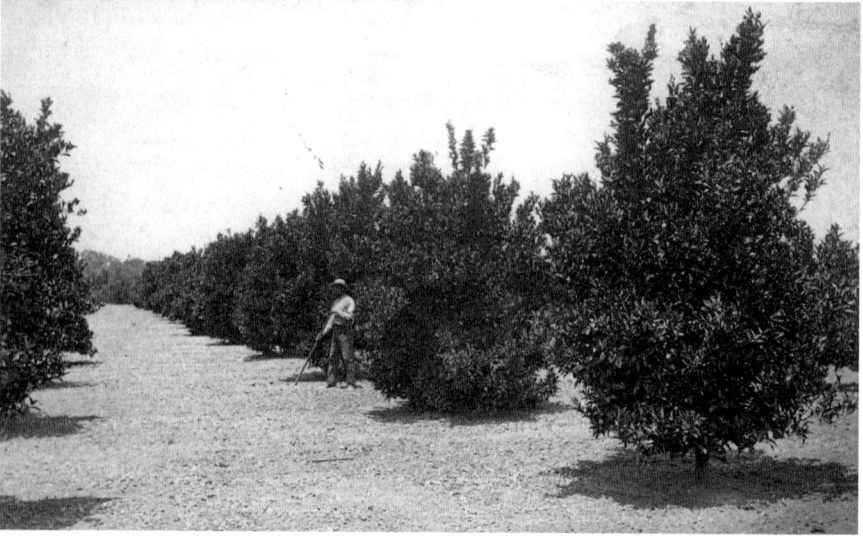

Yale Grove interior view with Diego Granillo. Watkins photograph, 1880.

not even gold—so great as water. A prolonged drought curled the orange tree leaves, and one almost despaired at their shriveled appearance, when one good run of water, if it only came in time, made them all fresh and crisp in a few hours. The troublesome gophers were also drowned, and it was said that the rich sediment in the river water was good for the trees.[91]

I have known as high as eighty hours of water on the place at one run, which was often secured by renting extra stock. Day water was fifty cents an hour, and night water half as much, so that with the services of two men to properly handle it, an irrigation [of the orchard] meant the expenditure of a good many dollars, not counting the labor of a man and team in preparing for it. It was certainly one of the great events in our life, as so much depended upon it. If the water came at night, lanterns were hung on the trees, and lunch, with hot coffee, provided for the men, for it required robust physique as well as good judgment and experience to be proficient in this ranch work. The faithful services, at an early period, of Diego Granillo, and later those of Jean Ramon Arguello, contributed greatly to the success of our orchard, and they always commanded our regard for their invariably respectful demeanor and lively interest in their work.[92]

CHAPTER 6

THE MASSACRE OF THE INNOCENTS

The years had flown apace, and while the orange grove was approaching bearing age, other expedients such as butter making, the raising of small fruits and the marketing of eggs—a somewhat uncertain proposition at times in every farmer's experience—were resorted to, to increase the family exchequer.

Instead of one, there were now three little sisters: Elsie, Marjory and Kate. Before the advent of Marjory, one brilliant August day [August 10, 1876], the kind neighbor who had promised to perform the first services for the child was most unfortunately dragged by her cow while staking the animal in the alfalfa patch. Consequently, there was suspense and wailing at "Yale Grove" until another neighbor, who had as a girl in a pink brocaded satin gown danced at Tyler's Inaugural Ball,[93] was called in and the baby duly initiated into the mysteries of life on an orange farm. The day before the third sister came along, in peach time, the mother canned forty quarts of the delicious fruit, so that Kate [July 17, 1879] always reminded us of a ripe peach—so delicately tinted were her round cheeks. Each child had her orange tree, and a real playhouse with a porch, two windows, a door and a low fence surrounding its garden had been built by the thoughtful father. On one side grew a Hermosa rose; on the other, a flowering pomegranate, while in front, a Chinese umbrella tree raised its green canopy to shade the little workers as they planted seeds in tiny beds, painted pictures in old magazines, had tea parties on their table or, best of all, played "ladies," wearing their mother's long dresses and flouncing in and out with their dolls.

Among other possessions we had raised a flock of forty hens which, with several pompous roosters and a gay turkey gobbler, plumed themselves in

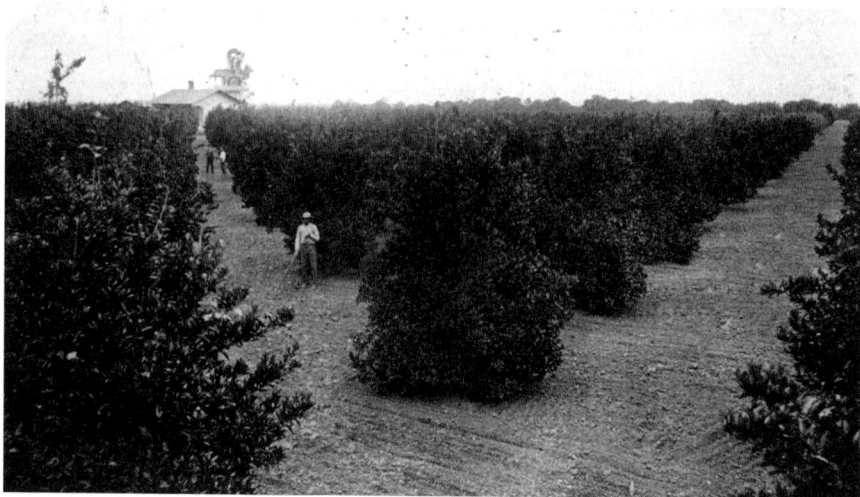

Yale Grove interior view showing Granillo in front, Clayton and friend to the rear and the ranch house in the distance. Watkins photograph, 1880.

the safely built extensive chicken yard near the barn, a considerable distance from the house. In the establishment was an ever faithful heathen named "Ah Chong" who alternately drove a one-horse plow in the vegetable garden, picked blackberries, boiled clothes on an improvised furnace in the backyard, scoured pots and kettles and made himself useful in all sorts of out-door work. An attempt had been made by Elsie, after her teaching in Sunday school, to convert Ah Chong. He listened politely to her plea, but all he said was, "You learn Chinese first," which settled the matter for once and all. He had in his small room adjoining the tool house a most mysterious glass jar, into which he cast everything from a sprig of parsley to a grasshopper to make what he called "heap good medicine." I have seen many a horned toad disporting itself in the depths of this wonderful bottle, which was every now and then well shaken up and taken in great tablespoonfuls for some probably imaginary ailment. Every Christmas, a silk handkerchief of bright color and generous proportions found its way to me from Chong's capacious padded jacket, and for the children, there were always Chinese lilies, nuts or wonderfully colored dangling paper lanterns with gay tassels.[94]

One spring morning, as we all sat at breakfast on the vine-covered porch enjoying the "Cloth of Gold" roses which hung in fragrant clusters about us and the yellow poppies that completely carpeted the long driveway, we saw Ah Chong, in white blouse and queer Chinese hat, running toward us, excitedly calling, "Chickee allee dead—coyote come—eatee him allee!"

Father, mother and children three all flew toward the barn to find every young hen in the chicken yard prone, the blood sucked out of the neck—coyote fashion—but not otherwise mangled. The animals had burrowed under the fence, and the poor chickens stood no show, as the gate was locked. Such wails as went up for Lady Dominick, Snowflake Leghorn, Princess Plymouth Rock and the Black Spanish Queen were seldom heard. It was indeed an occasion of mourning, for it meant that we must start all over again, and eggs were eggs at this time.[95] But the father, with an eye to the future, facetiously suggested that we form a procession and carry the hens to fertilize the orange trees. So we all followed the harrow and dropped the hens, which had come to such an untimely end, in the rows between the trees. The children were consoled by our assurance that the crop of fruit would be so greatly increased that more hens could be bought. The remaining roosters and the turkey gobbler, as well as the favorite blind hen with her dozen chicks which had escaped, were housed that night in the barn. And at midnight, we were awakened by fiendish yells of coyotes, who came back only to find themselves cheated of further prey and then retreated to their lairs in the Santiago creek bed.[96]

At this time, it was no uncommon occurrence to find a wiggling centipede in one's bed or to encounter a great tarantula crossing the path. In the absence of a man to dispatch them, a milk pan, with a stone on top, was quickly clapped over the tarantula, thus checking the career of this most poisonous of spiders.[97] Snakes were only occasionally met with, as the ground was being plowed and cultivated incessantly when irrigation was not going on. Mountain lions—a species of wild cat—were frequent in the foothills, as well as panthers, badgers, squirrels and rabbits. A curious, beautifully plumaged bird known as the "road runner," a native of Australia, interested us greatly as it glided along swiftly and gracefully in the middle of the road.[98]

There were a great many owls, from small ones living in the ground, known as the monkey-faced owl, to the larger species. A pair of barn owls took up their abode in our windmill tower and lived there unmolested for years, as their services to the orchardist are invaluable. They slept all day and hunted and screeched at night, making a great uproar from their eyrie home as they picked the bones of field mice and gophers. When I left California, I carried them with me stuffed, and one now looks down solemnly from its perch in the library, while the other graces the desk of an old friend in Chicago.[99]

As for bee culture, nearly every farmer had a hive or two, and the Santiago Canyon, the home of the white sage, was alive with bee ranches.

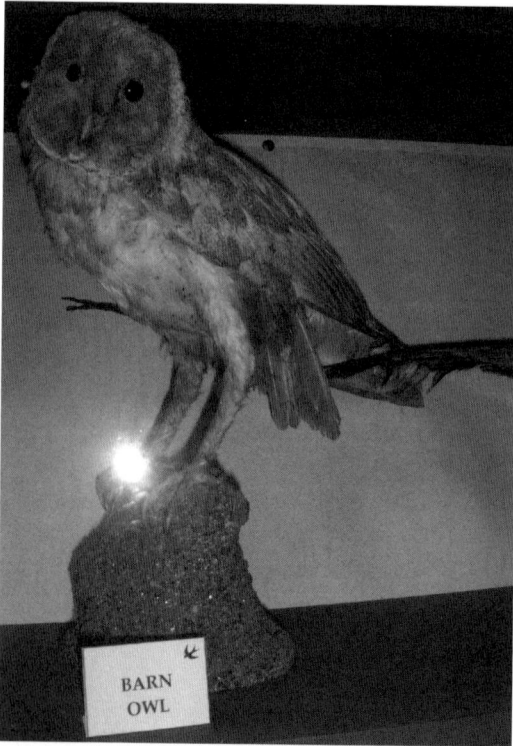

A stuffed barn owl, probably from the Yale Grove, displayed at La Porte County Museum and donated by Teegarden/Clark family. *Photograph by the editor.*

The fine honey was even then shipped to England. It was almost perilous to attempt to drive past these places in swarming time, as the bees would settle on the horses, nearly driving them frantic. About this time, a great flock of sheep went through the town. The children begged so hard for a lamb that I went out and offered to buy one, but the herdsman refused to take money and gave the children one which could not keep up with the flock. They joyfully seized it and at once began to build a corral for it in the alfalfa patch and chained the dog "Shot" by name there to keep it warm at night. But the lamb was delicate, and Marjory, in her great love for it, squeezed it too hard. And the nights were too cold, so one foggy morning, it was found stark and stiff, and this was the first real sorrow in the lives of the children. They had played under the lemon verbena tree, which was fifteen feet high and wide spreading, and had buried there all the dead birds they found. But the lamb was laid to rest under the favorite cherry plum tree, which was an immense bouquet of fragrant white blossoms every spring.[100]

Just here, I recall Elsie's first party, when she was stung by a hornet and had to go home before refreshments were passed—a very serious and never forgotten episode in the child's life. Soon after, we were asked to a small evening party—really the first and only one in years—which perhaps impressed the incident more firmly upon my mind. The guests had all arrived, and when the smiling hostess from the parlor side opened a door leading to the dining room, what a picture met our eyes! There in the middle of the beautiful table sat young Ivan, deliberately taking out the first slice of the frosted cake. He was quietly led away by his mother, and when she returned, the meal went on as peacefully as if nothing had ruffled her gentle spirit.[101]

Other friends must not be forgotten in these simple annals, and especially the brave, sweet Christian soul who, on the midst of all her own sorrows—and they were many—was a sister to me and a mother when my children needed her. There was also the gentle lady who always wore a soft, black gown in memory of him who died for his country on a foreign shore. Her house was a Mecca to the children—so filled with curious things from every clime—and no other flowers seemed so sweet as those she gathered for us in her stately garden. She, too, has gone the way of all the earth, but methinks heaven will be dearer for the presence of such a rare soul. Then there were the delightful Winslows from Cambridge, the home of Longfellow, which fact cast a glamor of romance over their personality.

The little doctor, in his equally small drugstore, was a great authority to us all, and we went there just as much to catch his jolly greeting and the merry twinkle in his eye as to buy his medicines. The search for health had sent this family to our country, and owing to vicissitudes, many treasures were left behind—but there was an old heavily carved sideboard whose mahogany contrasted strangely with the redwood walls in their dining room. There was also some colonial china—flaring tea-cups with green sprigs, and the most beautiful silver cake basket, which on occasions was piled high with delicate sponge cake, for which they were famous. Their hospitality was sweet and genuine, and they loved the children and made a round of pleasures for them. There was even a doll's wedding, with the bride resplendent in the white satin and real orange blossoms, while the groom wore a most ingeniously made suit of black broadcloth. This couple still reposes in the depths of an attic trunk, waiting patiently for the golden wedding which may be celebrated by the next generation.[102]

In an adjoining town, we discovered a family who had once lived in our suburb near Chicago and among them a treasure of a girl who was glad to come and be one of us and help with the care of the children. Her ability to make hair flowers, as well as worsted picture frames,[103] drew from her admiring charges many encomiums. And the fact that she baked excellent gingerbread and marble cake was even more of an accomplishment in their eyes. Then the Johnsons—also from Chicago—found us out, and what delightful trips we made to their home on the gravel land, where they lived temporarily in the most picturesque barn while their house was being built. To be invited to a meal there and to eat of Mrs. J [Johnson]'s unexcelled brown bread, with some of her home-gown strawberries, was indeed a treat. Two charming sisters proved dear companions for our own, and when they moved from the valley to the city, their treasured dollhouse was left at "Yale Grove" as a parting gift. Again, in turn, when we left Richland after many years, the dollhouse was carried all the way home by freight in safety until it reached the gateway of our new home in Indiana, where a careless drayman let it drop and broke it all to pieces.[104]

About this time, so many inquiries about our new home came from eastern friends there that, one day, I pruned my enormous rose geranium bush, and cutting up the wood, for it had really reached a great size, broiled a steak with it so that I could add one more California story to my vocabulary. For a long time, we had heard a perfect humming above our living room and so concluded to send a bee man to investigate. He came, saw and conquered and took one hundred pounds of dark honey from the little attic, where the walls were completely lined with it. We could not eat the honey, as it was dusty and old, but we made enough beeswax to last us the rest of our mortal lives. Our friends were many, and it is no lack of loving appreciation that others may not be named. The dearest associations of my married life are buried in the groves and rose gardens of my adopted state, and my heart beats warmly for her welfare—now and always.

CHAPTER 7

MAY DAY IN ORANGE COUNTY PARK

Acustom of the country was the holding of a great festival on the first day of May in the beautiful Santiago Canyon. This spot, then comparatively primitive and unknown, has since been heralded the world over, for Helena Modjeska's retreat, the "Forest of Arden," is situated beyond the picnic grounds. Here, under sylvan shade of vine and tree, with music of babbling steam, the famous actress found that true rest which only Mother Nature can bestow upon weary mortals.[105]

On this first day of May, forth the settlers fared from all the homes in great wagons or stages or on horseback—for to my certain knowledge, at this time, there was not a top buggy in Richland. All business was suspended for one day of enjoyment, and each family carried its basket, well filled with sandwiches, doughnuts and fruit; even flaky summer mince pies and delectable green gooseberry tarts were not lacking. Out we all drove through the small settlement, past the deserted blacksmith shop and general merchandise store which also served as a post-office.

Even the horses, with their bright harness and little flags, seemed gayer than usual as we dashed along the gravel road (for the natural roads of this country are beyond all compare with those of civilization) out toward the foothills, now so verdant and beautiful; past peach and almond orchards of delicate pink and glossy green young orange trees; then through vast fields of alfalfa and ancient vineyards, planted by the early Spaniards, until, at length, we came to the quaint adobe houses of Yorba, with great strings of Chili peppers brightening their dark walls. Little children in the

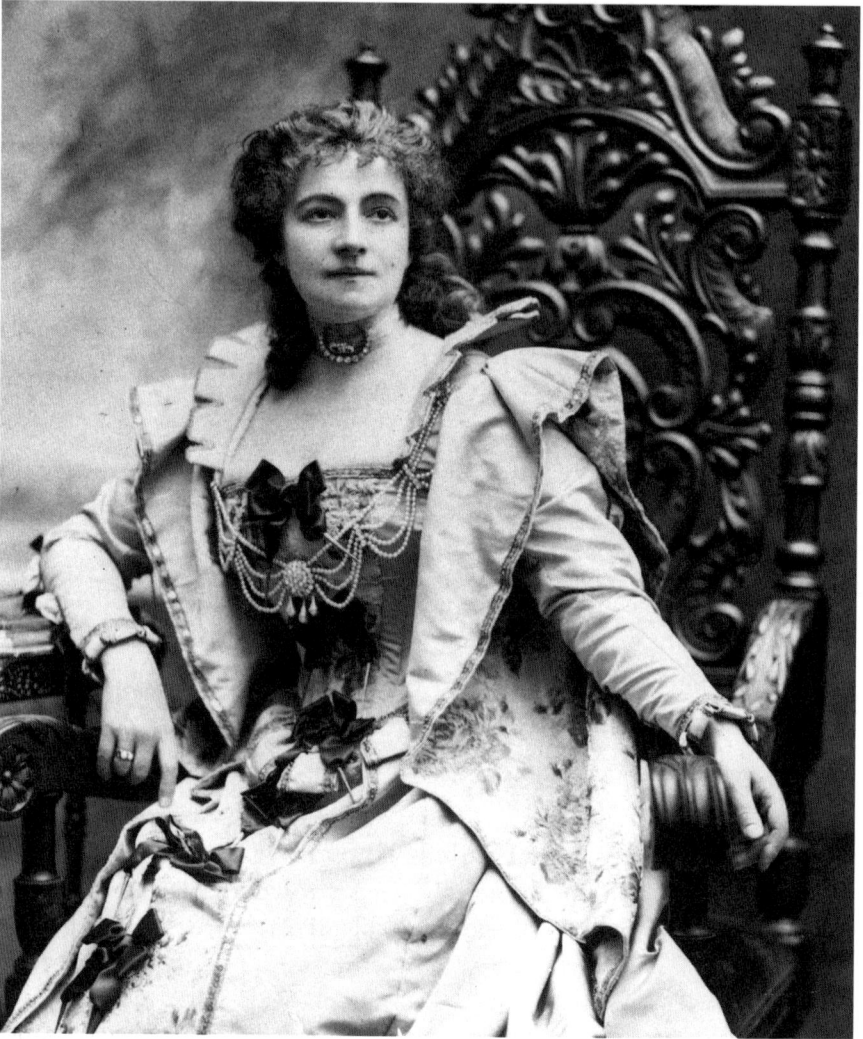

Helena Modjeska photographed in 1896. Modjeska's "Forest of Arden" existed in the upper reaches of Santiago Canyon. *Courtesy of Anaheim Public Library.*

doorways shouted "Adios" as we flew by, and ancient crones, sorting beans, looked curiously at us, while the gaily bedecked caballero, all booted and spurred, talked to a black-eyed senorita by the wayside, smilingly touched his sombrero and drew in his broncho as we passed. All along the roadside, among the chaparral, grew thorny cactus plants bearing blossoms of every hue and most delicate texture. And ever and anon, the children shouted with glee to see jack rabbits and cotton tails pricking up their ears in the clover patches and then hopping quickly away as only rabbits can. As we gradually began the ascent of the foothills and passed into the mysteries of the canyon, it seemed as if we were enclosed in a sort of fairy ring. There were the stones left from the druids' temples; the stream was framed in green watercress, and all about us, majestic sycamores and wide-spreading live oaks lifted their hoary heads, completely festooned with wreathes of mistletoe—truly a scene of pastoral beauty.[106]

As I recall these holidays, there was nothing at all formal. It was only a joyful reunion of all the settlers of Orange, Anaheim, Santa Ana, Garden Grove, Gospel Swamp and Westminster. Under the trees were groups of friends sharing their picnic dinners, while children ran about, playing the old games we all loved once—"London Bridge," "King William" and "Oats, Peas, Beans and Barley Grows."[107] The tired horses were staked at a distance in the moist grass, and faithful dogs guarded the wagons. Mirth and jollity were supreme, as veterans of both sides of the Civil War vied with one another in stories of camp and field and sang once more old songs which have since become immortal. Here college graduate and Texan farmer exchanged ideas on the ever-new subject of irrigation, while country pastor and layman, who had traveled the world over, discussed doctrine and church government.

There was seldom a day in the whole year except May Day when farm work was entirely suspended, as when it was too wet to plow, it was time to clean harness or make fruit crates as boxes, and when irrigation was not in progress, cultivation was going on. As for the housewife, she did the cooking, washing, ironing and baking of about fifteen loaves a week, single handed, unless her husband had time to aid her. I had nothing to complain of, for mine was a most able assistant, and he even left his plow for days, one busy season, to hold a crying child that I might get my work done. But it was a land of sunshine, and much of the work was done out of doors. The children took care of each other, and so developed the beginning of self-reliance. Newspapers, especially those pertaining to horticulture, were greatly appreciated, and dailies were not even thought of, but we devoured the weekly *San Francisco Bulletin*—a most excellent paper. Libraries were not yet established, but books and magazines were received from home, and we had fully as much reading matter as we had time to digest.

When the shades of night began to fall in the canyon, the air grew too chill for those in summer garb, so preparations for departure began on every side, and soon the road was a moving panorama of all kinds of vehicles. As for headgear, everything from a sombrero to a Chinese hat could be seen on

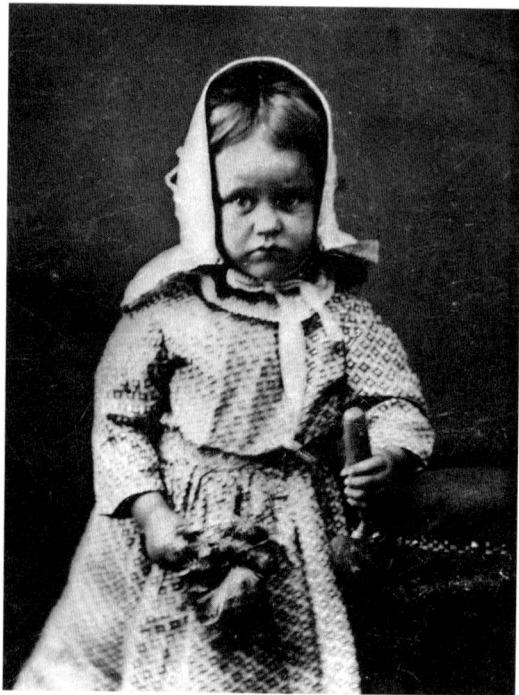

A very young Elsie Clark wearing a bonnet.

the men, and many more of the women wore neat blue or white sunbonnets rather than expensive hats. Dame Fashion had not yet invaded this peaceful valley, and to prove this, I only cite the instance of the same grey traveling gown that I wore out to California, being six years later re-made and worn on the first trip to revisit the old home. Until that time, my children had not been inside a millinery shop but always wore white sunbonnets or those caps of muslin and lace which form so charming a setting for young faces.[108]

It seems to me now, as I look back through the vista of time, veiled in a mist of tears, that life was very pure and sweet in those days. For we lived and worked out of doors, and our houses, while neat and comfortable, had none of the priceless furnishings and ornamentation of today to gather dust and vex the housewife. It was a simple life, for we rose early and worked all day. The children lived in the sunshine, and the names of bird, butterfly, ladybug or bee were as familiar as their own. We planted, often in utter weariness, and we did not always reap, but we lived too close to dear Mother Nature ever to grow selfish or sordid, as she gently let fall upon us that healing balm which, where love dwells, keeps all hearts young and pure.

CHAPTER 8

THE VISIT OF THE GIPSIES

The dew was pearling from shrub and flower, and the birds were trilling their mating songs while three little figures sat under a prickly lime hedge, industriously picking up the small yellow fruit, the proceeds of which meant a year's subscription to *St. Nicholas*,[109] whose stories were the delight of their hearts. I can see them now, one with dark braids, and two with flaxen heads, sitting on the floor, poring over "The Miller of Doe," "The Pedestrians" and such nonsense rhymes as:

> *There was a young man of Cathay,*
> *When a peddler called round, he would say,*
> *"The price is quite low, and I'd like it, you know,*
> *But I think I'll not take it today."*

> *And there was a young lady of Booking,*
> *Who had a great fondness for cooking,*
> *She made forty pies that were all of a size,*
> *And could tell which was which without looking.*

They were happy, favored children, for to them, twenty acres of orchard was a world in itself, and their father's companionship and training in the lore of nature better than books. They had at different times a variety of pets: once six kittens and a shepherd dog, then a bronco pony named "Fly," whose agility was such that no one could hitch her up without turning a double somersault in the operation. He took the older girls to school on his back, and at recess, all the little Mexicans were allowed to ride him as a special favor. Later on, there was a monkey direct from the Orient, a present from the soldier-uncle [Fred Clark], but Jocket's life was of short duration, as he committed suicide soon after arriving, or such was the conclusion when he was found one morning hanging from the branches of the pepper tree.[110]

Marjory called herself the boy of the family, riding on the cultivator and harrow on all occasions, while Kate preferred to rattle off the scientific names of shrubs and trees, as, for instance, her favorite flower was *Tacoma jasminoides*,[111] and the vegetable she liked best was "beefsteak." Like Wendeline of my own childhood, they often captured ladybugs, kept them

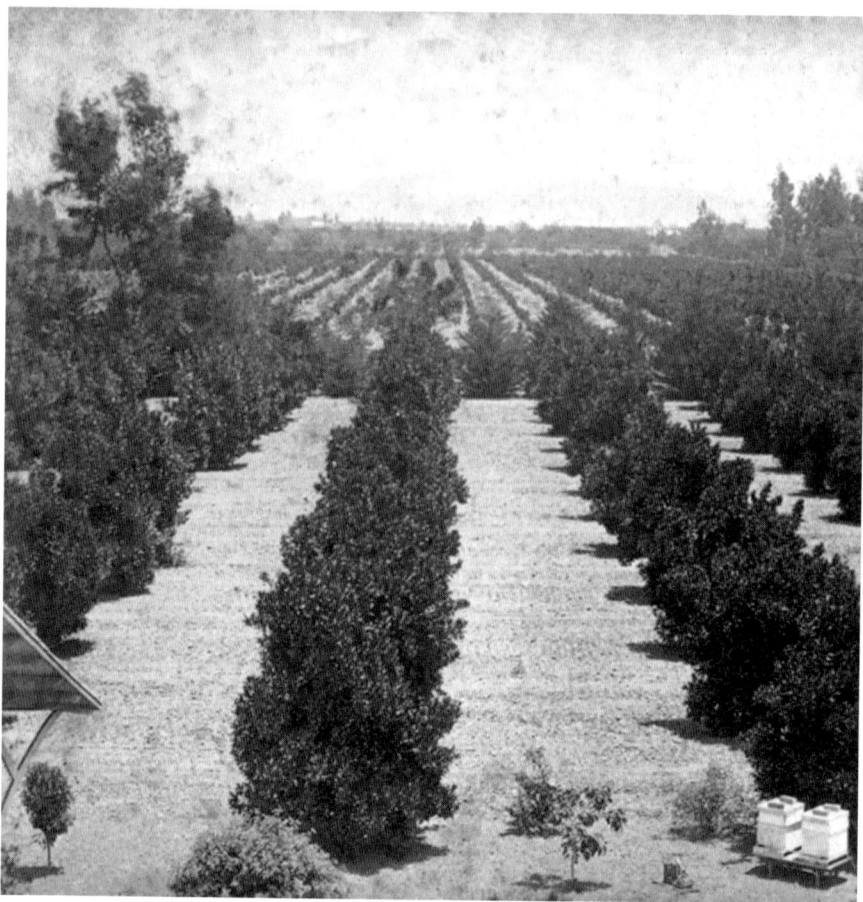

Yale Grove and nearby land viewed looking east from atop the ranch's observation tower. Watkins photograph, 1880.

under a tumbler and trained them to follow their fingers. Marjory and Kate had a colony of toads in their garden which they generously handled, and Elsie fussed because she feared they might get warts, of which she had a great horror.

One day, while the children were working and singing in the hedge, and I was shelling peas (now and then looking up and down the rows of orange trees at the "plowman wending his weary way"), a high top buggy came dashing along the driveway. This appeared to be the advance guard of a gaily decorated gipsy-van which had halted by the roadside. Wrinkled hags sat on the beds inside, and fat, shiny urchins peeped out of the openings, while scrawny dogs, with burrs in their tails, were tied with tin pails underneath. Helter-skelter came the frightened children, breathless and with flying hair, for had they not heard, over and over again, that gipsies carried off just such sprites as they? I dropped my work and took hold of their cold hands while they clung closely to me, their wondering eyes fixed on the two women who had tied their horse and were coming toward us. They were certainly picturesque, for they wore the traditional short black skirts, white bodices and aprons trimmed with broad lace, red bandannas on their elfin locks and in their ears great hoops of gold. A cheerful "good morning" from them somewhat dispelled the children's fears, and as the gipsies sat down on the steps, the children peeped from behind my chair at the first real specimens of the wandering tribes they had ever seen. It was nearly noon by this time, and preparations for dinner had begun by the setting of the table, as usual, on the wide back porch. The women still lingered and displayed their laces, and as one wanted to tell my fortune, I finally crossed her palm with a piece of silver. It was the usual tale of a letter to come, a journey to be taken and more children in store.

At this moment, the hungry husband came in to dinner, and rather than break the spell, he politely asked them to sit down with us. They, however, declined the roast lamb which we served with peas, saying that they preferred the good roast beef as well as the "greenery," as they called it, of old England. Southern California was not to their taste, as camping places with green grass and water were not easily found. There was ample chance, as we sat there, to study a real gipsy, who cajoled and flattered and, on leaving, asked me for a ham and a loaf of bread. I told her that hams were a luxury not often enjoyed by us and that bread baking was a task attended by too much labor for a woman without a servant to cast her loaves upon the waters. So they at length departed for greener fields, thus ending another episode.[112]

At long intervals, the sound of the fish horn resounded through the town. This was a signal for the children to run out and barter with the peddler for a small mess of smelts or a few sea perch, but as a rule, we did not get the best fish. We often longed for Eastern oysters, as those grown in the Pacific are too coppery to be delicious. So one day, when we were in Los Angeles, we bought two cans of Baltimore oysters, for which we most willingly paid the price of three dollars, that we might once more enjoy our old Sunday morning breakfast of broiled oysters on toast. When the cans were opened, they were, one after another, poured on the ground—even the chickens refused to eat them—and our disgust was so great that oysters never again appealed to us.[113]

We invested in a great black pig, hoping to cure our own bacon and hams, but when we found one morning that she had—cannibal-like—eaten up her young ones, we harnessed up and started with her for market, three miles away. Our destination was the then pretty little town of Santa Ana, but before we quite reached her borders, the pig squealed so terrifically that I dismounted with the children, and we sat by the roadside until she was delivered to the purchaser and the wagon returned to pick us up.[114]

Each year brought us visitors from the East who created a great stir in our quiet life. First, in early days, came one whom the children adored and nicknamed the "beautiful lady." She entered most gracefully into the new and somewhat trying life. She devoted herself to the children, made dainty dresses and aprons for them, renovated their dolls and took long strolls with them over the flower-carpeted meadows. More than one bachelor, and there were many in Richland, sighed as he gazed upon her fresh delicate beauty. And they vied with one another to escort her to the mountains or the coast on those jolly parties so common in that day. Every man of them could cook a fine meal of broiled quail, mealy potatoes and delicious coffee over the campfire.

Occasionally, as a family, we suspended work and drove to Trabuca Canyon, where we camped over night, gipsy fashion, while the fishermen coaxed the trout. The country was full of interesting places, and these little excursions greatly relieved the monotony of our daily toil.[115]

Soon after this, the soldier-uncle [Fred Clark] came down from the northern part of the state to inspect our orange farm. His first question was, "Albert, why in the world don't you plant bluegrass between the trees?" This necessitated a lengthy treatise upon all the details of orchard work, with which he, as a civil engineer, had no reason to be familiar. He laughed at our heavy calf-skin shoes and called us "grangers" and in his droll but perfectly pleasant way made no end of fun of our methods. He was very dear to the children, always doing nice things for them or telling them wonderful stories of his checkered life. One time, when he stayed a week, he mended all the broken furniture, tacked cloth on a room or two, put up shelves and, one day, sent us all off for a drive to surprise us with one of his fine-cooked suppers on our return. At times, the brothers seemed almost like those two happy boys who had worked years before at the turning lathe in the little carpenter shop which their Connecticut grandfather, Captain Abner Bailey, had built for them in Northern Indiana.[116]

The next visitor was the children's tall grandfather [Abraham Teegarden], who like all truly great souls, made himself a child with them. An ardent lover of flowers, he enjoyed their garden and sat for hours by the playhouse, listening to their childish chatter, for like many children, they had most vivid imaginations. And he, long in the storm and stress of life, gladly laid down his many burdens to enjoy the young life which had come to cheer his later years. His visit was a great event, so an evening gathering of neighbors was planned in his honor. All the morning, while I was busy stirring custards and pounding almonds for cake, baking biscuits and roasting chickens, the children stayed in the orchard, and at five o'clock, the grandfather carried out to the playhouse the little supper which he was to share with them. There were diminutive biscuits, cut out with a pepper box, all the hearts and livers of the chickens and very small cup custards and cakes, so that the children would be satisfied, after the feast, to go to bed and let the grownups have the evening. When the supper was finished and the grandchildren ready for bed, there were only a few little giggles, a pillow fight or two, then prayers and quiet. Later in the

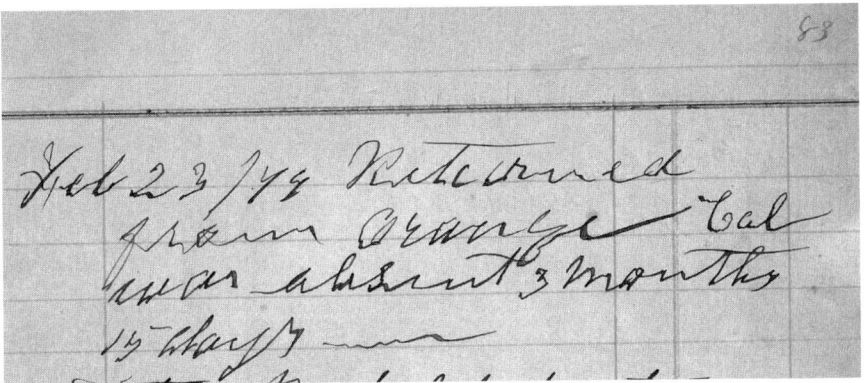

Handwritten entry by Abraham Teegarden in his *Ledger/Diary* documenting his return from Orange on February 23, 1879.

evening, the village doctor and his tall wife and rosy-cheeked daughters, the minister and his sister and the storekeeper and his wife came in out of the cool moon-lit night to sit by our blazing fire, with the latest trophy of the chase, a fine deerskin, lying in front of the fireplace, shot in honor of the grandfather.[117]

To this day, the grownup children talk of the delicious almond cake that was served that night, but if it was really deserving of praise, I have never been able to make it again. Perhaps it was the childish fancy, for I certainly never tasted such cranberry pies as my good Mother [Lura Treat Teegarden] used to make so long ago.

CHAPTER 9

CAMPING OUT

As the orchard grew older, more men and teams were necessary, and we purchased an expensive riding-cultivator and many other costly farming implements, as well as a pair of Clydesdale horses. As pests had been introduced from Australia on nursery stock, a spraying outfit was absolutely indispensable to exterminate these deadly red and white scale bugs. The first whale oil soap used in our orchard was imported by us directly from New Bedford, Massachusetts, and if I mistake not, the entire expense for this year's spraying was something like fifteen hundred dollars.[118]

At this time, orange growing took on a roseate hue, and great expectations, which were never fully realized, called for much outlay. Two extra men were hired for orchard work, as well as a girl to assist in the kitchen, and, as the house had become too small for the growing family, a carpenter was engaged to build several additional rooms. He no sooner brought his tools and went to work than a camping trip to the San Bernardino Mountains, seventy miles away, was agitated. We speedily decided, as no better opportunity presented itself, to all go, including the faithful Hilda, leaving the orchard and stock in the charge of a trusty Mexican—Diego [Granillo] by name.[119]

A lumber wagon was filled with straw, sacks of flour, potatoes, beans, sides of bacon, coffee, sugar, cooking utensils, bedding, feed for the horses and all the usual paraphernalia of camp life. The men were to drive on ahead with Hilda to supervise the older girls, while the father took Kate and me in the open buggy.

In the meantime, our house was to be finished and ready for us on our return, when lo and behold the bachelor carpenter set up a wail that he too must go as assistant cook. Of course his request was finally granted by the overly accommodating ranchman, while Hilda and I rejoiced over the prospect of less labor.

One bright June morning, our cavalcade set out, and I confess to a sigh as we left that sweet orchard home behind us. What would we find on that long dusty trip to compensate us for the loss of the vine-covered porch—so cool and inviting—all the comforts of the little house, the flower garden, the ripening peaches and berries and the refreshing trade winds which kept the mill wheel going? Above all, the cool splashing of water as it pumped up and fell into the great tank—music indeed in a land where it rained only once in nine months, and sometimes not even then.

At the end of the first day's journey, we reached Colton[120] and camped just outside the town by the dusty roadside. In the morning, we journeyed on, heat growing more and more intense. In fact, it was so hot on the mesa as we ascended toward the mountains that eggs could almost be cooked on the stones. When at last, on the second night, we reached our destination and unpacked our supplies, I discovered very near our camp a perfect dream of a trout brook over-hung by alder bushes. There was a great boulder in the middle, and later on, little Kate sat there for hours, kicking her bare legs against the cool stone, communing with a small green frog. As tracks of bear were discovered near our camp on the second morning, big bonfires were lighted every night afterward to protect us. If it had not been for the paddling in the brook and sleeping near it, where we were lulled to rest by its soft babble, we could hardly have endured the heat. In the day-time, the children lived in the water, and every morning, Hilda and I prepared the breakfast of bacon, eggs, fried potatoes and onions and coffee, while the men, who had promised to assist us, went off hunting or fishing.

A week of boiled potatoes, bacon and canned salmon became monotonous, when, one day, the hunter brought in a great deer with a young fawn. The fawn was at once appropriated by Marjory as a pet, and she declared that she would never be so cruel as to eat the flesh of the beautiful mother. We now had venison broiled, roasted and stewed and even jerked or dried in the sun on the tent poles.

As our butter had long since become oil, we began to sigh for the fleshpots of Egypt in the form of juicy melons and peaches. But as we were far from civilization, we contented ourselves with a box of our own oranges, as well as with dried fruit and pickles. The children teased for cookies, but as all our work was done over an open fire, built up with stones with a couple of sticks to hang the kettle on, baking was out of the question. If gasoline stoves were then in vogue, I, at least, had heard nothing of them and should have been afraid to use one if I had.

The most appetizing dish was a stew of venison with onions and potatoes and a dash of chili pepper. Coffee was good even with condensed milk, and Cross & Blackwell's jams spread upon bread made a rather dainty finish after a hearty meal.[121]

The days passed with the usual routine of camp life. The men hunted or fished, but it was too warm in this closely shut-in valley for the women to explore. Besides, the bear tracks had certainly cooled our enthusiasm for wandering away from the camp. Why should we leave the delights of our entrancing stream—so cool and shady—to be overpowered by wild cats or other unknown foes who might be hidden in their fastnesses? We sat all day by the brook, and I read *St. Nicholas* and *Wide Awake* to the three mermaids, thinly clad in muslin Mother Hubbard gowns. With flowing hair and bare legs, the children seemed indeed like water spirits.[122]

At last when our holiday was drawing to a close, the fishermen one day brought in three barley sacks of trout, wrapped in alder leaves to keep them cool. Every frying pan in camp was called for, and such a meal as we sat down to is beyond description. All who know the flavor of this little fish, whether caught in the streams of New England, the South or California, will agree with me that there is nothing in the whole family of fishes surpassing it.

The next morning, when the hour for departure came, the children, with one last look at their dear alder-fringed brook, with the green frog still occupying his cool stone, climbed regretfully into the high wagon which was to take them far away from "Bear Valley." Soon, ever ready for change, they were chattering like so many magpies of their pets at home, and the ripe apricots and peaches on their own trees.

As we journeyed along, we reached a desolate plain, with here and there a cotton wood tree, where an Indian funeral was in progress. Wrinkled old squaws stood over a great kettle, under which a fire was burning, stirring some concoction—at the same time wailing the death song in a low, whining tone, accompanied by a shrill whistle produced by blowing into the hollow leg bone of a dear. It was very weird, as their voices rose on the evening air and re-echoed from the hills beyond. The young men of the tribe circled around on their ponies, while to the crones was left the duty of accompanying the departed spirit to the Happy Hunting Grounds.[123]

I recall another delightful trip to the coast on which we went to spend the day. It was a wonderful drive over country more beautiful than I had expected to see. When, in the windings of our way, over hill and dale, we

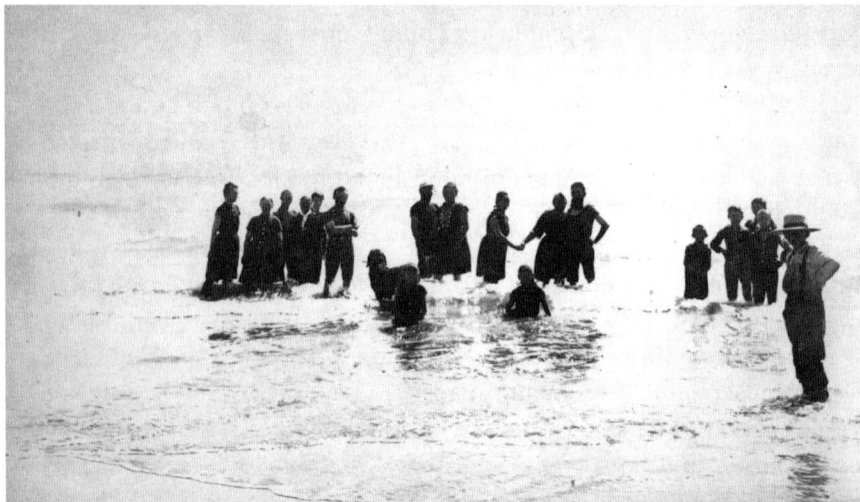

Victorian-era bathers wading on a Southern California beach. *Courtesy of Anaheim Public Library.*

came upon the first lake I had seen in Southern California, my delight knew no bounds. There were great crevices in the rocks full of bees, and everywhere bright yellow poppies were growing. Finally, we came out through a canyon to the beautiful blue sea and camped on a fine beach called Laguna. While the hunter was looking for game, for there was duck shooting on the coast in those days, and great sacks of canvas-backs were often the spoils, the children and I sat on the cliffs, gazing far out to sea, or hunted abalone shells when the tide was out or waded in the surf to our hearts' content.[124]

I cannot describe to you the primitive beauty of those early California beaches. There were no habitations then, only great stretches of glistening sand and flower-carpeted hilltops. I would not halt the progress of time, but often I wonder just how much natural beauty advancing civilization will leave for the children of tomorrow.

Forgetful of time, we, strange to say, failed to keep an eye on the horses, and when we looked for them, they were nowhere to be seen. They had quietly unharnessed themselves and gone halfway home before a passing fisherman had discovered and returned them to us. It was very dark when we were loaded up with ducks and shooting irons, with the tired children asleep on the blankets on the bottom of the wagon.

Then began our journey through a lonely country, always fascinating to me. Only once in miles would we see a tiny light flickering in the distance, as we passed some old Spanish ranch, with its neglected pear and olive trees. Its original owners had been a happy, pastoral people, with roomy adobe houses and sheep and cattle on a thousand hills. Their homes were the scenes of many festivities and the coming of their ministering priests occasions of great rejoicing. They had olive orchards and vineyards, making oil and wine after a primitive fashion, and looked with great pride upon their thousands of acres which you of today know as the Irvine Ranch.

Their family life was peaceful, their voices soft and they managed their Indian servants most kindly and admirably. The work of the house went on in absolute quiet, though at times, from forty to fifty people were housed and fed. Their hospitality knew no bounds, and if a passing guest had no money, his purse was filled before he went on his way. Now the scene is changed, with the coming of American greed, and the descendants of the old stock have lost or dissipated their inheritance. With that inevitable Spanish characteristic—mañana—never doing today what can be put off until tomorrow—they have lost the sweet, simple lives of their forefathers. Except for records preserved in the old Missions and those of song and story, one would in a few years lose all knowledge of the early life of the native Californian, by none so beautifully portrayed as by Helen Hunt [Jackson] in "Romona."[125]

CHAPTER 10

THE MARKETING OF A CROP

Before the orange shipping season arrived, everything was in readiness, as for instance, boxes all made and piled up in the fruit house, wrappers in great bunches, brushes on hand and tall stepladders mended. Boxes were hauled into the orchard and placed under the trees, while the fruit was carefully cut with pruning shears, culls thrown out, and only perfect specimens reserved for the fancy wrappers which were a guarantee of their excellence. Word had been dispatched as to the state of the orange market, and on receipt of telegrams to rush shipments in, all hands were set busily at work. This was, we must remember, in the days when every man handled his own crop. Whereas now, there are associations to protect the growers, and in most cases, the fruit is sold on the trees, and the owner has nothing to do but to receive the proceeds. Early growers were at the mercy of the market, and as that of San Francisco was soon flooded, we finally shipped to Chicago. To ensure the truth regarding its condition on arrival there, for I regret to say that the word of commission men was not infallible, we generally sent a few boxes to friends in the locality where the carload went, requesting them to report as soon as possible. They invariably responded that the fruit was received in excellent condition, so we really knew, even if we got unfavorable reports from the commission houses.

Freight charges at that time were ninety cents per box by the carload, which, added to the cost of 1,500 trees, their cultivation, irrigation and spraying and pruning until they finally came to bearing, which was about ten or twelve years for seedling and six for budded fruit, made orange growing

To Orange Shippers.

———o———

HAVING CONTRACTED FOR A LARGE QUANTITY OF

Orange Boxes,

WE SHALL KEEP THE SAME

Constantly on hand at Market Prices. and will furnish in Car Load Lots at Mill Prices.

WE HAVE ALSO RECEIVED A CAR LOAD OF

MANILLA TISSUE ORANGE WRAPPERS

In the various sizes, which we will sell

CHEAPER THAN EVER,

In Lots to Suit Purchasers.

Give us a call and get prices before buying elsewhere.

SANTA ANA VALLEY FRUIT CO.

An advertisement for citrus shipping supplies, including "Manilla Tissue Orange Wrappers."

a costly business. While we were safe from frost, ravages of the Santa Ana winds often deprived us of a good many boxes, for those oranges which were not blown off were pierced by thorns and made unsightly and unsalable. At first, black scale was a menace, but not a circumstance in its pernicious effects to the red and white varieties which appeared later. I am certain that we could have bought all the oranges we cared to eat, for a mere trifle, compared to the expense of raising them at this period.

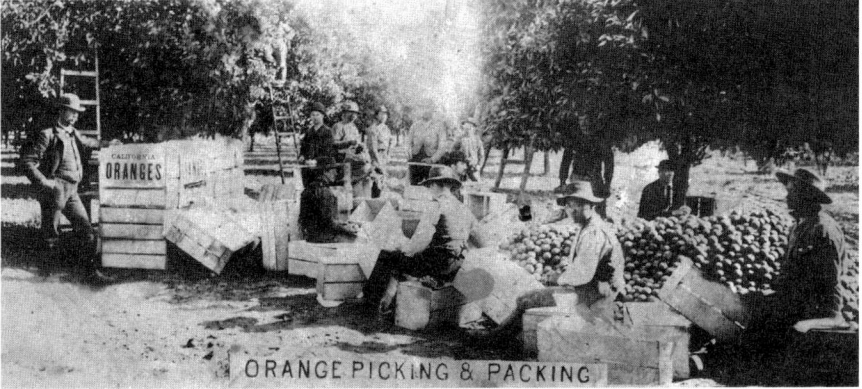

Orange pickers and packers in an orchard. Note the multiethnic nature of the crew. *From Orange, Cal., Illustrated and Described (1886).*

Often prices were very fair for Seedlings, while Navels brought as high as four dollars a box, which greatly encouraged us. On one occasion, when hope ran high in our hearts, when extra pains had been taken, and only experts employed to do the work of selecting, wrapping and packing, a fancy carload was dispatched, with a joy which no words can express. Weeks elapsed before we even heard that they had reached their destination, and for all we ever knew, they may have been dumped into the Chicago River— so meager were the returns which we at a very late date received.

After this, fruit was sold on the trees. And one season in order to facilitate its speedy shipment, we were induced to take the agent who bought it for his commission house with his family to board. Judge of my surprise when the newcomers arrived with canary bird, sewing machine, baby and dog—not to mention a sister-in-law. One of the ladies was a fine musician, so the piano which we had just bought was thrown into the bargain.

The smallest number of oranges that we ever put into one box was sixty-five—Navels, of course, and of extra size. The average box contained from two hundred to two hundred and twenty-five or forty. Culls were often sold in the orchard at a dollar a hundred to campers or others traveling through the country for their health in covered wagons—at one time quite a fad in California.[126]

This reminds me that, one day, as I was ironing on the back porch, one of these wagons stopped at our entrance, and from it alighted a pleasant-voiced, ruddy-cheeked man who approached and addressed me by name, though, at first, I did not recognize him. He had been a neighbor of the Clark boys and had often worked in their carpenter shop, which had been a rendezvous for many whose paths now lay far apart. His errand was to get some fruit, as he and his wife and son, dog and parrot were making a leisurely trip through the southern country in search of health and recreation. As they had a long day's journey ahead, we could not prevail upon them to stop overnight.

At an early stage in our ranch life, as we were eating a simple breakfast on the porch, a tall man on a white horse came riding in. And great was our surprise to find him an old friend and also a well-known general of the Civil War, under whose flag many of our best young men had served their country in her time of need. The general had already breakfasted at the hotel in an adjoining town, but he took a second cup of coffee with us and then, with kindly words of farewell, rode away into the world, which was, after all, not so great but that we might almost any day have some passing guest who had known and loved the dear old home.

A new public school building had now been erected, and the little girls, having learned to read at home out of their mother's first reader, arrived at the dignity of scholars and went every morning, three-quarters of a mile, to the Lemon Street School. At recess, the children dug steps in the dirt banks nearby, and these steps led up to fascinating houses and tents made of pepper-tree boughs. The playground was as a rock and very interesting to them because it was full of the strange little homes of the trap-door spider, made in the hard earth.[127]

In those happy days, every vacant lot was a wildflower garden, gay with yellow poppies and Indian pinks, and one could gather armfuls of blossoms almost at their very doorstep. Another favorite pastime, also one which I delighted in as a child, was the making of "flower ladies" from geranium blossoms and leaves and also the art of knitting upon spools, pleasures of such simple and inexpensive play. The tumbleweeds also afforded them great amusement, as when dry, they literally tumbled everywhere, with the happy children in hot pursuit. When we drove through the country, great buzzards hovering over some deserted sheep camp attracted them, and the far-away blue hills were living pictures of sheep and cattle, browsing on the rich, green fields, while one of the most beautiful scenes was the change which the first rain brought in the landscape. There was snow upon the distant mountaintops, and the hills, before so brown and bare, blossomed with the verdure of richest green. We sat on our porch on the Fourth of July and saw the snow glittering on San Antonio. I remember one time only when we had a very light fall of snow in our valley. It so excited the children that, seizing every milk pan at hand, they ran to catch it and kept it long enough for me to make them a taste of the ice cream which old fashioned children made, stirring the sugar and milk and flavoring into the snow and calling it delicious.[128]

For books, my children always had *St. Nicholas* and *Wide Awake*, Hans Christian Anderson and Juliana Horatia Ewing's charming stories of *Mary's Meadow*, *Jackanapes* and *The Story of a Short Life*. An old book of my own childhood—*The Rose and the Ring* by Thackeray—was resurrected, and they pored over the adventures of Giglio, Bulbo, Betsinda and Gruffanuff with never-ceasing delight. When the wind blew and played havoc with their orange trees, they got out the *Wind Spirit* and the *Rain Goddess* or the funny *Bee Book*, translated from the German, in which Hans Dralle figures so delightfully. *Under the Window* by Kate Greenaway, presented by the grandfather, was handed down from one child to the next, while the old-fashioned Franconian stories by Jacob Abbott and

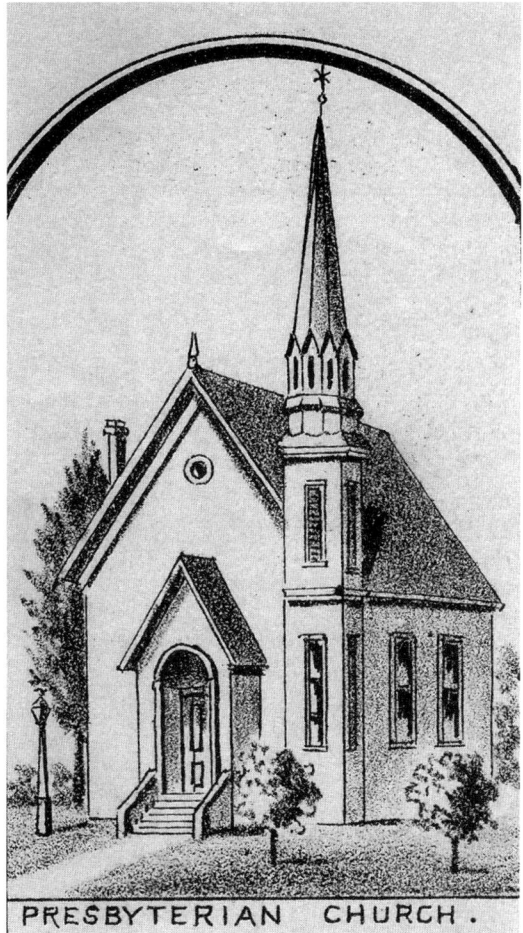

Drawing of the Orange Presbyterian Church building. *From* Orange, Cal., Illustrated and Described *(1886)*.

the Harper's Story Books were only second in their estimation to *Hans Brinker, or the Silver Skates* and the charming, wholesome Alcott stories.[129]

A Presbyterian church had now been built in addition to the Methodist, and it was here that the children first went to Sunday School. Their teacher was a dear lady who will always hold a tender place in our hearts. Her house was none too large and her means but moderate, yet she was never without some homeless orphan child, in whose care and training she exemplified the worth of practical religion, which is, after all, far above mere professions of faith and forms of doctrine.[130]

CHAPTER 11

THE RAID OF THE BANDITS

It was an early spring evening [March 3, 1880] when returns from first shipments of oranges were due. Supper of baked macaroni, tomato omelet, fresh strawberries and cream was over, and the children were snug in their beds while the anxious orchardist had gone to the general store for his mail. It was an unusually dark night, favorable to nocturnal prowlers, but as none ever came around, I had no fear. Besides, a fish horn hung on the porch, with which Diego [Granillo] could be summoned from his quarters in the barn, if necessary. I had been in and out all the evening, spreading linen on the grass to bleach, and looking at the threatening weather, which indicated rain. Hour after hour passed by. It began to rain and blow—still no sound of footsteps or the cheerful whistle which had always been our countersign. When, at last, the missing man came slowly and silently in, not a word would he say concerning his adventures, except that he, with other orange growers, had been unexpectedly detained at the store. The true story did not come out until the next day, when it flew like wildfire over the settlement.[131]

It seemed that five or six friends were sitting in the rear of the store, examining their receipts for fruit shipped at Christmas time, when, on looking up, they saw one of their number, who had just come in, struggling at the door with several masked men who were pointing revolvers at him and threatening to shoot at once if he did not throw up his hands. The other men at first thought they were only mischievous village boys playing tricks, but it soon developed that they were Mexican bandits of most desperate character.

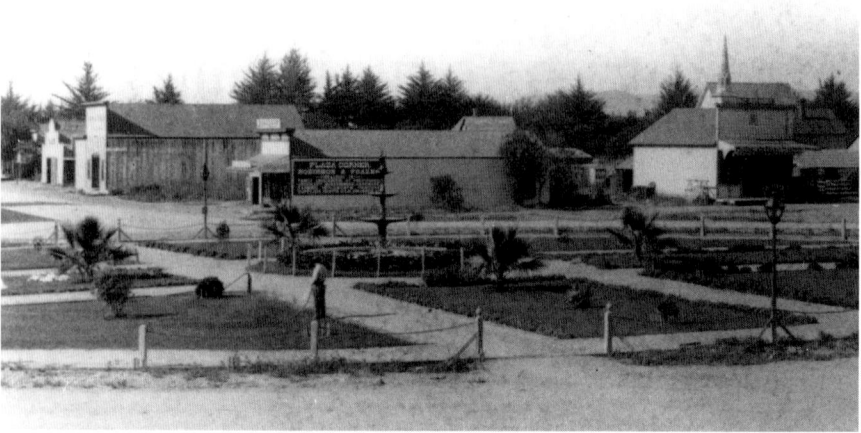

The Plaza looking northeast, 1889. The "Plaza Corner" building, center, was Crowder's Store and likely the site of the 1880 bandit raid. *Courtesy of Orange Public Library, Local History Collection.*

So without firearms or police protection, the ranchmen made the best of a bad matter and offered no resistance. One by one, they were roughly thrown to the floor, knocked with revolvers, their hands and feet tied with strong ropes and barley sacks put over their heads.

Their pockets were gone through, watches and money removed and the best overcoats taken. The storekeeper's wife [Marian Crowder] was summoned from her rooms in the rear and made to reveal the combination of the safe, from which money belonging to her husband, as well as others who had deposited their savings there in the absence of a bank, was taken. Then a goodly supply of crackers and bacon, canned goods, coffee and sugar, as well as blankets and other household articles, was hurriedly strapped together and thrown on the waiting horses outside. In the meantime, the men on the floor were bandying jokes at one another, as he, with the old coat and cheap watch, had fared better than the one with the silk-lined overcoat and gold repeater. Finally, after the rogues had secured all the booty they could well carry, the merchant's wife was told that in an hour she might cut the ropes and free the prisoners, provided she promised to give the Mexicans time to escape. What a situation! In the back room lay her sleeping child [Mamie Crowder] in its cradle, while her husband was tied on the floor with the rest!

It was midnight when the raiders sprang to their saddles and sped away in the darkness through the quiet village, all enwrapped in peaceful slumber and unmindful of the presence of such uncanny guests. As the bandits disappeared, they shouted back "adios" with the promise to pay another visit at some future time. At the allotted hour, the ropes were unloosed, and the men, stiff and somewhat undone by their adventure, dispersed and went to their homes.[132]

This proved to be a very well organized raid on three or four lonely settlements, each of which had a similar experience, and the sheriff of Los Angeles County, with his deputies, was aroused to do his best to apprehend the thieves. One by one, after a long time, the fellows were caught or shot in the pursuit and eventually landed where they belonged, behind the bars at San Quentin.[133]

Very soon after this, we had a strange Mexican irrigating for us. Just as I had set out his dinner on the kitchen table, he grew very white, for he saw one of the deputies riding by and looking into our place. Immediately, the man disappeared as if the earth had swallowed him up. As he neither ate his dinner nor asked for his pay, I always thought he had been guilty of some misdemeanor. Otherwise, I could not explain his hasty exit at a time when his services were greatly needed. This bandit story has been told and retold to tourists and handed down to the younger generation until it has become a part of the early history of Richland.[134]

"Robbers' Cave," within the entrance to the Santiago and overlooking the entire valley, was, in the early days, the rendezvous and hiding place of horse and cattle thieves and bandits. Among the most noted of the latter were Juan Flores, Tiburcio Vasquez, his lieutenant [Cleovaro] Chaves, Pedro Lopez and Diego Navarro. In the *History of Los Angeles County*, published in 1880, will be found a full account of their exploits.[135]

CHAPTER 12

GLIMPSES OF THE OLD HOME

In the meantime, we decided to revisit the old home in the East, as an aged grandmother, of whom we were all very fond, was filled with longing to see us again. As it bid fair to be a very busy summer [in 1880], with a large crop of northern fruits to be cared for, an excellent superintendent was engaged [William H. H. Clayton] to take charge of the entire place and occupy the house, and we began to prepare for the journey across the continent. The replenishing of my neglected wardrobe was no easy task, but what woman ever lived who loved pretty clothes less than plain ones? And I confess to a great joy at casting aside for a season useful garments for more dainty and becoming attire. At this time, the older girls had their first hats, from a San Francisco milliner, one with a garland of daisies, the other with forget-me-nots, and there were never more delighted children. After waiting so long, it was good to at last experience such genuine happiness over a little thing.[136]

By securing a stateroom, we traveled very comfortably with our three small Californiana, who were keenly alert to everything on the long journey. In fact, their anticipations were so great that I almost feared they would never be realized. When at last we reached the familiar town, and the loving and ever generous grandfather [Abraham Teegarden] enfolded them all in his arms, I knew that the most vivid imagination could not begin to portray all the delights in store.

There were the uncles, aunts and cousins and the little great-grandmother [Elcy Tracy Treat], who still kept her small house, with its tall cherry, glass-knobbed highboy which had been my envy as a child when she sent me there to get out her best cap, crape shawl and parasol. The old Connecticut clock, with a picture of Napoleon on its face, still guarded the door, which was never locked for fear some neighbor might need something. But we loved best of all to wander in her old-time garden, with its oak trees and tall mulberry bushes, cling-stone peach and Siberian crabapple trees and the clumps of black raspberries from which she still made such delicious pies. Little white and yellow roses, as well as the red and striped ones of York and Lancaster, rows of pink and white sweet peas, bachelor's buttons, Johnny jump-ups, velvety double buttercups, ragged ladies, bouncing Bets, celandines and big single red poppies grew there in great profusion. In the herb garden, there was always sage, pennyroyal and spearmint, besides horehound, from which she made syrup for our colds. How the children trooped through it all, ever finding new surprises—even a gooseberry bush growing in the cleft of an oak tree and a fascinating rain barrel full of "wigglers." In the kitchen was a big, old cupboard which smelled of allspice; and on the top shelf, a mysterious green-and-white china teacup, in which she kept her money. On Independence Day, she always baked the most delicious plum cake I ever tasted. She loved strong green tea and served it to the children, but when she was not looking, I watered the rose bushes with it. In fruit time, the boys, taking advantage of her deafness, sneaked into her garden and ate her fruit, so it was hard for her to get any peaches. It was here that the children made dolls out of hollyhocks and cheeses out of what the grandmother called "Little Harriets," a species of Malva. There were balloon vines and canary bird flowers in the garden, as well as gay zinnias, which little Kate admired beyond measure. Of course, the grandmother's morning glories were bluer than any others, and her four o'clocks and lady slippers, with their snapping seed pods, not to mention what she called "sturtions," all revelations to these little denizens of a semi-tropical country whose flowers, while rich and rare, are not hallowed by the old associations so dear to us all.[137]

In the grandfather's garden, a most wonderful playhouse, shaped like an Indian wigwam and built by him of bark and shingles, awaited the children. There was a swing inside for the two babies, Kate and Lura [Lura Treat Bradley], her cousin, and a row of seats all around, with drawers underneath which, when pulled out, revealed picture books, slates and pencils, boxes of paints and every known device for amusing children. Also, there was a little table, rocking chairs and stools, besides a flag waving from the peak. A photograph was taken of the entire family—the grandfather, Uncle John [John Henry Bradley], Aunt Myra Bell [Myra Bell Teegarden], all of the children and ourselves, besides jolly Betsy Black, the cook, and flaxen-haired

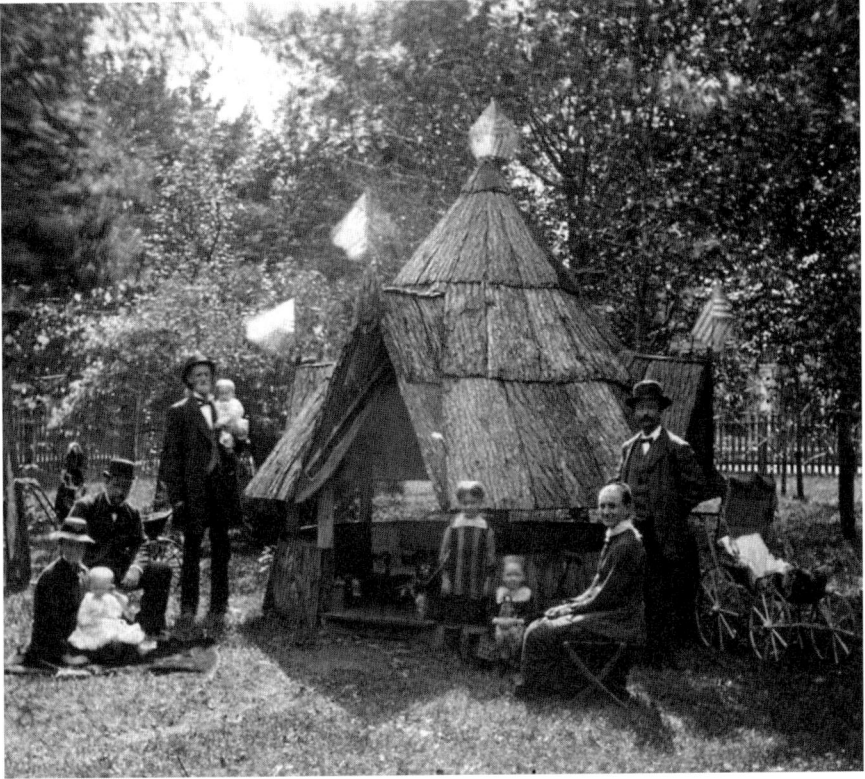

The children's playhouse in La Porte, Indiana, 1880. Dr. Teegarden is seen standing and holding the baby. The other unidentified persons are members of the Clark and Bradley families.

Amanda, the nurse, with the picturesque house in the background. Across the street, another uncle and aunt and some older cousins lived, and between them all, the children had very lively times. Aunt Kitty made most delicious lemon pies, but it took so many to go around that she often felt discouraged. And the baskets of peaches which she provided were emptied so soon that she remarked one day that she "never did see children eat so much fruit."

There was great Aunt Caroline, whose house was full of curious books and pictures, albums, old daguerreotypes and toys made long ago by one of her sons. There were dolls' cradles, bureaus and little washing machines, and the children were allowed to play with them all, as well as to have tea parties with the aunt's flaky doughnuts and harvest the apples which grew in her front yard. Across the lake was another aunt who used to invite them over to play under her big catalpa tree. At six o'clock, she served them a delicious supper of hot biscuits, cold tongue and sweet strawberries from her garden. Then beloved cousin Katherine made them some of her famous molasses candy, and if they happened there in the morning, she baked those waffles for dinner, for which she was noted. There was a continual round of pleasures and, last but not least, were drives with the grandfather after his sorrel horse "Frank," and the birthday parties, when new children were asked and came even in hail storms, to bring presents, which, while most unexpected, were very acceptable.[138]

At the last was the three weeks visit in Chicago, where dear little cousin Rebecca, whose children had long since grown up, allowed the little girls to concoct and cook dishes on her fine new range, and Josephine, her daughter, made their dolls some very fashionable dresses and hats and gave them no end of good times. They next went to Englewood, of the Chicago suburbs, to visit their father's dear cousin, who had married a literary man who, as a boy, was often willingly locked in the grandfather's library when the family went driving, to devour books until their return. He too had been a soldier in the Civil War and was also a man of varied accomplishments. He could paint a creditable picture, play on the violin or write most entertaining stories of adventure. From his plans, the exterior of the little house at "Yale Grove" was first evolved. He and vivacious cousin Flora made the visit most delightful; and to this day, they are idolized by Marjory, whose constant chatter and mischief made their days somewhat strenuous.[139]

CHAPTER 13

CHANGES

Summer [of 1882], with bright sunshine, cool nights and an occasional refreshing fog, had come again. Tree spraying was on; soap boiling in vats to be afterward loaded into tanks, with either the ranchman or his stout Mexican helper, as might be, sitting on the high seat, manipulating the long hose and drenching scale bugs and red spiders. There was no end to orchard work in this fair land, where the sun shone nearly every day in the whole round year and left no room in one's anatomy for a single lazy bone. If it were not spraying, it was irrigating or fertilizing, pruning, summer plowing and cultivating or gathering, sorting, packing and shipping fruit.

Even the women and children were, in their way, as busy as bees in clover. With sweeping and dusting, churning, working over butter, frying doughnuts and baking bread and pumpkin pie—or between times hanging out lines of washing, which gave color to the landscape, as pink and blue aprons and sunbonnets waved in the stiff breeze besides snowy tablecloths and pillow cases. As the water was soft and the sunshine clear, with no sooty smoke to blacken, laundry work was a pleasure instead of a task. I had learned from an old housekeeper that to wash the clothes clean and dry them in the sun, carefully folding them afterwards, was better than heating ones blood by polishing with flat-irons, excepting, of course, the starched garments, which had to be ironed.[140]

Elsie, now seven years old, had learned to make good bread, and Marjory often achieved success in plain cake and pudding without eggs, simply because she generally forgot to go to the chicken yard for the eggs. The

Mary Clark's signature included in a letter written to Mary Orme in 1914.

children studied German with me in the evenings from the little primers sent by my dear old teacher in Chicago, and I called in a native lady of Castile who gave us, twice a week, lessons in the liquid Spanish tongue. It was no unusual occurrence for the children to be chattering in three languages at once—not in all with equal facility, of course, but fairly well for beginners.

When Frau Weber came (for she had married a German and dropped her pretty maiden name of Serano), she often brought her bouncing daughter Juana, who created quite a stir in our usually quiet house when, one day, she went through an inner glass door and shivered it into fragments, a daring feat which put a temporary quietus on the Spanish lesson. There were music lessons later, from a black-eyed Washington lady, and she, as well as the Sunday School teacher, frequently asked the little girls to tea, feasting them upon delicious raisins made in their vineyards. The children's pleasures were simple and wholesome and their home life most carefully sheltered.

As the summer waned and the pressure of work was somewhat over, the children and I went to Long Beach by the sea while the tired ranchman joined an excursion to Alaska. We now sat idly on the beach and whiled away the summer hours with pleasant friends. The children paddled, bathed or played in the sand. It was as if a new life of ease and pleasure had stretched out its arms to me, begging me to forget, for a season, all that was hard and discouraging in our somewhat isolated existence in a new country.

One afternoon, while I was deeply immersed in a tragic love tale which was being poured into my listening ear, a big wave came and washed Kate well out to sea before I realized her predicament. She was soon rescued, however, at the expense of a pair of new shoes and a fresh muslin gown and carried dripping up the long flight of steps to the hotel, where she was restored and returned to the beach.

Little Hal and she were of one age and always played together in the sand, while the older girls went swimming. Hal's sweet mother [Mary C. Orme] reminded me of the violets which grew in her dear garden in the heart of the then small city of Los Angeles. The cool deliciousness of her little house, with curious Japanese vines shading its windows and the fragrant myrtle, which I have never found elsewhere, comes to me now and then, as it were, in a dream. I have never forgotten her, although our paths now seem so far apart that we have apparently lost all trace of one another. Alida, her only daughter, the delicate bloom of whose cheeks I have never seen equaled, was Elsie's idol; and it was because the older girl had that fine sense of courtesy and consideration for younger children which is seldom met with.[141]

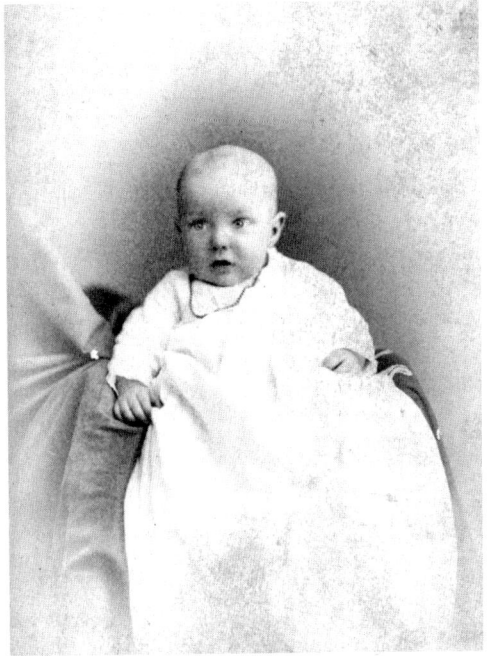

A baby photograph of Donald Clark taken in Oakland, April 1883, just prior to his father's death.

Another Christmas found little Donald asleep in his clothesbasket, under a fig tree near the house, with some one always at hand lest he should suddenly open his big blue eyes upon a strange world. The birds fought and chattered in the boughs above, and occasionally, a ripe fig dropped down to disturb his slumbers. His coming had been a great joy to the sisters, and in a little book, which was carried around in the father's pocket, had been written a list of fifty names from which to choose one for the new brother. Donald, always good and substantial and full of pleasant associations, was finally decided upon.[142]

There had been sickness in the home, and the beloved grandfather [Abraham Teegarden] had been with us. Both Marjory and her father had fallen ill with typhoid fever, which often prevailed here, and it was only the services of good doctors and kind neighbors that helped to pull them through. No trained nurses were available, but the kind who know instinctively what to do were not lacking. Marjory was very delirious and pulled out all her hair but finally recovered. It was a cause of great regret to her sisters that she was too ill to even look at her Christmas presents, and Elsie and Kate wandered sadly in the orchard, talking of her who had always been the life of the house.[143]

A few months more, and even greater changes had fallen upon the little household at "Yale Grove." The dear father had passed away in the very prime of his life, but the sun still shone on mercilessly, the roses bloomed and the birds sang as joyously as ever. In the midst of sorrow and temporary loss, we sought the silver lining in the dark cloud which hung over our home, while the gentle ministrations of friends helped us to take up the broken threads of life once more.[144]

CHAPTER 14

RECOMPENSE

A s Browning says, "It's a long lane that knows no turnings," so one morning, when the Bon Silene and La France roses nodded across the path at the sweet peas and carnations and luscious apricots and nectarines hung on the orchard boughs, a stage stopped at our entrance. The children were almost wild with delight, and even old Rover wagged his tail with unusual expressiveness, for the newcomers, who brought sunshine and helpfulness with them, were the New Hampshire grandmother [Harriet Crosby Clark] and the artist aunt, Rose [Harriet Candace Clark] by name.[145]

Now there were lessons in sewing, as well as other things which had been neglected, and the cooking, under Aunt Rose's management, took on daintiness hitherto unknown. We had delicious salads and entrees, and the grandmother insisted upon trying her hand at bread-making with the famous California flour, which was never known to fail. She reproduced for us New England cornmeal puddings, as well as other delights. Every feature of our life appealed to her—first the climate and scenery, then the children, the flowers and the oranges, of which she never tired. We had fancied she would be strict to live with, but we found her delightful. And greatly to our surprise, she enjoyed a good novel as much as anybody.

Some new friends had lately come to us. They were an elderly couple which had settled on a vineyard in the adjoining village of Tustin[146] and had built a barn and a windmill tower, which being connected, served as a house also. Many a picnic dinner was enjoyed under their stately Sycamore trees, and the choicest of melons and grapes were always kept for us. The Yale

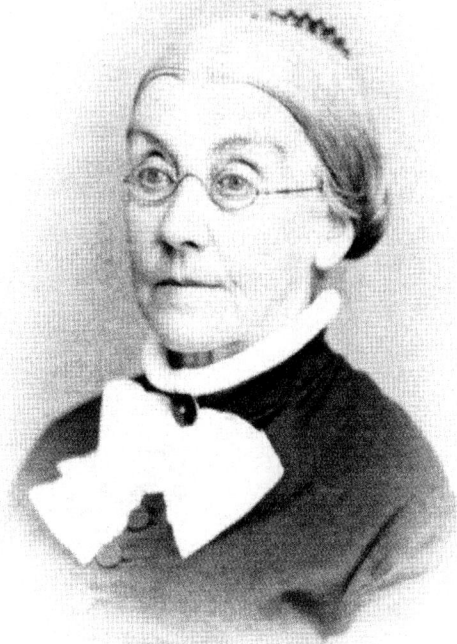

Harriet Crosby Clark, the "New Hampshire Grandmother." *Courtesy of La Porte County Historical Society.*

bond was strong between us, for the father, as well as his three sons, had graduated within those classic halls. How many times have they driven into our place, in the easy old phaeton [open carriage], with "Petty Bay"—so gentle and well cared for—and how sadly we missed them when the close tie which bound us together was severed!

When Donald arrived at the age of two years [December 4, 1884], he one day took his little saw and sallied forth like "Jack of the Bean Stalk" to conquer new worlds. He went to work very quietly and laid low a hedge of scarlet geraniums, which had attained the height of several feet. He was not punished, as we had plenty of choicer flowers. And who could, with reason, chastise him for displaying his skill as a carpenter? Presently, however, we felt the need of curtailing his liberty, so [Ah] Chong built a corral of lath under the pepper tree, and we tried to keep him there. But he soon climbed over the fence and continued his tours of discovery—either in chickens' nests or blackberry patches, from which he brought back traces of resistance in the shape of sharp pecks on his tender cheek from a hen's bill or bloody scratches from thorns.

This year, at Christmas [1884], Santa Claus did not come, because Elsie had told the other children that such a person did not exist, and this having been whispered in Aunt Rose's listening ear, she at once put herself into communication with the jolly old elf. As a result, he flew quickly past with his reindeer, leaving the children sadder but wiser.[147] Now that there was more ease and rest, with a good German girl to help with the housework,

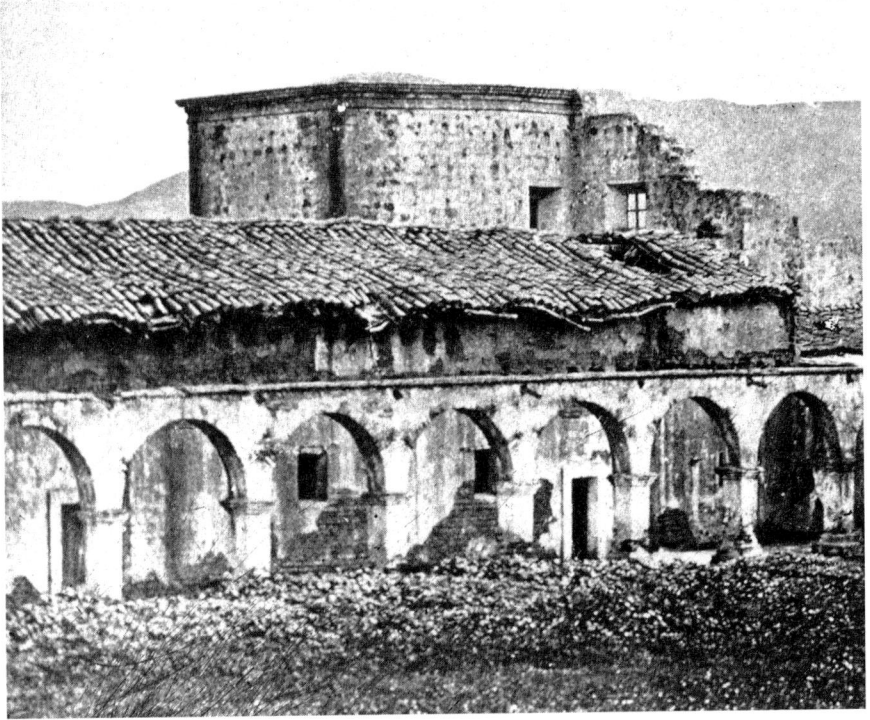

A deteriorated Mission San Juan Capistrano around 1890, about five years after Mary Clark's visit. Restoration began in 1895. *Courtesy of Phil Brigandi.*

our faithful horse "Prince" took us on many pleasant excursions—among others to San Juan Capistrano, some twenty miles away. An all-day drive brought us to the quaint village in time to see the sunset's rosy light. The old bells still hung in the Mission—a sad reminder of the time when they called the Indians to worship on the feast day of "La Purísima," December 18, 1812, thirty-six years after its establishment. In the midst of the devotions, a dreaded trembler came down, like a thief in the night, and laid waste to the beautiful and picturesque structure. The bells were still rung daily by the padre in charge, but the ivy-covered ruined arches, as well as the neglected olive trees, produced a pathetic impression upon us. There were originally eighty fertile acres of orchard and garden and four hundred olive trees. As the padre was absent, ministering to some isolated members of his flock, we did not see the old chapel which alone remains intact.[148]

The next day, we called upon the remnant of a once wealthy and powerful Spanish family whose extensive possessions had been subdivided and sold, and they had come to live in the town, amid most incongruous surroundings. There was the mother, with delicate features and soft voice, who could speak no English; the children, with dark hair, lustrous eyes and quiet demeanor— so different from the young Americans; and the aged grandmother, whose wrinkled face was a study in sorrow, as she bent over, telling her beads. There still remained that fine sense of courtesy and hospitality, for we were shown, without solicitation, beautiful old gowns, laces like cobwebs, rare jewels and tortoiseshell combs and fans which had been handed down and kept as heirlooms. Aunt Rose, artist-like, coveted the soft, tinted silks and filmy laces for her studio, but as we were only privileged to look, not to buy, we folded away the touching mementos of a happier day and showed our appreciation by expressing our thanks in Spanish. The living room contained a piano and some rich furniture, but we could see the gradual letting-down of that family pride, which had in years gone by, extended over thousands of acres, with servants at every beck and call. The only thing left was that unvarying politeness to one another, as well as to strangers, which showed that their gentle breeding had been preserved in the midst of all their vicissitudes.

Southern California was fast becoming a favorite winter resort, and hardly a day passed without tourists driving in to see the orchard. Some would be friends or acquaintances, to spend a few days en route, and often, when there were washouts on the railroads, they would pass a week or more with us. After their stay in hotels, they seemed to find our simple life pleasant by contrast. When they asked what they could do to help me, I brought out a pile of dresses to be mended or let down, which, thanks to their skillful fingers, were soon as good as new. It is a matter of great regret that I did not keep a guestbook all those years, as we had visitors from nearly every quarter of the globe, and it is this cosmopolitan characteristic which makes California so fascinating to the student of human nature.

The children were most anxious for new people to come; and one day, when they were cleaning out their playhouse (for I had advised them to be ready for visitors), Mr. [Edwin A.] Honey, the stage driver, who was also the owner of a bee ranch, which made his name all the more appropriate, handed in a mysterious telegram. This was the signal for Hannah, the capable German girl, to begin preparations for visitors, and [Ah] Chong was at once dispatched to the store for flour and sugar. The butcher was apprehended as he drove by and a leg of lamb secured, while the children were sent to pick as many green peas as possible. Photographs of the expected guests were resurrected and put on the walls. Their room was made ready, and a general air of "something unusual about to happen" hung over the place. Faces were washed, clean aprons put on, porches swept and stray toys relegated to the playhouse. At the appointed hour, "Prince" was hitched up to the two-seated buggy, while "Fly" was put to a cart, and the procession started for the station of the Southern Pacific. Mr. Brown, the agent, looked out of his window smilingly as he saw us coming, and Mr. Honey was on hand with a baggage wagon.[149]

When the train pulled in, there stood the little flaxen-headed children by their mother's side on the rear platform, waving frantically. Marjory had decided to stay at the head of her tricky little pony, lest he should take to performing and upset the cart, so the rest of us lined up at the station to greet the newcomers. By distributing ourselves in the two vehicles, we reached home in safety, but before the trunks had been unloaded, the boys disappeared and were not discovered for some time, as they were hidden under the tomato bushes, from which they finally emerged, looking like two small Indians, their faces, hair and garments completely dyed with the juice.

The four little girls played very happily either in the house, orchard or playhouse, but for Henry [Henry Teegarden Bradley] and Donald, there were many escapades—for instance, hunting eggs and playing ball with them, climbing the windmill tower and trying to jump off or playing havoc with the paint pots in the shop. Aunt Myra Bell [Teegarden] would scold a little, while Uncle John [John Henry Bradley]—handsome and dignified—looked on with a twinkle in his eyes, for his great heart had a tender spot for the children who had lost their father so early in their lives.[150]

One of our jolliest excursions was a fine picnic in the Santiago Canyon or Orange County Park. In Uncle John's carriage, with a dashing team, were his family and Kate, while the rest of us went in our buggy with Vicente, a Mexican who sometimes worked on our place as driver. As the reader has already, in an earlier chapter, taken this charming drive, I will only say that the day passed very happily, with a dinner under the live oaks and an afternoon of play, when the children crossed the streamlet on stone bridges which they built and gathered ferns or flowers or played at hide-and-seek behind the trees, canopied with mistletoe.

When it was time to start for home, Uncle John went on ahead, and his fleet horses soon out-distanced us. Vicente must have been drowsy or absent-minded, as when we were crossing a narrow place in the road, we suddenly began to slip down an embankment which I knew to be thirty feet deep. Luckily, Donald was in my lap, and I quickly got down with the children on the bottom of the wagon and held them there, while we continued to descend, until at last the horses stopped because there was no farther to go. Somewhat scared, we all got out and climbed up the bank, while Vicente repaired the damage—a broken harness. He then led the horses up, dragging the wagon after, and we went on our way rejoicing. It was so late when we arrived home that the family were growing alarmed, but as Shakespeare says, "All's well that ends well," so we were most thankful that there were no injuries and that our pleasant excursion left only happy memories.

CHAPTER 15

A TRIP TO THE YOSEMITE

One day, behind the roses on our porch, while the children were away, Aunt Rose and I talked it all over, and that night, a bag was packed with necessary changes for a two weeks trip. We were really going to the far-famed Yosemite Valley, leaving Kate and Donald in the care of the grandmother [Harriet Crosby Clark] and a dear friend whom we all called "Aunt Nelly." Arrayed in wool dresses strong enough to resist wear and tear, with stout shoes and sensible hats, we started on our journey via the Southern Pacific from Los Angeles to Madera. Here we took a six-horse stagecoach to the Mariposa Big Trees, and arrived at night [November 1, 1884], to find the message from Uncle Fred [Fred Clark] that he would meet us there the next day. What joy for Elsie and Marjory to have for a pilot through this wonderful spot, their soldier-uncle![151]

After a night spent in the shadow of these monarchs of the forest, we continued on into the Valley, and such a journey! At every turn, some new beauty met our wondering eyes, either grandeur of mountain peak or silvery music of waterfall. There was the filmy "Bridal Veil" or "Po-ho-no," meaning night wind, the Yosemite or "Large Grizzly Bear" and the Vernal and Nevada Falls, whose Indian names were indescribably charming and whose rippling waters, falling from great heights, reminded us of fairyland— so beautiful yet so unreal.

The little hotel, built around a great tree, had board partitions so thin that every sound could be heard, and the Englishman's shout for "hot water" for his "bawth" first greeted us in the morning. The children were much amused at the literary woman—also English—who sat on the veranda from morning

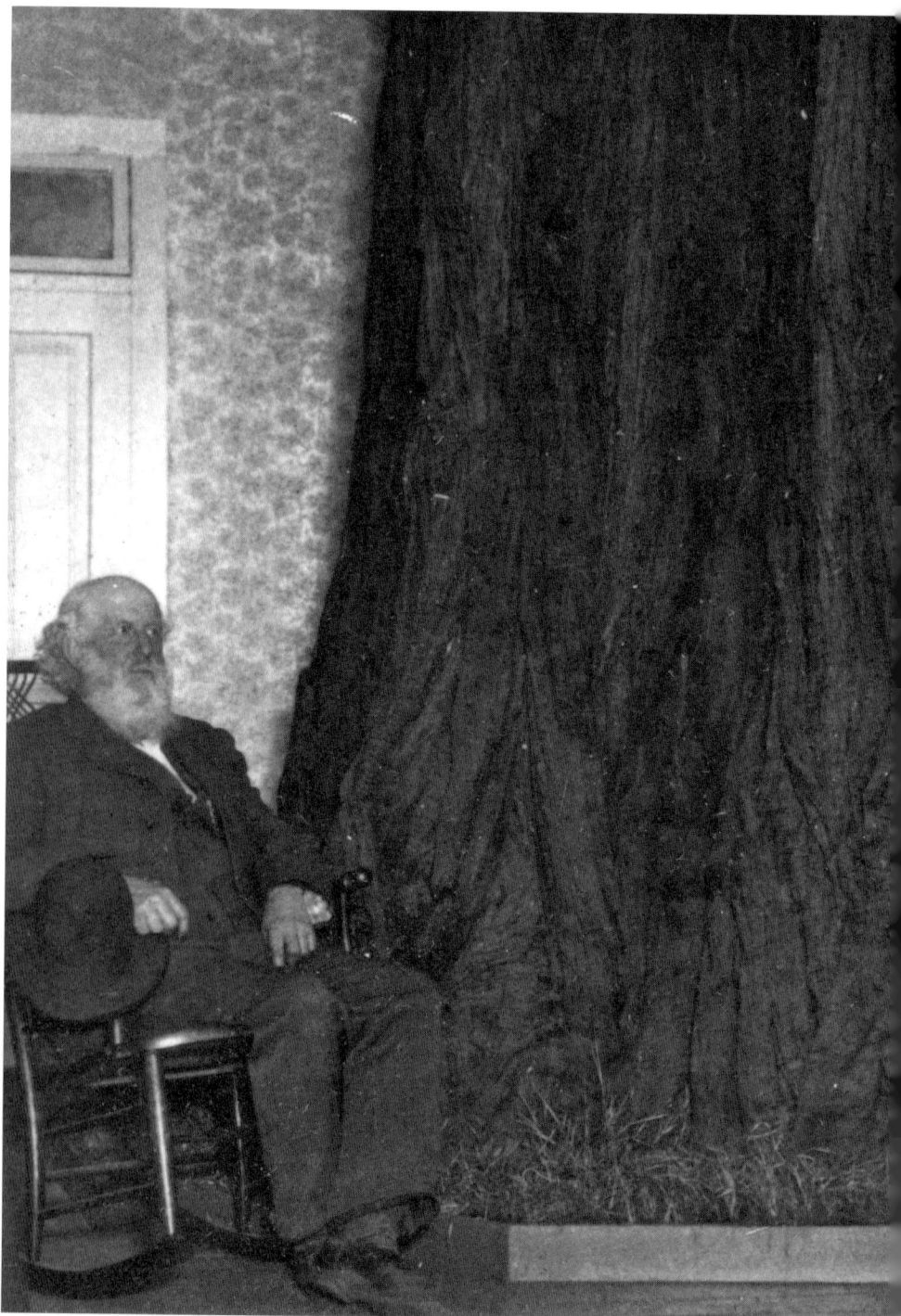

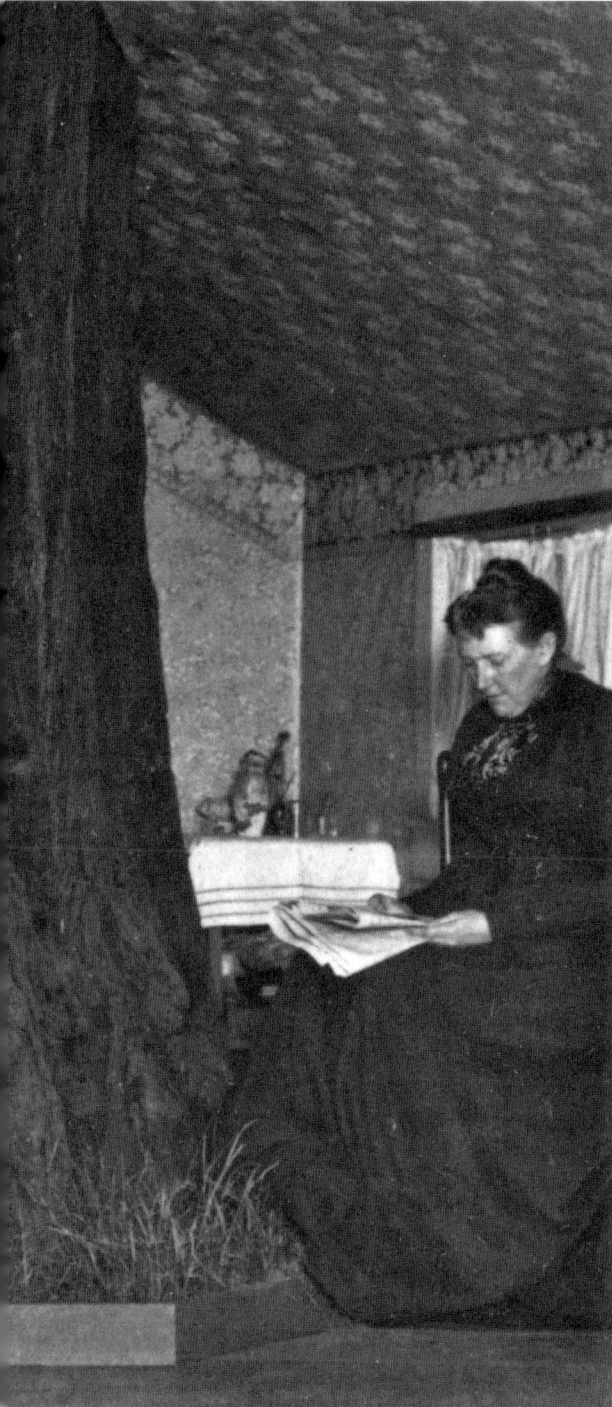

until night, paper and pencil in hand, gazing at the distant mountains and getting statistics from us all in order to write a book, without unnecessary and fatiguing exertion on her part.[152]

Every morning we mounted our burros or donkeys and started out, with guides, of course, to ensure safety. In this way, we visited all the places of interest; and on our last trip—to Glacier Point— Aunt Rose became so dizzy during the ascent that she was forced to dismount on a plateau, halfway up, while I in going down tremblingly recalled the fact that burros sometimes lay down on the trails. As I gazed down the awful abyss, the sensation of "jumping off" which some people experience at great heights came to me. The children were plucky little mountaineers. Elsie was only nine and Marjory seven, and Galen Clark— the celebrated scout—acted as their guide.[153]

The Big Tree Room at Yosemite's Upper Hotel. Mary Clark remembered it as "the little hotel built around a great tree." Persons shown unrelated. *Courtesy of Yosemite NPS Library.*

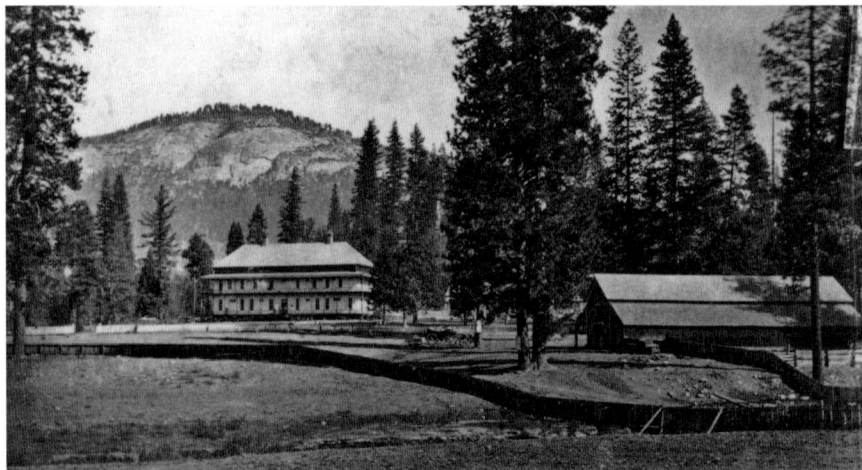

Wawona Hotel at "Big Trees," where Mary Clark stayed in 1884 and watched for the "lost" Fred Clark and British Colonel. *Courtesy of Yosemite NPS Library.*

We returned to the Big Trees to spend the rest of our time, and we had a very exciting experience there. One night, two of our party, the Uncle and a Colonel of the British Army, who had gone on a hunting expedition, failed to return at the appointed time. Guns were fired, bonfires built and searching parties went out, for the country was wild and frequented by dreaded grizzlies. The hotel was alive all night, and one searching party after another came in, with no clues whatever, until we all feared that the worst had happened to the intrepid Major [Uncle] and his companion, the Colonel. We sat all night on the porch listening to the guns and watching the fires which lighted up the enchanted forest with spectacular effects. About noon the next day, the missing men walked calmly in, but no amount of coaxing could get the story from them. All they said was that they had slept overnight in a deserted cabin, which, by the way, no guide could locate. It remains a mystery to this day where the gallant pair spent the night—whether up a tree, to escape Bruin, or wandering like the lost tribes of Israel, all the long hours of the night. As there were no signs of game, I sadly suspect that they were really lost in the mountain wilds but feared to acknowledge the fact, lest it might be a blot on their escutcheon.[154]

CHAPTER 16

THE FLIGHT OF THE DUCHESS

She was active, stirring, all fire—
Could not rest, could not tire—
To a stone she might have given life![155]

It was the epidemic of whooping cough, with even [Ah] Chong coughing sympathetically, which brought the "Duchess" to our rescue from her home in San Francisco. Her capable eye at once took in the situation, and good nursing, along with the mild climate, brought speedy relief. The "Duchess" had tired of her former profession of teaching school and liked our outdoor life and the children, so we persuaded her to remain for a time as a member of our family.

Finally, the two older girls went north to visit their Aunt Rose, and many were their delightful experiences, as for instance, French with Mdlle. Grandjean and dancing lessons and tea parties in Mrs. R's beautiful garden, under great snowball trees, or in her studio, where Marjory posed for a portrait. At this time, they went to their first fancy dress ball, at the house of the dear cousin [Susan Louisa Teegarden-Smith] who had always been kindness itself to us, and had for companions Henry and William, Arthur and Doris and pretty, rosy-cheeked Susannah. In the neighborhood was the boardinghouse where lived the voluble boy who kept declaring that "Spanish was the champion language of the globe," and whose fat father sat and slept after meals, with a napkin over his bald pate to keep off the flies. There was a Fourth of July with Uncle Fred [Clark], when he took Marjory

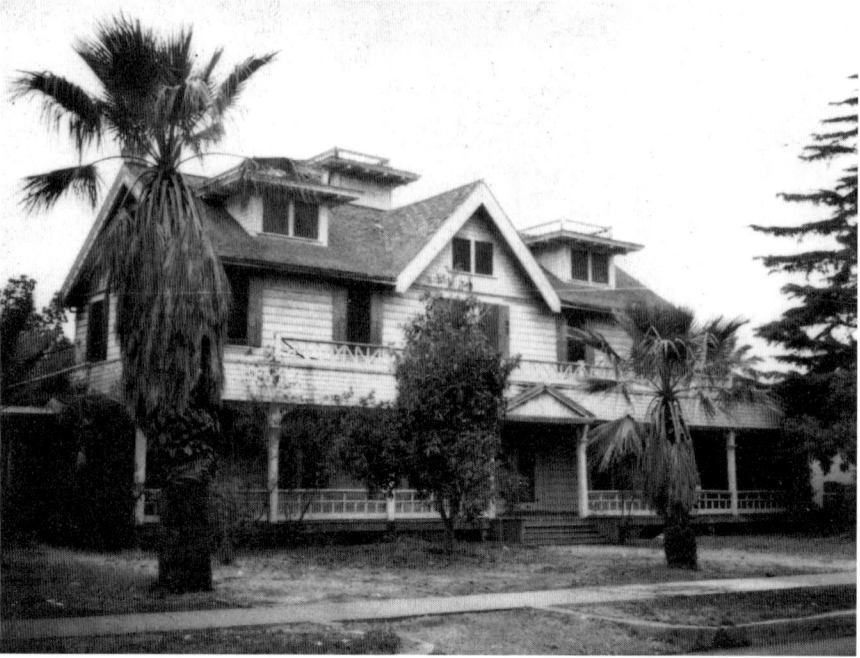

The Palmyra Hotel in later years. Built in 1887 at great expense, it soon symbolized the "Boom of the Eighties" parade of excess speculation.

and Susannah to see the fireworks, with ships of every nation in the harbor. They also visited the Geysers and the Petrified Forest and had a jolly time at Cloverdale with some more cousins [Francis Josephine Teegarden-Bowman].[156]

After the girls returned, Dick and Gevie and their mother, who was the sister of the "Duchess," spent the holidays with us, and what a wonderful Christmas we had, with three doctors, the day after, to heal disordered stomachs and bind up broken heads, for both Dick and Donald fell off the porch and gave the mothers no end of fright. Elsie, who was naturally hospitable, made lemonade on all occasions, and amusing Marjory filled the gaps, while Kate's oft-repeated "good night" produced laughter. Old Rover, a dog who came to us years before to take the place of "Shot," who was poisoned, allowed Dick and Donald to tumble all over him and seemed to enjoy their tricks beyond measure. Gevie was so sweet that a favorite doll still bears her name. Although the sunshine of her little life— as well as Dick's—went out very early, they are sacred in our memories, and our hearts still bleed for the mother who gave up her darlings when she so sorely needed them.

C. Z. CULVER,

Santa Ana Valley Immigration Agent,

No. 34 North Spring Street,

LOS ANGELES.

Called the "Prince of Speculators" by historians, C.Z. Culver's promotions eventually failed, and he took "flight to Mexico," as remembered by Mary Clark.

In the meantime, a "boom" struck Richland, which left in its wake more of disaster than benefit. To be sure, new settlers came, and property changed hands, but the sudden inflation in prices did not keep up, and many who had labored hard for years to secure a compensation lost it "in the twinkling of an eye." Under the management of speculators, special trains, in palatial style, were run from distant eastern cities. A modern hotel called The Palmyra was built and expensively furnished, and every traveler who had dollars to invest was sought out. Much of the money had been secured from Richland people—either struggling ranchmen or widows, as well as department clerks and school teachers at a distance. So great was the impression produced by all this parade that even one's banker advised loans to help it along. Finally, the bubble burst, and those who had to pay the fiddler lost thousands of dollars. It was only another instance of the old story of deceit and mismanagement, with a flight to Mexico at last.[157]

After the "boom" had passed over[158] and things had begun to slowly adjust themselves, one day, when the "Duchess" and I were talking over the future of the children, she suggested that I should go East with them for a couple of years, or for an indefinite time, if I liked. She promised to manage the place, with [Ah] Chong to do some of the outside work, and to rent rooms in the house. It really seemed plausible, and after consideration, I decided it would be a good thing for us all.

Meantime, our preparations went on, and several sewing machines were kept busy fitting out the four children. Aunt Rose very kindly sent Donald an artistic suit of her own making, and as the "Duchess" was a fine seamstress in addition to her other accomplishments, she proved invaluable at this time. How blind I was not to look ahead and realize that some bachelor would find my treasure, even as a widower had, many years before, cast longing eyes at another member of the household!

I had built a small cottage on the northeast corner of the place which had been occupied by several tenants. The gentleman for whom it was built, with his lovely wife, made ideal neighbors, but his business soon called him to a larger field, so some newcomers from Bonnie Scotland came next. They had a very interesting family of little children—Bella, Alice and Simeon, called "Simmy" for short—and their blooming cheeks were good advertisements for the oatmeal porridge upon which they had been brought up. Kate thought their quaint language beautiful and asked me one day why we did not call the bugs "beasties," as the little Stewarts did. With these children so near, we hoped that our departure would not leave an aching void in the heart of the "Duchess," but we were much mistaken. When the time came for us to start, the "Duchess," [Ah] Chong and Old Rover stood in line, and a more downcast dog I never saw, for there were actually tears in his expressive eyes. It was noon, and "Whiteface," the cow, standing in the green alfalfa field, gave a parting "moo." The red roses by the playhouse seemed to nod their heads, and the great windmill wheel swung slowly around, as to say good-bye. The stage—late by ten minutes—came dashing in, and the little Stewarts, who had by this time arrived, took their places in the line, and everybody waved us away. Mr. [Edwin A.] Honey, in his haste, drove so recklessly that the children lost hats and hair ribbons in the flight, while the luggage bounded from side to side, and we barely reached the station in time, as the conductor had just shouted, "All aboard!"

When we reached the old home in Indiana, a house was rented, and the children were placed in school. Everything was moving on quietly, when one day, a startling letter came from the "Duchess." Her virtues had been discovered by a most desirable bachelor—the possessor of a lovely home—and she wished to be released from the contract made with me. It must have been a case of "love at first sight" to progress so fast, but I did not withhold consent or congratulations, and the "Duchess" did not take flight until she had settled affairs to my satisfaction.

We have stayed on not one year or two but nearly twenty, and the life at "Yale Grove" had become only a precious heritage of memory. The pink crape myrtle tree still carries high its rosy head, though he who loved it walks no longer through earthly gardens, and the Catalonian jasmine drops its pure snow on the walk, where little tots played so long ago, picking up its petals for a chain. The old pepper tree, with its unused swing, looks in vain for the children who romped beneath its leafy shade, and the one mocking bird that ceased to sing when the dear master left is seen and heard no more.

People may come and go, but like Tennyson's *Brook*, the trees and flowers will "go on forever" to make some heart glad. And who shall deny that its early impressions may not be made to blossom in the third generation? For even now, two dear little children [Norton W. Barker and Margery Barker], in their country home near the shores of Lake Michigan, wander among the arbutus and wintergreen in the early spring, listening to the song of the meadow lark or studying, with intense interest, in the winter time, great flocks of snow birds in the millet fields. So, in the midst of my loneliness and longing for the sweet old garden, I try to find consolation in the thought that its mission has not been in vain.[159]

> *The clear spring, that 'midst it herbs*
> *Wells softly forth and visits the strong roots*
> *Of half the might forest, tells no tale*
> *Of all the good it does*
> *—Bryant*

1906.

CHAPTER 17

THE FULFILLMENT

The story which you have just read was laid away unfinished over twenty years ago. When the dear mistress of "Yale Grove" recently passed into the Great Beyond, she left the last chapter, which she had planned to sometime add, unwritten. Many changes have come to pass since she first began her story. At that time, Donald had just graduated from Yale, and in the course of later events, he returned with his mother to "Richland" to aid her in the disposal of the old home and orchard. Here Cupid quite unexpectedly played a hand in the formation of his career, and sixteen years ago [1909], he became the owner of a part of "Yale Grove." He set out a new orchard and married his sweetheart [Celia Mable Nunn], and a wonderful family of children came one by one and two by two into the little grey house in which Marjory, Kate and Donald were born.

The first six children remember their dear grandmother [Mary Teegarden Clark], who came often with Kate to see them from her home in the East. She was such a young grandmother in spirit, so straight and slender of form and quick in mind and step. I can see her now, coming down the long driveway, past the fifty-year-old giant eucalyptus tree, her arms full of the books her own children loved. Soon, the little blond, rosy-cheeked grandchildren gathered all about her, and the "story hour" began. She told them many of the tales you have here before you and others of her own childhood, which they will never forget.[160]

Each Sabbath morning, under the white hawthorn tree, they met for Sunday School, sitting demurely in a row on a small wooden bench,

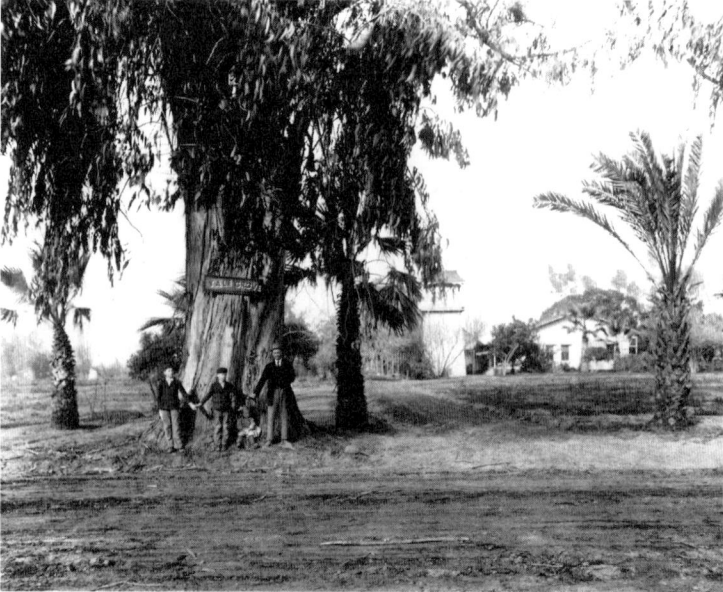

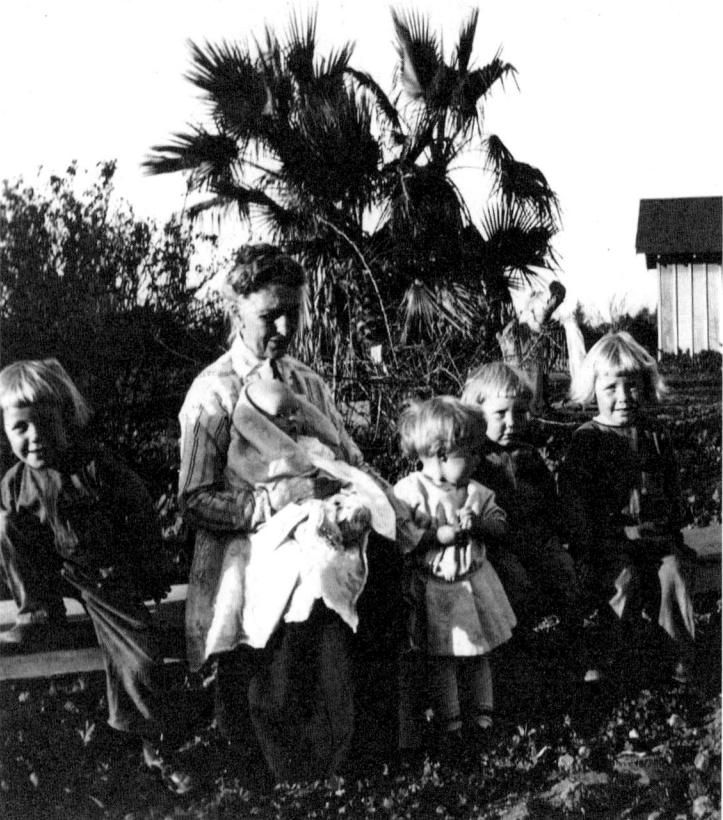

while their dear grandmother taught them the first simple truths of the Bible. There were many happy excursions with her to the beach and the mountains, and whole Kodak albums were filled with the "snaps" Kate took of them all during the first ten years of those visits. Her passing away was to them a great sorrow, for she held a most cherished place in their tender little hearts. But she left behind to her children and grandchildren the heritage of a memory so perfect that only joy and inspiration can follow them all the rest of their lives.[161]

1924 K.C.

Opposite, top: Yale Grove as seen from Palmyra Avenue in 1910. Donald Clark, standing at right beside the "giant eucalyptus tree," soon planted a second orchard. (The children are unrelated neighbors.)

Opposite, bottom: Mary Clark in 1916 at the Yale Grove with five of her grandchildren.

APPENDIX A

MARY CLARK READS A BRIEF HISTORY OF EARLY ORANGE

Orange Star
January 16, 1917

The meeting yesterday of the Woman's Club of Orange was one of the most interesting held in recent times. The program was on "Landmarks" and was in charge of Mrs. Billingsly. Mrs. Billingsly read an exhaustive paper on Landmarks, taking her hearers back to the constructive period and bringing them gradually to the present. Her treatment of the missions was particularly fine. Mrs. J.E. Parker, who is a member of the older families in the community, read an excellent paper, hers being descriptive of the period between 1873 and the present and telling of the changes wrought through these older families from a veritable wilderness. Mrs. D.C. Pixley, the president, gave an impromptu talk concerning the Plaza, comparing its passing from a dump heap on which were found many articles from a tin can to dead chickens, when the Pixleys came here, to the present beauty spot now enjoyed by tourists who come from all over the world. The paper which follows is from the pen of Mrs. Mary T. Clark and tells stories of human interest that concerned the more intimate happenings of those early days, hers being from 1875, when she and her husband first saw Orange.[162] *At the urgent request of the many who enjoyed and heard the paper, Mrs. Clark consented to its publication:*

In the fall of 1875, a worn-out court reporter of Chicago, with his young wife and eighteen months' old little girl, set out for Southern California, seeking an out-door life. The little house which they hoped to build had been planned by an architect friend the night before they left Chicago and is now standing intact in an orange grove on West Palmyra Avenue, for many years known as the "Yale Grove," in honor of the original owner's alma mater.[163]

Our first stop was at Vallejo, to visit some cousins, and here I had my first glimpse of "John Chinaman," otherwise "Ah Fong," the cook at the hospitable Starr home. An air of mystery hung about him always, for he had on his right hand an extra finger. My cousins' garden, with its lovely roses, fuschias, heliotrope, laurustinus, honeysuckles and pepper trees, was a delight to me. Leaving Vallejo, our boat waited to take us to Santa Barbara, where we drove to beautiful Montecito Valley for a few hours' visit with our old-time friends—the Bonds. Then resuming our journey by water, our next stop was Wilmington, thence by rail to Anaheim and by stage to Orange, which was destined to be our future home.[164]

When we reached Orange, the stage halted before a square cement building known as the "Hygiene Home" and kept by a Dr. Larkin [Larken]. It stood in a large enclosure, surrounded by pepper trees, about where Ehlen and Grote's store is now located. It was absolutely the only refuge for travelers and was miserably furnished with poor beds and worse meals, with only ditch water to quench one's thirst.[165]

Upon arising early the next morning to gaze upon the boasted orange trees, I found them little whips among the corn stalks. The only welcome I received was the bow of a diminutive owl, perched upon my window sill. There were some fine vineyards of Mission and Muscat grapes, and the young orchards of almond and walnut, but much of the country was covered with cactus and sage brush, presenting a desert-like appearance.

When it became known we were in search of land, we were driven over the country by interested parties, many of whom had large tracts of land in sheep and bee ranches, which they were eager to subdivide. It was an uncommon occurrence in 1875 for eastern tourists to seek out Orange. I can recall but one family stopping at the Hygiene Home while we were there. They were from Boston and did not remain. The Collins brothers, with their mother, as well as Dr. [James N.] Truesdell and family, the Sibleys, Yarnells, Fraziers, Shaffers, Joslins, Armors, Rusk, Walter [L.] Witherbee and Mr. [George C.] Hager came about the same time, and the Harrow family a year or two later. The Lockharts, Parkers, Travises, McPhersons, Andersons, Crowders, Gardners, Mosbaughs, Chadborne,

P.D. Youngs, Haywards, Harwoods and the two Beach families were already settled here. Pioneer days appeal strongly to me, but absence and the lapse of years dim my memory, and some names have escaped me.[166]

To return to my story, after searching the country for a piece of land with a house on it and finding none, my husband, solely to satisfy me and relieve my constantly increasing home-sickness, decided to remark our goods, which were still at Newport Landing, and return to the east. I wrote to my devoted father [Abraham Teegarden] of my troubles, and he replied at once that he would put a country place of ten acres, with a small home on it, at our disposal in case we returned to Northern Indiana and still sighed for country life.

The morning came for our departure. I had said good-bye to kind Mrs. Beach, who had sent me flowers and fruit from her little garden as a parting gift, and I was sitting on the hotel porch, with the baby on my lap, all ready for the journey when the stage drove up. A jolly man named Neal [Henry Neill] was on the box, who, with the bystanders, looked askance at the homesick lady saying good-bye. All at once, I was overtaken by the most dreadful remorse and shame for the lack of courage I had shown, and turning to my husband, I disclosed that I would stay on and do the best I could. The stage drove on, and I began a search for an abiding place.

The town was very small—not a room or house to rent, only the Grange store operated by Mr. J.W. Anderson and Crockett Bowers, the post office being in this store. Next was the establishment of Mr. R.L. Crowder, who kept a general stock of dry goods and groceries and was also a moneylender.[167] Then there was the blacksmith shop, the little water office and the Methodist church.

One of the most picturesque features of Orange, in those early days, was the old Chinese wash-house, located near the Presbyterian church. Here the Chinese congregated in their native costumes with the queues, which were afterward banished. It was very amusing to hear them chattering so fast in their indescribable pigeon English. On Chinese New Year, they always presented their friends with nuts, lilies in pots, silk handkerchiefs and those wonderful tasseled lanterns which so delighted my children.[168]

Fortunately, in my search, I came across a kindly Irish woman who rented me a front room and gave me the privilege of using her kitchen stove. It did not take long to get a few necessary articles unpacked, and we were quite comfortably settled before the winter rains set in. In the

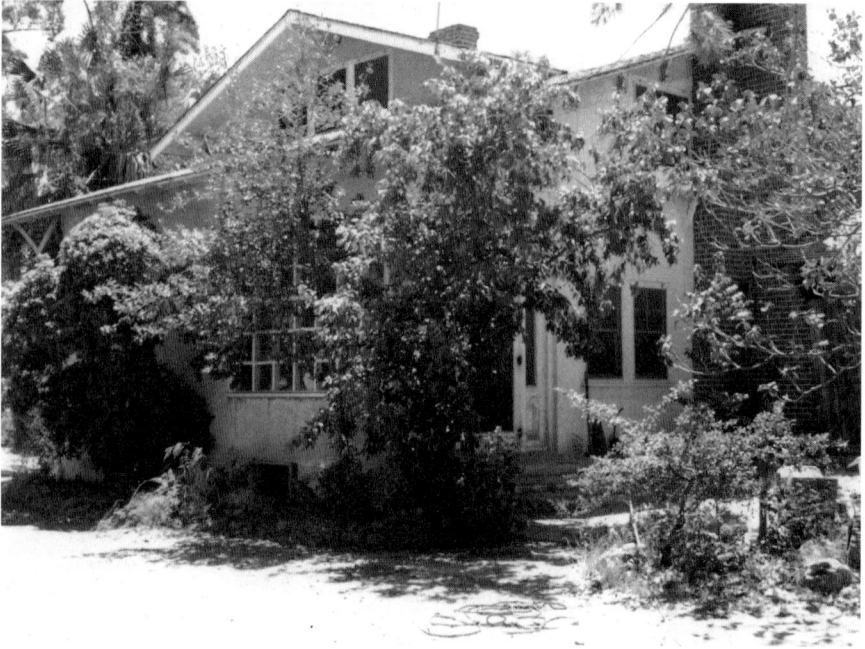

The Yale Grove ranch house just before its removal in 1976. *Courtesy of Christine Clark.*

meantime, we secured twenty acres of land, three-fourths of a mile from the town, on what is now West Palmyra Avenue. My husband bought a team of horses and swung his hammock under the pepper trees near the hotel, where he slept to ward off horse thieves, who were rampant at this time.

Christmas day approached, and horses Bell and Rattler were hitched to the drag to clear the land, yellow with mustard stalks, for a home. Little Elsie and I sat on the ground, making garlands of baby blue eyes, spring beauties and lupines, for at that time, there were acres and acres of the loveliest wildflowers. All at once I sighed for the fleshpots of Egypt, remembering the Christmas feasts at the old home. I begged the tired ranchman to give the horses a rest and take us over to Anaheim to get something good to eat. At length we set out, and finding in a neat little shop in Anaheim some mutton chops, drove home through the fast falling darkness. The baby was given her cup of milk and put to bed. A fire of corncobs was kindled in the stove, and the table was set with a wheaten loaf and a pat of fresh butter. And when the chops came off the coals, it was a feast for the gods.

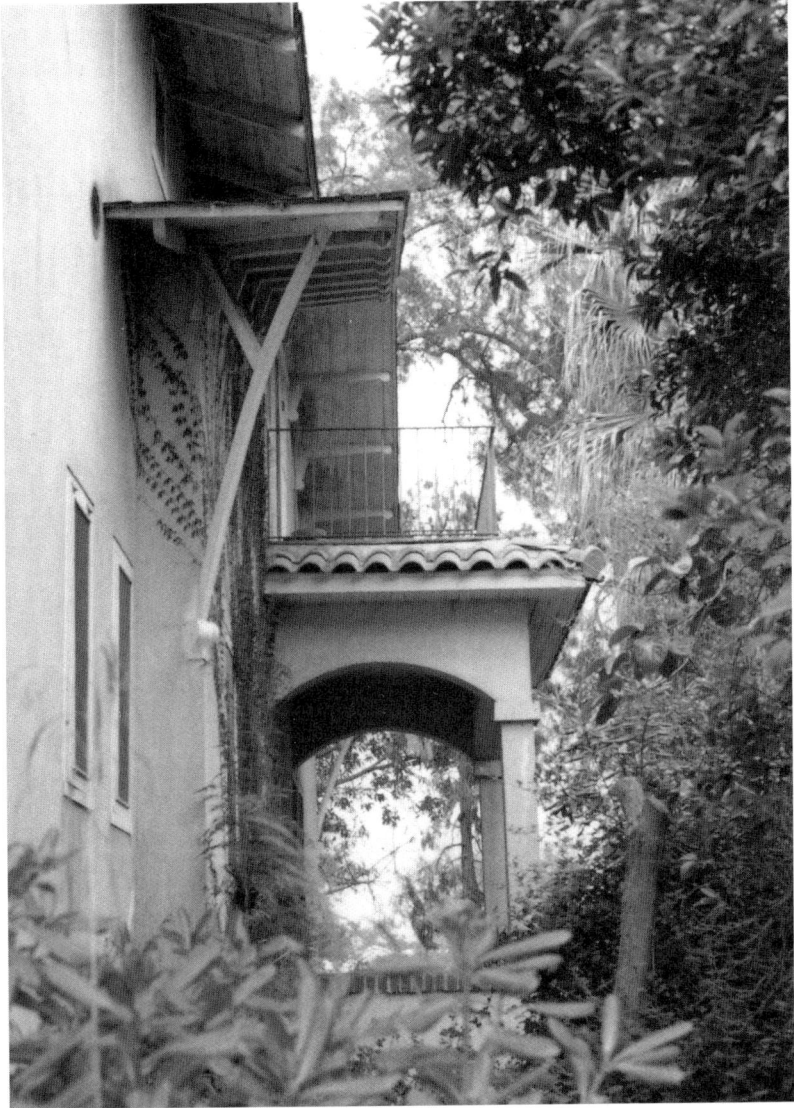

Side view of remodeled Yale Grove ranch house in 1976. Notice the eave decorations from the original home. *Courtesy of Christine Clark.*

So time passed, the lumber for the house was hauled from Newport Landing, and often, the baby and I went and returned on the load. We were so happy when the little house was complete, the deep well driven and the orange trees set out. Then there was a Jersey cow and some chickens, vegetables growing and berries. The only misfortune about the chicken business was the destruction of forty young Plymouth Rock hens in a single night by coyotes, leaving only a turkey gobbler and one Leghorn rooster to people the carefully built chicken house.

There was no more home-sickness, for we had our books and pictures. Life was very busy, and we were making new friends. The firewood was willow poles, and a man could cut and haul a year's supply for about $8 or $10.[169] There were no luxuries such as gas and electric stoves, automobiles and moving pictures; no worry about fashion in hats or gowns, except to be neat and comfortable. We all worshipped for several years in one small church and shared each other's joys and sorrows.

One of the most exciting events of this time was the raid of Mexican desperadoes, which occurred one dark rainy night in 1878 [1880]. Among those who figured in it were our neighbors, Mr. [George J.] Mosbaugh, Mr. Samuel Rusk, Mr. [Henri F.] Gardner, Mr. [J.] Colman Travis and Mr. [Albert B.] Clark. As I was alone with my children, I became very uneasy, as the hour grew so late, and my husband did not appear. It was his custom to go down to the Grange Store for his mail and to discuss orchard and irrigation matters with those who gathered there. This evening, as they had gone from Anderson's (where Woods' store is now) over to Crowder's store and were busily talking in the rear, a commotion at the front door drew their attention. Upon investigating, they encountered a number of desperate Mexicans holding revolvers in front of them. Some of the ranchers were inclined to resist but being unarmed were finally overcome and thrown to the floor.

Barley sacks were tied over their heads, their hands and feet were bound securely and their pockets gone through. Overcoats, if not too well worn, which was the case with Mr. Clark's, were taken, as well as watches and all valuables. In the meantime, Mrs. Crowder, with the baby, in the rear of the store, where she lived, was called in and made to reveal where the money and valuable goods, such as blankets and men's clothing, were to be found. After overhauling the stock, which they bundled on their fast horses, the bandits told Mrs. Crowder to untie the men in about an hour and let them go home, thus giving the desperadoes ample time to escape. This raid was only one of many on several adjoining settlements, but the old History of Los Angeles County, published about this time, says that the robbers were finally apprehended and punished.[170]

Though it is thirty years since I left Orange with my four children, after their father's brilliant and promising life was cut short by illness and death, tributes to his memory still come to me and are greatly cherished. His vigorous work as first president of the Santa Ana Valley Irrigation Company, at a most trying time in its history, will not soon be forgotten. Forty-one years after the first Christmas spent in our new home in Orange, my little grandchildren gathered about the same fireplace to open their tiny stockings and share the joys of Christmas with their eastern grandmother.[171]

The following postscript is from the *Orange Daily News*, April 30, 1938:

It is interesting to learn that the former home of Mrs. Mary T. Clark at 607 West Palmyra, Orange, has remained in the Clark family for sixty-three years [in 1938]. *After the death of Albert Clark in 1883, his widow,*

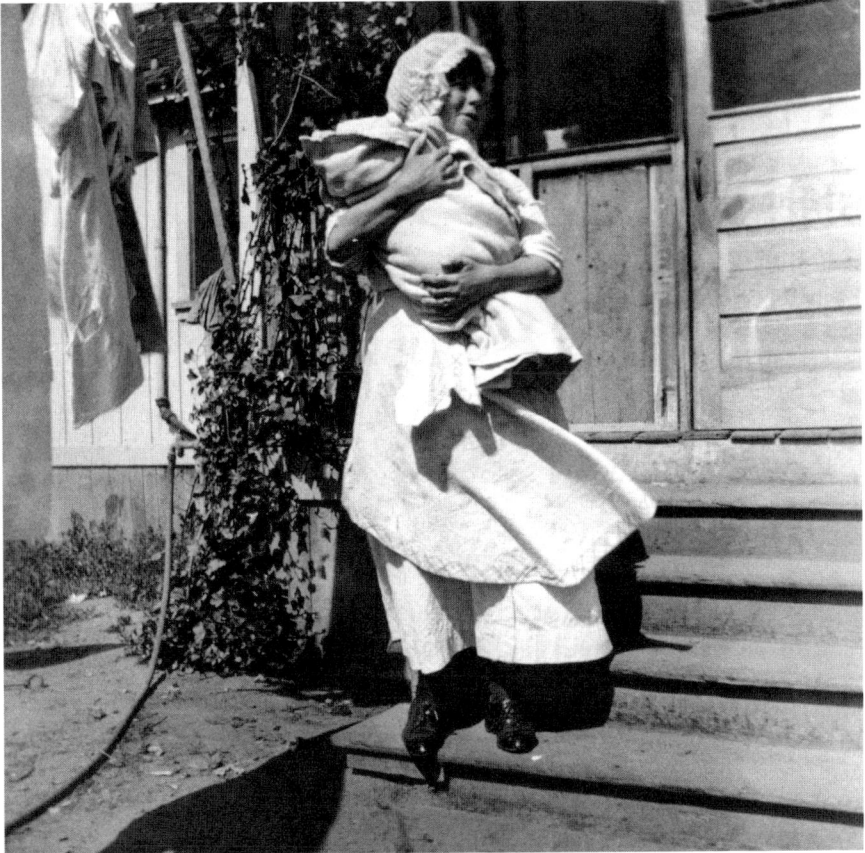

Celia Nunn Clark, wife of Donald Clark, holding a child at Yale Grove.

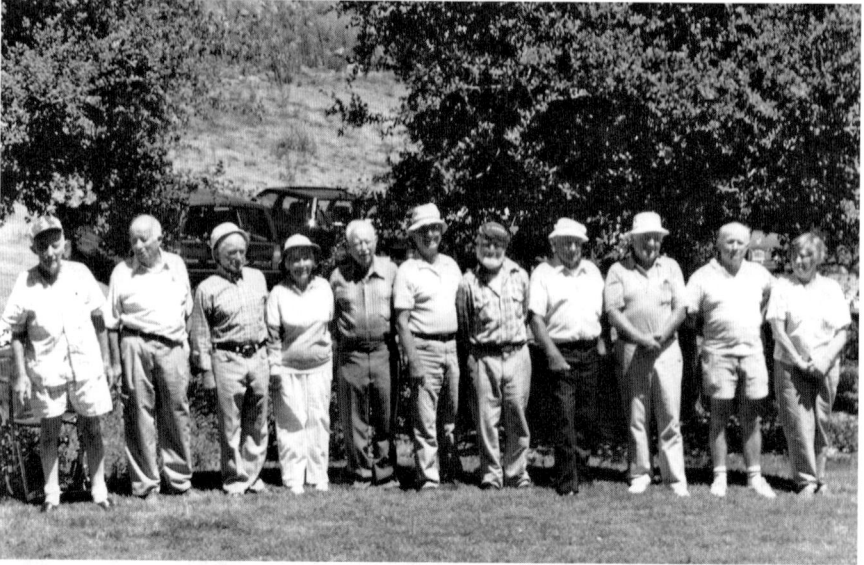

The "Children of Yale Grove" in 1990. *From left to right*: Donald Teegarden, Duncan, Albert, Suzanne, David, Stuart, Robert, John Neil, George, O. Joseph and Celia Rosamond.

Mrs. Clark, returned in 1887 to her old and childhood home in La Porte, Indiana, and there reared her four young children.

In 1910 [actually 1909], *her only son, Donald Clark, a 1905 Yale University graduate, returned to Orange and has lived since on part of the original twenty-acre tract that had been the home of his parents and the birthplace of their three younger children. He married Celia Nunn of Orange on January 22, 1912, and Mr. and Mrs. Donald Clark have owned and occupied the old place for the past twenty-six years. Here they have successfully reared their family of eleven children, namely: Donald, Duncan, Albert, Suzanne, David, Stuart, Robert, Neil, George, Oliver and Rosamond.*[172]

The original orange orchard was replanted about 1910, but the little home built by Mr. and Mrs. Albert B. Clark in 1875 remained practically unchanged until 1924, when it was enlarged and modernized for the need of a growing family of another generation.

MARY CLARK TELLS OF HER FAMILY LIFE AND FATHER IN INDIANA

The La Porte *Daily Herald*
January 9, 1907

The January meeting of the La Porte County Historical Society, adjourned from New Year's Day, was held at the city library last evening. A good attendance was present, and several new members were taken in. The feature of the evening was Mrs. Mary Treat [Teegarden] *Clark's paper on the life and character of her father, Dr. Abraham Teegarden, who began the practice of medicine in La Porte in 1837 and became one of the most notable figures in the community. Curiously enough, the first patient he was called on to treat professionally, Robert White, was at the meeting. He spoke of the circumstances and of the friendship which, commencing then, endured so long as the doctor lived. Others who spoke of Dr. Teegarden and of his skill and humanity were Dr.* [George M.] *Dakin, John W. Ridgeway and William Niles.*[173] *Mrs. Clark's paper, which is of exceptional value, follows:*

Let me bring before your mind's eye a beautiful portion of eastern Ohio known as Columbiana County. It is a land of hills and dales, of brooks and ravines—picturesque in the extreme. It borders on Pennsylvania, and hither, at an early day, came many settlers from the Keystone State.[174]

Among them was a sturdy, pious farmer named William Teegarden, with his helpmeet, Susannah Rafelty, who, as their names would

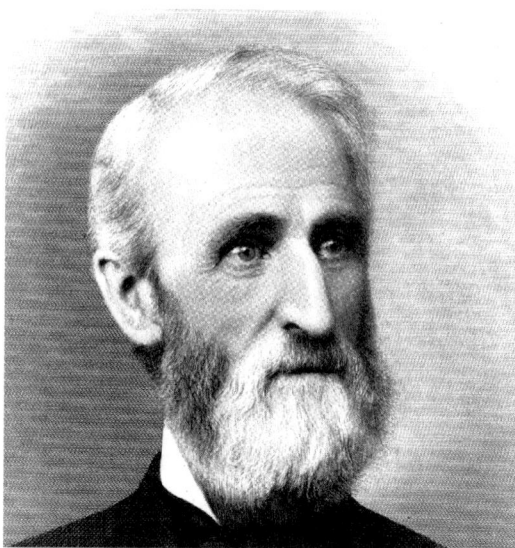

Portrait of Abraham Teegarden.

indicate, were both of that excellent stock known as Pennsylvania Dutch.[175] As the years of pioneering went on, they tilled a large farm and brought up a family of seven sons and five buxom daughters.[176] That these children were trained to obedience, reverence and piety stands to reason, as the course of their after lives will show. Family prayers were never omitted, and if tasks were shirked, punishment awaited the offender.

As my grandfather became more prosperous, he built a large cream-colored brick house which still stands in good repair—a monument to those who in an early day built wisely and well. Under the eaves are carved the initials "W.T. S.T.," as was the custom at that time. It was substantial and stately, with a wide hall running through the center, on one side, a spinning-room for the girls, who were expected to weave all the cloth used by the family, and on the other side was a shoemaker's and tailor's shop for the boys. It is true that at times, when the exigencies of farm work prevented, workmen came and plied these trades, but as a general rule, the children as they grew up did the bulk of this work.

A few years ago, it was my privilege to visit this ancestral home, to find it, much to my regret, in the hands of strangers. Remains of the orchard and picturesque stone springhouse were there, but on the shelves of the latter I found no traces of the pans of rich cream and spicy pumpkin pies which were a tempting bait to the children of long ago. I also made a pilgrimage to the ruins of the log schoolhouse, where, for a few weeks only in the year, each child got the requisite amount of schooling. My grandfather was somewhat of a hard taskmaster and, like many of this day and generation, did not think a great amount of education necessary, especially when it interfered seriously with other tasks.[177]

Abraham, often called Abram, the fourth son, was rather a delicate lad, and instead of being put at severe farm labor was, through the intercession of a kind mother, allowed to herd and care for the sheep, besides doing light chores and often assisting in household tasks. I am sure it was here that he learned to cook, for he could always broil a steak to perfection and roast a pan of coffee to just the right degree of brownness.

As the years rolled on, one by one the boys escaped, as farmer boys will. Eli was the first to go to a medical college in Cincinnati, then followed Aaron, later Abraham, then Matthias and Albert, leaving only Uriah and William to carry on farming as their chosen profession. It seems rather an unusual occurrence for four brothers in one family to become physicians. That they were all successful, California, Ohio, Indiana and Wisconsin can testify, for in each of these states, they were honored in life and lamented in death.[178]

It was in the year 1837 that a lank, light-haired horseman of about 26 years, Abraham by name, said good-bye to his tearful mother and sisters and rode from his Ohio home across the country through the wilderness of Indiana to the trading post at Fort Dearborn. He had his good horse and gun and $100 in money, and his saddlebags were distended by all sorts of remembrances, among the rest a Bible from his mother. Chicago, with its stretch of desolate prairie and its impassible mud, did not attract this young Buckeye, who had been raised among stately forest and running brooks, so he retraced his weary way and after viewing the little hamlet of La Porte, he stopped there, boldly hung out his shingle and waited for patients.[179]

As the electic school of medicine, in which he had won his diploma, was then comparatively unknown, in this section at least, he was not pleasantly welcomed by the regular practitioners of the old school. They frowned upon him and his methods—such as compounding his own remedies from roots and herbs. Still, he went on making his famous pills and distributing them, for it was in the time of fever and ague.[180] And right before me now (on the secretary's table), you may see his old mortar and pestle, which I esteem one of my greatest treasures. Gradually, he won his way, and the new settlement afforded a good field for his ministrations.

He rode day and night over the country, alleviating misery, and by his skill as a nurse, restoring many to health who had been given up by other doctors. He was a fitting type of the pioneer physician whose praises have been worthily sung by Leroy Armstrong in his novel The Outlaws:

"There was unconscious pathos in the practice of those old doctors. Above all men these were the public servants, subject to any hour of the dark or daylight to any call from any distance; rousing from needed sleep in blessed bed to such exposure as cannot now be estimated, driving or riding unmeasured miles, and fighting death in many forms, with weapons simple and inadequate, with shrewd guessing instead of demonstration, with careful estimating of remedy instead of well-established formulas or ready preparation—these were the doctors in that early day. They opened the eyes of the newly born, they cared for them through the besetments of infancy, and healed their hurts in the accidents of youth. They knew these patients, the maladies that lay in wait for each, their power of résistance and the medications to which each would respond. And they died just as they had established a sound generation, and went to their rest forgiving a myriad debts that money could pay—but did not, and a legion of obligations that no cash could cover. And they sleep under sod as silent as the sons and daughters whose health was in their keeping. Heaven rest them, for they earned it when the land was young."[181]

To return to my father, I will say that he finally came out victorious, though tradition has it that he fought several pitched battles to achieve it. His strict integrity and uniform courtesy, together with his professional skill, finally won him great respect from those who had at first opposed him. By this time—in 1840—he had found a wife in the eldest daughter [Lura Treat Teegarden] of Samuel Treat, a pioneer from Plainfield, N.Y., who was affectionately known in the settlement as "Uncle Sammy." It required no little courage and ability to become the helpmeet of a country doctor whose practice had now so increased that he had built a large house on Main street, containing offices and living rooms, as well as accommodations for students who were eager to profit by his instructions. The attic was devoted to skeletons and dissecting rooms, and as a child, I had very gruesome ideas of this forbidden spot.

Among the pleasantest recollections of my early childhood were the visits paid with my father to one country house which always seemed like fairyland. It was none other than the beautiful home of General Joseph Orr (now the Dick farm), whither the doctor went regularly

An ad for Abraham Teegarden's hotel in La Porte, Indiana, where alcohol was said to have been forbidden. *Courtesy of La Porte County Historical Society.*

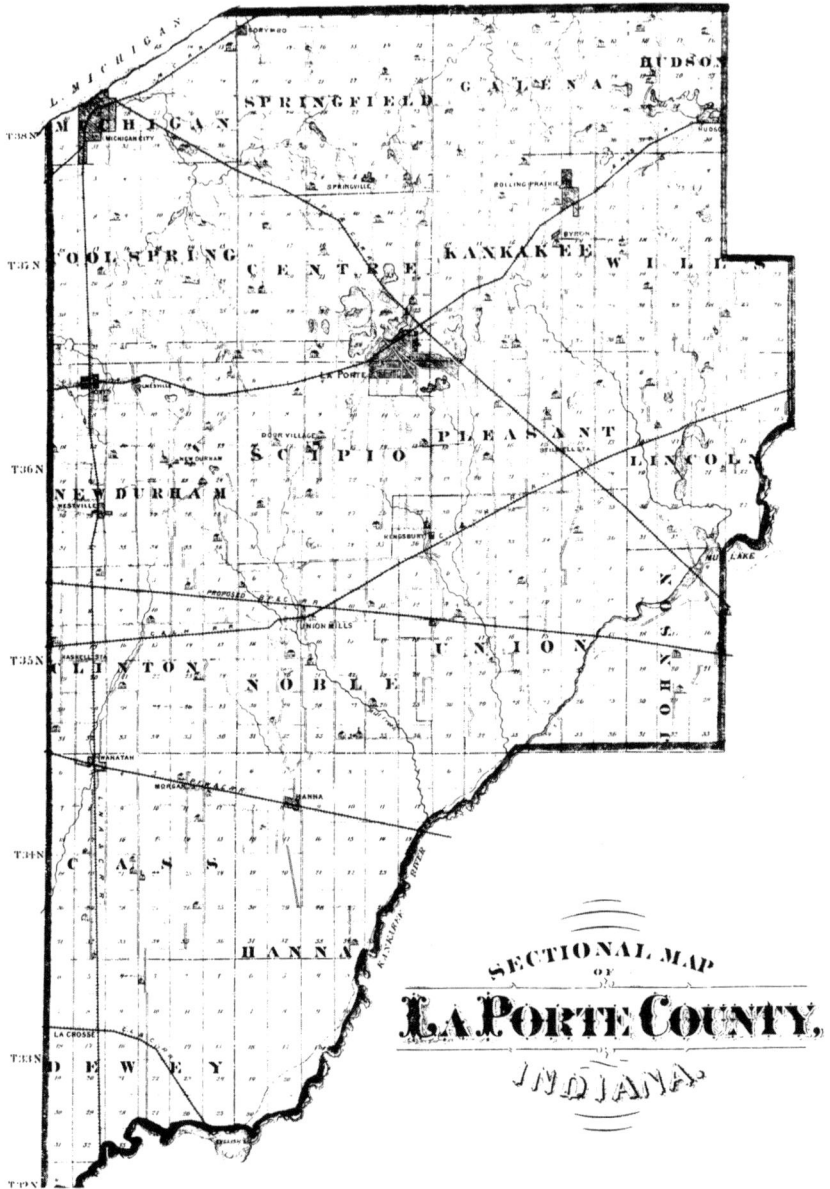

Map of La Porte County showing the city of La Porte in the center with surrounding townships. *Courtesy of La Porte County Historical Society.*

to minister to the general's invalid son. There were always geraniums blooming in the windows in winter, as well as remarkable little Jerusalem cherry trees in pots. And on the shining mahogany sideboard were plates of red apples and slices of pound cake for a good little girl. In summer, the cherry trees were laden with rosy clusters of "Ox-Hearts" and "May Dupes," while from pear and peach boughs gleamed golden fruit of wonderful perfection. The general, a florist and horticulturist far ahead of his times, received a great many premiums at county fairs, and on one occasion, there was a life-sized figure of a child on a wire frame done in dahlias of every color. This was presented to the doctor, and it became one of the greatest treasures of my young life. Even after the flowers dried up and faded away, I still seemed to see those waxen petals of rich crimson, purple, gold and white.[182]

There was another homestead, the Crane farm in Scipio Township,[183] where our butter was made for over 25 years. In the dooryard was an old-fashioned well with bucket and sweep, which produced the coldest water I ever tasted. The treat at this place was a thick slice of fresh salt-rising bread, well spread with delicious yellow butter cut from a roll suspended in the well bucket to cool it.[184]

After these visits, there was the long drive home, either in sleigh or carriage, according to the season, and at the end, the smiling face of my mother at the door awaiting us with a simple but wholesome supper of creamed dried beef, poached eggs, hot biscuits and honey or the delicate preserves upon which housekeepers of that day prided themselves. Afterward came the goodnight hour in the great office redolent of orange and lemon peel, stick cinnamon, cloves and raisins. All of these ingredients went into some very excellent bitters which made the doctor famous. On the counter were the scales, and in one corner stood a great desk piled with most mysterious ledgers in which accounts were kept, which, I fancy, did not always balance in favor of the generous doctor, who never pressed his poor patients.[185]

My father loved children and flowers. From the time of his first coming to La Porte, he always carried in a famous pocket some little treat for his child patients, while in his garden grew every conceivable herb of healing and flowers of every hue, which he bestowed upon his friends. Whether they were choice roses, clove pinks, sweet peas or hollyhocks, they were equally prized by those so fortunate as to receive them. Simplicity was one of his most striking characteristics, and though he lived to the age of three score and ten, he kept the heart of a child in all its charm and purity. He left his impress upon this community as a man of honor and lofty patriotism; of everyday Christianity and unfailing kindliness and charity to all, whether rich or poor, black or white. In times of sorrow, his presence was a benediction, and his keen pleasantry made him a welcome guest at joyful feasts. The lesson of such a life cannot be lost; it must outlive its day and generation, and in the words of Ruskin, "It is better to be nobly remembered than nobly born."[186]

NOTES

Introduction

1. Orange County split off from Los Angeles County in 1889.
2. Los Angeles *Daily Herald*, July 24, 1880. To say "absolutely nothing in the shape of habitations" existed in 1873 arguably reflects a newspaper editor's hyperbole. These places saw families settling, but the sparse population no doubt caused outsiders to wonder about their prospects, as demonstrated by Mary Clark's own account of her early homesickness for the well-settled areas of the East.
3. Together, Los Angeles and Orange Counties contain over five thousand square miles. By comparison, La Porte County, Indiana, where Mary Clark grew up, covers about six hundred square miles and counted around 27,000 persons in 1870 and 31,000 in 1880. Chicago held nearly 300,000 persons in 1870 and over 500,000 in 1880. The entire U.S. population in 1880 was about 50,000,000. In 2010, Los Angeles and Orange Counties embraced over 12,800,000 persons.
4. Orange first appeared in 1870 newspaper notices under the name of "Richland"; see *Anaheim Gazette*, November 10, 1870 and Los Angeles *Daily Star*, December 14, 1870. The name Richland was short-lived, as it was replaced by Orange when the community sought a post office in 1873, at which time postal authorities mandated another name since a town called Richland already existed in California; see Leo J. Friis's *Orange County Through Four Centuries* (Santa Ana, CA: Pioneer Press, 1965),

63 and Phil Brigandi's *A Brief History of Orange, California: The Plaza City* (Charleston: The History Press, 2011), 15–19. Orange's population when the Clarks arrived reportedly stood at about 250; see *Anaheim Gazette*, March 4, 1876. Orange incorporated as a city in 1888.

5. Other Southern California memoirs from late nineteenth century exist alongside Mary Clark's. Within Orange, another female voice is that of Margaret Gardner (1888–1970), who spoke eloquently in the "The Community of Orange" in *Orange County History Series, Vol. II* (Santa Ana: Orange County Historical Society, 1932), 149–195. Gardner relied on family and other sources for earlier events she told. Florence Smiley (1893–1979) vividly recalls domestic ranch life in Orange from the late 1890s in her oral history interview with Milan Pavlovich, 1970 (Fullerton: Oral History Program, 1977).

6. Pioneer settlers began arriving in northwest Indiana around La Porte in the late 1820s, with a major rush of home seekers following final land cessions by the indigenous Potawatomi tribe in the late 1830s. La Porte incorporated as a city in 1852 with a population of over five thousand.

7. Various sources discuss women during this time, including Ellen M. Plante's *Women at Home in Victorian America: A Social History* (New York: Facts on File, Inc., 1997).

8. In the original typescript, Albert Clark is given the fictitious name of John. For additional biographical information, see Paul F. Clark's "Albert Barnes Clark: A Pioneer Community Leader" in *Orange Countiana*, Vol. 6 (2010) and "Albert Barnes Clark" in John Steven McGroarty's *California of the South: A History, Vol. IV* (Chicago: S. J. Clarke Publishing, 1933), 667–69. Suzanne Clark Struck held the Alaska letter that appeared on Richard Clark's former Yale Grove website. A copy exists in the editor's possession.

9. E.D. Daniels, *A Twentieth-Century History and Biographical Record of Laporte County, Indiana* (Chicago: Lewis Publishing Company, 1904), 414.

10. Mary Clark's abridgement of her California life appeared in the January 16, 1917 edition of the *Orange Star* as "Early History of Orange Read before the Woman's Club." It is reproduced here in Appendix A. The *Orange Star* reprinted this again on January 30, 1917, as "Orange in Early Days." A later reprint appeared in the *Orange Daily News* on April 30, 1938. Another paper prepared by Mary found publication in the La Porte *Daily Herald*, January 9, 1907, as "Mary Clark Tells of Late Dr. Teegarden," reproduced herein in Appendix B.

11. La Porte *Daily Herald*, October 31, 1922.

12. The Teegarden family's American origins begin with an Abraham Teegarden who reached Philadelphia from Germany in 1736. See Helen E. Vogt, *Descendants of Abraham Teegarden* (Berkeley: Consolidated Printers, Inc., 1967), 19–22.

13. The eclectic, or electic, school of American medicine made use of botanical remedies and physical therapy practices. Reaching its peak of popularity in the 1880s, this profession ceased to exist by the 1940s. These doctors opposed the early medical techniques of bleeding, chemical purging and the use of mercury compounds, then common among "conventional" physicians.

14. The Treats constituted Mary Clark's New England heritage, tracing their line to Matthias Treat of Wethersfield, Connecticut, from around 1650. Like many New England Yankees, the Treats journeyed westward to New York and then followed the Great Lakes into the Midwest. See *Genealogical Notes on Twenty-four Families of East Hartford, Connecticut* (Connecticut State Library, 1933).

15. See "Mary Clark Tells of Late Dr. Teegarden" in Appendix B.

16. Vogt, *Descendants*, 77–79.

17. A letter dated January 30, 1976, from Harold B. Kristjansen, registrar at Vassar College, verifies Mary Clark's one-year attendance at Vassar. See also obituary information in the La Porte *Daily Herald*, October 31, 1922, for her early education. She never graduated from Vassar.

18. See *Diary of Dr. A. Teegarden's Western Trip*, Item # 81.110, in the Teegarden/Clark Box, and "From the Great Lakes to the Pacific" by Dr. A. Teegarden, printed in the La Porte *Daily Herald*, undated. Both are held by the La Porte County Historical Society at the La Porte County Historical Museum in La Porte, Indiana.

19. Swedenborgianism represents a religious movement developed from the writings of Emanuel Swedenborg (1688–1772). Swedenborg claimed revelations from Jesus Christ over a twenty-five-year period. His writings predicted the establishment of a "New Church" following a more traditional Christianity. The American branch organized in 1817, and Teegarden helped form the La Porte congregation in 1859.

20. Biographical information on Abraham Teegarden appears in a number of places, including Vogt, *Descendants*, 77–79; Daniels, *A Twentieth- Century History*, 414–15; *History of La Porte County, Indiana* (Chicago: Chas. C. Chapman & Co.: 1880), 661–62; *Biographical Sketches of the Members of the Forty-First General Assembly of the State of Indiana* (Indianapolis: Indianapolis Journal Company, 1861), 22–24; and Abraham Teegarden's handwritten *Ledger/Diary*, 1874–1883.

21. Heman R. Timlow's *Ecclesiastical and Other Sketches of Southington, Connecticut* (Hartford: Case, Lokwood and Brainard Co., 1875) includes a complete genealogy for Amzi's branch of the Clark family. The children of Amzi and Candace Clark were Edward Payson Clark (1835–1908), Catharine Bailey Clark (1837–1916), Frederick Augustus Clark (1840–1920) and Albert Clark. The children of Amzi and Harriet Clark were Harriet Candace "Rose" Clark (1852–1942) and Walter Amzi Clark (1854–?).

22. Albert Clark's scholastic records, as well as those of his brothers Fred and Edward, may be found at Wabash College's Lilly Library in the Robert T. Ramsay Archive Center. The *Order of Exercises of the Commencement of the 1864 Anniversary of Yale College* (New Haven: E. Hayes, 1864) documents Albert's graduation from Yale, where he received the honor of "colloquies," the lowest honor a student could receive. His college life and later biographical information are found in various reunion publications of the Class of 1864 held at the Yale University Library and Alumni Records Office.

23. Documentation related to Albert Clark's Civil War service include the *Register of the Commissioned, Warrant and Volunteer Officers of the Navy of the United States* (Washington, D.C., Government Printing Office, 1865), 177, and in the USS *Pampero*, Muster Rolls (1861-1866) and the Logbook of USS *Pampero*, Records Relating to Service in U. S. Navy & Marine Corps, Record Group [hereafter, RG] 24, National Archives Building (NAB), Washington, D.C. Albert's medical condition is documented on page 203, June 1842–January 1896, Volume 44 (1865), and on page 224, Box 131, Hospital Tickets, Records of the Bureau of Death, Disability, Pension and Medical Survey, RG 52, NAB.

24. Clarence King, *Mountaineering in the Sierra Nevada* (Lincoln: University of Nebraska Press, 1970), 224–245; Yale 1864 Class Publications. Associated with Albert Clark in the Geological Exploration was his brother Fred Clark, who probably helped secure Albert's employment with King. Both Clark brothers find mention in National Archives Microfilm Publication M622, roll 3, Records of the Geological Exploration of the Fortieth Parallel, U.S. Geological Survey, RG 57 [hereafter, National Archives M622]. For Albert's employment as a "barometrical aid and general assistant," see King to Humphreys, September 2, 1870 (page 195), National Archives M622. On July 12, August 18 and August 30, 1871, the *Chicago Evening Journal* printed his western travel letters.

25. Albert Clark's U.S. Senate work is indicated in Yale 1864 Class Publications, the July 30, 1879 issue of the Los Angeles *Evening Journal* and

in a business card in possession of the editor. His Chicago court reporter business appears in several city directories, including *Edwards' Directory of the City of Chicago for 1873, Vol. 16* (Chicago: Richard Edwards, 1873), 255. Rose Clark's letter is Item #39.978, Clark File, La Porte County Historical Society.

26. The *Teegarden Ledger/Diary*, March 26, 1875, records payments for Albert Clark's California trip; *Anaheim Gazette*, June 12, 1875, notes Clark arriving in Anaheim. For the anti-saloon demonstration in Orange, see the June 12 and June 19, 1875 editions of the *Anaheim Gazette*.

27. The September 26, 1875 issue of the Los Angeles *Daily Star* reported the steamer *Orizaba*'s departure from San Francisco with passengers "A.B. Clark, Mrs. Clark." On September 29, the *Star* noted the *Orizaba* docking in Southern California. The land purchase appears in the office of the Los Angeles County Recorder, Book 40, Page 51, of *Deeds*, between Henry Page of San Francisco and Mary T. Clark of Orange. In exchange for $1,600 in gold coin, Mary received Richland Farm Lot Nos. 54 and 58. The easterly ten acres remained in the family for over one hundred years. The *Teegarden Ledger/Diary* indicates that Abraham Teegarden, Mary's father, gave Albert and Mary $700 total in 1875, and he sent Mary a birthday present of an additional $100 on January 1, 1876.

28. *Anaheim Gazette*, November 3, 1875. The Yale Grove ranch house existed within the easterly ten acres of the original twenty-acre site. For property improvements, see the *1886–87 Los Angeles City and County Directory* (Los Angeles: A. A. Bynon & Co., 1886), 139.

29. The SAVI Board Minutes are housed at the Sherman Library in Corona del Mar, California. For SAVI water history, see Clark, "Albert Barnes Clark," 18–21; the *History of Los Angeles County, California* (Oakland: Thompson & West, 1880), 163; and William H. Hall, *Irrigation in Southern California* (Sacramento: State Printing Office, 1888), 622–33. The January 14, 1871 *Anaheim Gazette* estimated the water volume of the Chapman Ditch system at 260 gallons per second, or 936,000 gallons per hour. By comparison, the SAVI main ditch, completed in 1878, delivered 900 gallons per second, or 3,240,000 gallons per hour.

30. For Albert Clark's run for state senator, see Clark, "Albert Barnes Clark," 21–23, and California State Archives, Sacramento, California, Los Angeles County Final Canvas of Vote, September 3, 1879. The SAVI Board Minutes, November 5, 1879, documents the start of Albert's second SAVI term. For confirmation of Albert's appointment as Orange Postmaster, see Postmasters–Los Angeles County, Volume 50 (1877–1891)

(National Archives Microfilm Publication M841, roll 11), Records of the Post Office Department, RG 28. Albert's horticultural society board service appears in the January 30 and October 30, 1881 issues of the Los Angeles *Daily Herald*. The September 3, 1881 issue of the *Anaheim Gazette* noted Albert's state division conference appointment. A promoter of the state division effort, the *Daily Herald* (September 9, 1881) listed Albert among the conference attendees without further mention. The *Herald* complained, "For the present, state division seems to have been killed in the house of its friends. The refusal of several of the southern [California] counties to send delegates, and the like mindedness of some of the delegates who were sent, has robbed the movement, for the time being, of all impending features." And so, happily has the California state division question remained.

31. *Anaheim Gazette*, September 5, 1879. The Clarks managed a busy summer with the political campaigns and Yale Grove improvements. Notably, Albert Clark's political episodes find no mention in Mary Clark's memoirs.

32. *Anaheim Gazette*, January 24, 1880; Los Angeles *Evening Express*, March 19, 1881; *Riverside Press and Horticulturist*, August 27, 1881; and *1886–87 Los Angeles City and County Directory* (Los Angeles: A. A. Bynon & Co., 1886), 139. The April 2, 1881 issue of the *Pacific Rural Press* recorded Albert Clark's Los Angeles Citrus Fair display, which featured "photographs of his orchard and homestead"—almost certainly the 1880 Carlton Watkins Yale Grove photographs.

33. See the *History of Los Angeles County*, 167, and the February 21 and March 6, 1880 issues of the *Pacific Rural Press*. The *Riverside Press and Horticulturist*, April 3, 1880, coined the term "Yale Wrappers" in describing Albert Clark's tissue-packaged fruit. Citrus wrappers are briefly discussed as part of the Sunkist shipping business by Douglas C. Sackman in *Orange Empire: California and the Fruits of Eden* (Berkeley: University of California Press, 2005), although he does not mention the origin of this technique in California.

34. The May 26, 1882 issue of Santa Ana's *Semi-Weekly Standard* announced Albert Clark's first boast of one dollar a scale bug, while *Riverside Press and Horticulturist*, September 25, 1882, reported the increase to ten dollars per bug.

35. The *San Francisco Chronicle* posted announcements for the Alaska excursion during July 1882. Albert Clark's embarkation appears in the *Chronicle*, July 29, 1882. The *Los Angeles Times* notes his return south on September 2, 1882. See the *Riverside Press and Horticulturist*, October 14, 1882, for the final published record of Albert before his sickness.

36. The November 5, 1882 issue of *Los Angeles Times* and the *Teegarden Ledger/ Diary*, February 26, 1883, document Teegarden's movements and Albert Clark's condition. Mary Clark received two letters of concern, dated October 25 and November 2, 1882, from Issac W. Tener, the Orange postmaster. Tener wrote of "inquiring daily with much anxiety about Mr. Clark and was much pleased he has at last got a turn for the better." Tener said during the time that Albert's "life trembled in the balance; I could not help sympathizing with you as if he were a blood relative. Oh! What a blessing if his life is spared." Copies of the Tener letters are held by the La Porte County Historical Society and the editor.

37. *Los Angeles Times*, April 10 and April 25, 1883; *Riverside Press and Horticulturalist*, April 28, 1883. Albert Clark's death certificate shows the cause of death as a lung infection. The SAVI Board draped the Orange water office in mourning for one month and recorded a formal resolution expressing condolences, stating, "It was through his energy and ability, so unstintingly devoted, that this ditch enterprise was brought to a successful conclusion."; see SAVI Board Minutes, April 28, 1883.

38. The May 1, 1883 issue of the Los Angeles *Daily Herald* lists "A. Teegarden, Ind." among railroad arrivals.

39. *Los Angeles Times*, May 17, 1883.

40. *Pacific Rural Press*, April 25, 1885; Los Angeles *Daily Herald*, April 4, 1886.

41. The April 3, 1886 issue of *Orange Tribune* reported, "Mr. H.N. Elliott, of San Francisco, getting up a beautiful illustrated pamphlet of the valley, and will canvass Orange shortly in the interest of his work." The term "canvass" likely referred to seeking money subscriptions, which Mary Clark likely provided. Elliot's final product was *Orange, California, Illustrated and Described* (Oakland: W.W. Elliott & Co., 1886). In 1886, structural improvements at Yale Grove reportedly cost Mary $800; see *Santa Ana Herald*, January 15, 1887. Various local directories listed the Yale Grove, or Yale Place, in promotional terms.

42. Wayne Dell Gibson, *The Olive Mill: Orange County's Pioneer Industry* (Santa Ana: Orange County Historical Society, 1975), 23; Phil Brigandi, *A New Creation: The Incorporation of the City of Orange*, 1988, 40.

43. *Los Angeles Times*, February 5, 1887; July 19, 1888; and April 3, 1889; *Orange Tribune*, December 1, 1888.

44. For the whiskey-instead-of milk comment, see Chapter 4, "Development of Water." Mary Clark's biographical sketch in Vogt's *Descendants* (page 80) states that she "spent a large share of the inheritance from her father's estate in a legal battle to keep taverns out of Orange." However, discussion

with other Orange County historians and a review of newspapers of this time reveal no court actions against saloons in Orange.

45. The July 3, 1887 issue of the *Los Angeles Times* printed, "Mrs. Mary T. Clark, with her children, has gone East for the summer." In fact, Mary remained in Indiana; see *Orange News*, November 27, 1895, and *Orange Post*, October 14, 1909, for her later Orange trips. Mary's La Porte home appears in *Images of America: La Porte, Indiana and its Environs* (Chicago: Arcadia Publishing, 2002), 15.

46. La Porte *Daily Herald*, October 31, 1922.

47. Elsie Clark received the fictitious name of Elizabeth in the original typescript. See also Vogt, *Descendants*, 80, and Daniels, *A Twentieth-Century History*, 415.

48. Marjory Clark was given the fictitious name of Polly in the original typescript; see Vogt, *Descendants*, 80. In telephone communication with the editor (2011), staff at the Abbott Academy confirmed Marjory and Mary Kate's attendance. Marjory's Michigan City home lies within a thirty-five-acre forest preserve known as "Barker Woods"; see *The Beacher*, January 10, 2002, and December 18, 2003. Marjory Clark's undated 1974 letter to the editor will hereafter be referred to as the *Marjory Clark Barker letter*.

49. Mary Kate Clark assumed the fictitious name of Kitty in the original typescript; see Vogt, *Descendants*, 80. Kate's personal history of her La Porte childhood, which lists Hollywood, California, as a residence in 1932, can be found at the La Porte County Historical Society. Other biographical information can be found in the 1926 and 1928 Orange County voter registration rolls and the 1932 *Orange County Directory* (Long Beach: Western Directory Co.).

50. Donald Clark received the fictitious name of John in the original typescript. He was the editor's grandfather. His post-Yale life is detailed in the *Five Year Record: Class of Nineteen Hundred and Five Sheffield Scientific School* (New Haven: Yale University, 1910). The February 1, 1944 issue of the *Orange Daily News* heralded, "Eight Stars Adorn Service Flag of Pioneer Orange Family," describing his sons' military service. Attached to the 1917 *Orange Star* article (Appendix A), an excerpt from the 1938 *Orange Daily News* article provides a listing of his children. Celia Clark's parents were James Nunn (1854–1908) and Mable McNeil Nunn (1861–1942). The *Orange Daily News*, January 22, 1912, records Donald and Celia's marriage. City of Orange building records document the construction of suburban homes on the Yale Grove site in October 1976.

51. Fred Clark was given the fictitious name of Richard in the original typescript. His Civil War records are found under Frederick Clark, Twenty-Ninth Indiana Infantry, Compiled Military Service Records, Entry 519, Box 6462, Records of the Adjutant General's Office, RG 94, NAB.

52. Fred Clark appears in National Archives M622 and in numerous secondary sources related to the late nineteenth-century geologic explorations of the West, including Richard A. Bartlett's *Great Surveys of the American West* (Norman: University of Oklahoma, 1962) and James Gregory Moore's *King of the Fortieth Parallel: Discovery in the American West* (Stanford: Stanford University Press, 2006). Sarah Dutcher is discussed by Harv Galic in *Chronicles of Early Ascents of Half Dome, Part I: Anderson's Years* (www.stanford. edu/~galic/history/halfdome), which includes an Appendix devoted to Fred Clark. The San Francisco *Evening Bulletin*, December 20, 1880, announced the marriage of Sarah L. Dutcher to Fred Clark of the "U.S. Geological Survey." Their divorce notice appears in the January 9, 1886 issue of the *Daily Alta California*. Clark's West Point employment finds confirmation in a letter from Susan P. Walker, USMA Archives, September 24, 1991, along with biographical and obituary information from unidentified newspaper clippings in the editor's possession.

53. Rose Clark was given the fictitious name of Sophia in the original typescript. She adopted the name Rose, or sometimes Rosa, at an early age. Sources for her life include several unidentified newspaper clippings in the editor's possession and communication (2011) to the editor from staff at the Forest Lake Academy, successor to Ferry Hall School, confirming her graduation.

Chapter 1

54. The ten-day journey suggests that they left Chicago for California on September 8, 1875. The *Daily Alta California*, September 18, 1875, listed among transcontinental rail passengers in Nevada on September 17, "A.B. Clark and wife, Chicago." The *San Francisco Chronicle*, September 18, 1875, records their arrival. A deeper context for Mary's comments regarding Native Americans at train stations can be found in Karen M. Morin's *Frontiers of Femininity: A New Historical Geography of the Nineteenth-Century American West* (Syracuse: Syracuse University Press, 2008), 141. Here Morin describes the routine (and often condescending) observations by other Victorian travel writers regarding poverty-stricken "native

peoples begging, performing feats of skill, or offering 'peeps' at their babies for a nickel or dime." These behaviors stemmed, Morin said, from tribal social disarray following warfare defeat and the imposition of the reservation system.

55. The crinoline, sometimes called a hoop skirt, was a woman's undergarment used to extend the dress and was popular from the 1830s to the 1860s before eventually being replaced by the bustle dress.

56. The "blot of Mormonism" comment by Mary Clark very likely derives from a shared hostility among the Victorian middle class to polygamy, which in 1875, was a practice associated with the Church of Jesus Christ of Latter-day Saints, or Mormons. The Mormon Church ended polygamy in 1890. Mary's reference to Japan probably reflects her awareness of the Russo-Japanese War ending in 1905, in which Japanese victories over Russia caused reappraisals of Japan's position in the world. This was one of the premier events of the first decade of the twentieth century, a decade sometimes called an "age of expansion," as Mary notes.

57. The cousins greeting Mary and her family in San Francisco could be Thurza Belle Teegarden (1852–1935) or her husband, Patterson A. Campbell (1838–1893). Campbell operated a grain and flour mill in San Francisco, and Thurza was the daughter of Aaron Teegarden (1808–1874), brother of Mary's father, Abraham; see Vogt, *Descendants*, 70. The Vallejo "hospitable home" was owned by Mary Anna Teegarden (1838–1914), another cousin of Mary's, who married Abraham Dubois Starr (1830–1894). Starr built up a successful milling and shipping business, and they maintained a substantial home in South Vallejo, built in 1869, which today is used as a bed-and-breakfast. Mary Anna was the daughter of Eli Teegarden (1809–1884), another brother of Mary's father, Abraham. Eli came to California in 1850 and became a farmer, businessman and politician in Marysville; see Vogt, *Descendants*, 71–75. The Starr's employed a Chinese cook named "Ah Choo," who is possibly the "Ah Fong" referenced by Mary Clark. The Occidental Hotel served in the 1860s as a leading San Francisco lodging but no longer exists. The Cliff House site contains a modern tourist restaurant perched on headlands above the Pacific Ocean on the westerly side of San Francisco. The Cliff House visited by the Clarks burned in 1894. Seal Rocks, adjoining the Cliff House site, famously provided habitat for sea lions.

58. Ada Deborah Starr (1861–1931) married Johan Bernt Borchgrevink (1847–1910) of Norway; see Vogt, *Descendants*, 75.

59. Silas Bond from Indiana settled at Montecito in 1868 and engaged in a horticultural business on fifty acres, according to the *History of Santa Barbara County, California* (Oakland: Thompson & West, 1883), 471. Mary Clark also mentions the Bonds by name in the 1917 *Orange Star* article (Appendix A).

60. The Los Angeles *Daily Star*, September 29, 1875.

61. The Hygean Home, the first hotel in Orange, appeared in the *Anaheim Gazette* on July 25, 1874, as a planned "retreat for invalids" by a Mrs. Dr. Larkin from San Jose. The September 26, 1874 issue of the *Gazette* noted, "Its walls are of concrete, a mixture of sand and lime. This will afford cool and pleasant rooms." On May 1, 1875, the paper reported Dr. Larkin accepting guests, who together with the well-insulated rooms, also found themselves, by Mary Clark's account, living in a fleabag. Spelling of the site's name varied, including Hygiene Home in the 1917 *Orange Star* article (Appendix A), in which Mary Clark also names "Dr. Larken" as the proprietor (Larken spelled "Larkin" in contemporary press). The reference to a "Dr. Clapp" implies a later fictional name. Torn down in 1905, the two-story structure stood adjacent to the Plaza Square at what is today 100 South Glassell Street and was also known as the Orange Hotel. Mary no doubt slept on uncomfortable straw ticks, a mattress made from a coarse cotton material filled with straw or other rough material.

62. Several descriptions in the *Anaheim Gazette* list early Orange businesses. The paper's November 28, 1875 issue related, "The town contains two large stores, one hotel, one blacksmith shop and no saloon!" A community hall and a real estate office rounded out this description. On December 10, 1875, the *Gazette* added a bookstore, drugstore, livery stable, Chinese washhouse and meat market to the previous inventory. Given Mary Clark's reference to seeking fresh meat in Anaheim, the Orange meat market likely offered very limited wares.

63. See the reference in the 1917 *Orange Star* article (Appendix A) to a Mrs. Beach as the "dear lady from New York state." Two Beach families lived in Orange at this time, and both included members from New York. One family, according to the 1880 census, included Matilda Beach (born in New Jersey), the wife of Charles Beach of New York and their two children, who were born in California. The other Beach family included Eliza Beach (born in Vermont), the wife of Joseph Beach of New York, and their son, who was born in New York. Given the stronger New York connection, the editor suspects the "dear lady" was Eliza Beach. Picking "Clove pinks" refers to *Dianthus caryophyllus*, the wild ancestor of the garden carnation.

CHAPTER 2

64. Don Meadows, *Historic Place Names in Orange County* (Balboa Island: Paisano Press, 1966), 97, 105; *Los Angeles Evening Express*, March 8, 1877. The "steamer landing" refers to Newport Landing, a small port developed in 1870 in Newport Bay (within today's City of Newport Beach) also called McFadden Landing.

65. Henry Neill fits this person. Neill engaged in a number of ventures aside from stagecoach work in early Orange, including working at the local water company and a livery stable; see *Anaheim Gazette*, June 15, 1877.

66. Several of the preceding comments by Mary Clark should be reviewed. First would be her reference to keeping meat and yeast. These were kept in a "meat safe." The *Pacific Rural Press*, July 8, 1876, described them in an article entitled "Meat Safes or Closets." These pioneer household accessories encompassed an area of about four feet in length by three feet high and were kept in a cool, northern exposure free from direct sunlight. "Many housewives will feel the necessity," explained the *Pacific Rural Press*, "wherein various kinds of food can be kept from the flies, and also receive a good supply of fresh air, and not be so damp as to promote mold." Wirework, mosquito netting, strainer cloth or a sheet of perforated zinc metal would be tacked onto a wood frame, along with a hinged door, to provide the needed circulation of air without insect intrusion. Mary also spoke of a lack of basements or cellars in Southern California. The whisper to housewives about ice prompts the editor to point out to twenty-first-century housewives that "ice boxes" served as home refrigeration in 1906, when Mary Clark completed this memoir, daily ice delivery being a necessity, as electricity was rare.

67. Orange was closer to five than three years old in 1875. Orange's first organized congregation, the Methodist Church, existed on Orange Street south of Chapman Avenue in 1875; see Brigandi, *A New Creation*, 16–18 and the *Orange Star*, January 30, 1917. For additional information on Le Roy Armstrong and his book *The Outlaws: A Story of the Building of the West* (New York: D. Appleton and Company, 1902), see Mary Clark's comments found in the "Mary Clark Tells of Late Dr. Teegarden" article in Appendix B.

68. On November 20, 1875, the "Orange Items" correspondent for the *Anaheim Gazette* reported stolen horses around Orange and added, "A committee with its colors stamped 'Death to Horse Thieves' would be beneficial." The trouble persisted. The July 24, 1876 issue of the *Los Angeles*

NOTES TO PAGES 50-52

Evening Express reported horse thieves "on the rampage" and suggested a "taste of Arizona law" to stop the problem.

69. Actually, the Franciscans were the first Catholic order of missionaries in what is today the state of California. While the Jesuit order did begin missionary work in Baja California, it was replaced by the Franciscans in 1767. The Franciscans expanded the missions north and, perhaps in legend, spread the mustard plant (*Brassica alba* or *Sinapis nigra*), a common weed with yellow flowers.

70. Gail Hamilton, a pseudonym for Mary Abigail Dodge (1833–1896), wrote poetry and essays from a female perspective, often promoting the equality of women.

71. The January 3, 1875 issue of the Los Angeles *Daily Star* reported that Anaheim contained two hotels, several restaurants, two blacksmiths, one tinsmith, two shoemakers, two tailors and seven general merchandise stores.

72. "London Graphics" probably refers to the British publication *The Graphic*, which ran from 1869 to 1932. A competing newspaper, the *Illustrated London News*, was published from 1842 to 1971. These periodicals employed vivid pictures that were greatly appealing to wide audiences in both England and America.

73. Additional holiday stories by Mary Clark appeared in the November 22, 1939 issue of the *Santa Ana Register*, quoting her from now-lost letters, one regarding Christmas in 1876: "I will give you our bill of fare for tomorrow: Entrees, roast beef with macaroni, spring chicken stewed in cream, green peas, new potatoes, string beans, new tomatoes, radishes, Muscat grape jelly, wild grape jelly, grandma's currant jelly, tomato pickles and catsup; Dessert: squash pie, English plum pudding, sliced oranges, apples, raisins, coffee, bread and butter, nearly all raised at 'Yale Grove.'" The article also described an incident during Christmas 1879 in which Mary Clark "wrote to her father and sister of driving to Santa Ana to buy a turkey only to find both turkeys and beef all gone. A fearful wind had come up, she wrote, and blew and froze until it was necessary to keep fires going night and day. In driving to Santa Ana, she states, she put on her velvet coat, a shawl, as well as her husband Albert's overcoat."

74. While state-chartered banks existed in Los Angeles, the only Southern California bank with federal government approval to issue gold certificates was the National Gold Bank of Santa Barbara, established in 1873. The Clarks probably sought reliable gold-backed currency, as gold coin or gold nuggets were then the preferred money in California, a holdover from gold-rush days; see G.D. Hancock, "The National Gold Banks," *The Quarterly*

Journal of Economics, 22 (August 1908) and Ira B. Cross, *Financing an Empire: History of Banking in California* (Chicago: S.J. Clarke Publishing Co., 1927).

75. Saleratus, a leavening agent made up of potassium or sodium bicarbonate, mixed together with flour, butter, sour milk or vinegar and baked immediately, produced such biscuits.

76. See the note regarding John William Munday in Chapter 12, "Glimpses of the Old Home."

77. The Willows lay southwest of Orange on the Santa Ana River; see Phil Brigandi, *Orange County Place Names A to Z* (San Diego: Sunbelt Publications, Inc., 2006), 106. Mary Clark also notes the Willows in the 1917 *Orange Star* article (Appendix A.)

CHAPTER 3

78. Mary Clark shows her training as a botanist at the hands of her father, the herbalist doctor, in naming the various flowers that filled the California open spaces at this time. She catalogs by name such plants as *Nemophila menziesii*, or "baby blue-eyes," a native of the western United States, and Indian pinks (*Spigelia marilandica*), which produce tubular flowers that are bright crimson with a yellow lining. Could the "lady with the little child" have been Mary Clark? Probably so. Similar enthusiasm found expression from even hard-nosed newspaper editors, such as that of the Los Angeles *Daily Star*, which noted on January 24, 1878, "The last rains have not only made our hills and plains verdant with growing grass and luxuriant grain, but they have put a broad smile of contentment and hopefulness upon the faces of our people." Meadows's *Historic Place Names* identifies Temescal Peak as a name sometimes applied to Santiago Peak (elevation: 5,687 feet), the highest point in the Santa Ana Mountains east of Orange. Meadows states that the name finds use primarily on the easterly, or Riverside County, side of the mountain. Mary Clark obviously lived on the west side but perhaps felt Temescal more poetic.

79. The reference to "New Church" points to the Swedenborgian Church. While not associated with the Swedenborgian Church, Pastor Charles Wagner (1852–1918) was a French reformed preacher and author of the book *The Simple Life*, which was published in English in 1901.

80. With regard to bananas, some experimented to commercially grow these and other tropical exotics in Orange. Among them was James Huntington, who also served as one of the first directors of the SAVI.

The December 4, 1876 issue of the *Los Angeles Evening Express* reported Huntington's farm as containing "several thousand of the Sandwich Island dwarf banana, and also five or six thousand pine apple plants." Unfortunately, both plants failed to be climatically suitable for profit. Mary's reference to a lime hedge may be clearly seen in the 1880 Carlton Watkins photographs of the Yale Grove. Pioneer Orange commonly exhibited such border hedges, as noted in the *Los Angeles Evening Express* on September 10, 1880: "Most of the lots are surrounded by either cypress or lime hedges, and on the outside of the hedges along the roadsides there is generally a row of trees, mostly orange or Monterey cypress. Then the sides of the roads are kept cultivated and free from weeds. This adds greatly to the beauty of the landscape." In later years, the strength of the Santa Ana winds led most ranchers to plant protective windbreaks around their groves. These windbreaks consisted of closely spaced rows of cedar or eucalyptus trees standing at imposing heights when mature. Such views dominated the Orange streetscape until urbanization.

CHAPTER 4

81. A description of the early Orange water system appeared in the May 18, 1872 issue of the *Anaheim Gazette* with an article entitled "Richland and its Resources" by W.T. Glassell. Glassell wrote of iron pipes studded with access hydrants placed in the town streets radiating from a main reservoir filled with irrigation water from ditches. The Santa Ana River served as the water source, channeled to the early settlement by the Chapman Ditch. This ditch appeared in the *Gazette* on January 14, 1871: "The construction is progressing rapidly. The idea entertained by C. [sic] B. Chapman, Esq., of running a tunnel through the hills [near Olive] and thus saving a distance of about one mile has been abandoned, owning to the expense." Water ran in this ditch around the end of April; see *Anaheim Gazette*, April 22, 1871.

82. Other individual wells and windmill combinations existed in Orange prior to the Clarks. For example, the August 29, 1874 *Anaheim Gazette* noted, "Mr. Hayward has a good well with water in it," and mentions another site with a well and windmill combination. Clark's drilling attracted notice when the *Gazette*, February 12, 1876, reported, "Mr. Hulse has begun boring a well for Mr. Clark." A week later, on February 19, the *Gazette* followed up, commenting, "Clark struck water in his well at sixty

feet and has twenty feet of water." The *Gazette*, March 11, 1876, seemed impressed with the Yale Grove improvements, advising, "Mr. Clark is erecting the first windmill in this immediate vicinity. It will be in running order by the middle of the week. He also has a 5,000 gallon tank and pump, the whole cost being $350."

83. Many sources describe the California citrus industry and the development of the Washington Navel variety in particular, including Douglas Sackman's *Orange Empire*, published in 2005.

84. In *Orange Empire*, Sackman describes private gardens as a quintessential feature of California citrus ranches. The Clark's garden certainly emulated this pattern. The Chinese saucer peach (*Prunus persica*), also known as the Saturn or donut peach, came to America in 1869 and produces an unusual flat shape. The evergreen Camphor tree (*Cinnamomum camphora*) arrived in America in 1875 from East Asia, and the crushed leaves find use for scent, cooking and medicinal purposes. Magnolias came from the Marysville nursery of William Smith, husband of Mary Clark's cousin, Susan Louisa Teegarden, according to Vogt, *Descendants*, 75. The *Teegarden Ledger/Diary*, October 21, 1876, records Abraham Teegarden sending bulbs, roots and cuttings of hyacinths, lilies and roses for the Yale Grove.

85. For a puzzling but contrary gopher reference, see the September 10, 1880 issue of the *Los Angeles Evening Express*, in which a local promoter advised, "The soil here [in Orange] appears to be peculiarly unfavorable to the operations of the festive gopher." To this day, the gopher, festive or not, stubbornly hangs on throughout Orange despite any idiosyncratic soil quality.

86. The gift of the churn, a hand-operated device once used to convert cream to butter, probably coincided with Mary Clark's January 1876 birthday, as she previously spoke of "working over butter" during the well drilling, which occurred in February that year.

CHAPTER 5

87. The SAVI Certificate of Incorporation, signed on July 30, 1877, was filed with the California Secretary of State on August 6, 1877; see SAVI Articles of Incorporation, California State Archives, Sacramento, California. Clark's election as SAVI president occurred on September 8 at the SAVI Board meeting following the stockholder bylaw adoption on September 6. Previously, Clark had served as the company's acting

secretary and W.C. McClay as the acting president; see SAVI Board Minutes, August 8 and September 8, 1877. The SAVI Board Minutes on September 8 do not specify a meeting site. Customarily, the first minutes noted their locations at Joseph W. Anderson's store in Orange. Since no reference appears in the September 8 minutes, this may be the meeting that Mary Clark said happened at Yale Grove, although meetings prior to incorporation are also possible.

88. The August 18, 1877 SAVI Board Minutes authorized stock sales beginning "as soon as the acting secretary could furnish" the certificates. Clark oversaw sales in Orange, where Mary Clark would have observed the opening of the books. Droughts of serious proportions did exist in Southern California, with less than five inches of rain falling during the 1876–77 season, well below the more than fourteen inches received the preceding year; see *Anaheim Gazette*, December 16, 1882. The June 9, 1877 *Los Angeles Evening Express* reported a regional heat wave compounding the drought, with many places recording extreme temperatures, including 104 degrees at Anaheim.

89. Some irrigation terms used by Mary Clark deserve clarification. A miners' inch represents a measurement of the amount of water flowing through a hole of a given size and at a given pressure. Another irrigation term is a head, or hydraulic head, which is a specific measurement of water pressure above a geographic surface point. These terms determine the fair allocation of irrigation water. The SAVI construction costs coincide with Albert Clark's estimate appearing in the *History of Los Angeles County*. Contrast the 1878 SAVI tunnel achievement near today's Olive community to Chapman's ditch built in 1871 minus a tunnel due to financial constraints. As summarized in Clark, "Albert Barnes Clark," 22–23, disgruntled persons brought allegations of irregularities, which marred Albert's later state senate campaign, although many local citizens rose to defend him; see Los Angeles *Daily Herald*, August 12, 1879, and *Los Angeles Morning Journal*, August 20 and August 26, 1879. Mary was correct in her overall statement that small landowners dominated the SAVI stock ownership; see SAVI records at the Sherman Library and the California State Library, California History Room, Sacramento, California.

90. The SAVI main office always operated in Orange. The original wood-frame building was eventually replaced by the brick structure standing today at 154 North Glassell Street. SAVI stockholders voted to cease operations in 1977.

91. Mary Clark left Orange permanently in 1887 and completed her personal history in 1906. The Chicago Ditch followed West Almond Avenue in Orange, delivering water to the most northerly side of the Yale Grove. SAVI Board Minutes, July 3, 1878, noted the acceptance of this canal into the SAVI system. Visible concrete structures from the Chicago Ditch exist today along West Almond Avenue. The "festive gopher" fared poorly during irrigation, which perhaps was the limiting factor, rather than soil, as indicated in the Chapter 4 note above.

92. The April 17, 1880 *Riverside Press and Horticulturalist* reported a new state law requiring counties to fix irrigation rates, and Los Angeles County specified the hourly SAVI rates at fifty cents per head. Of the Yale Grove help, Diego Granillo, is the best known. He appears in the 1880 Census as living in the Clark household and is described as a twenty-eight-year-old farm laborer from Sonora, Mexico. He shows up the following year as an Orange resident in the *Los Angeles City and County Directory for 1881–82* (San Francisco: Southern California Directory Company).

CHAPTER 6

93. Although Mary Clark specified John Tyler, Tyler became president upon the death of President Harrison in 1841 and under those circumstances did not have formal inaugural ceremonies. Perhaps Zachary Taylor in 1849 is the president who entered office enjoying traditional celebrations.

94. Ah Chong may have been the individual listed in the 1880 Census as "Chung," as no other Chinese are listed under the Orange "C" or "A" listings. Chung was born in China about 1861, which would have made him about nineteen at the time the census was taken.

95. The Los Angeles market prices for grocery commodities often appeared in the local press, for example, the March 24, 1881 issue of the *Los Angeles Evening Express* noted, "eggs 20 cents/dozen, coffee 28 cents/pound, cheese 20 cents/pound and chickens 50 cents each." Prices such as these may seem inexpensive by today's standards, but one must remember that skilled laborers were often paid two dollars per day, or less than fifty dollars per month, in Mary Clark's time.

96. Problems with coyotes plagued early California residents, as rudely rediscovered by many pet owners today. For example, the December 10, 1877 *Los Angeles Evening Express* warned, "It is said that the coyotes, as a result of the famine which pervades their country quarters, are hovering

about the southern suburbs of our city, picking up stray chickens, etc." Given that all three Clark daughters are mentioned, this event likely occurred after 1879.

97. The *Marjory Clark Barker letter* provided additional tarantula comments: "Porch—hard clay door yard. Incident of giant tarantula—grave daughter—Chinese Ah Chong hastily ran from kitchen—giant size dish pan—trapped—disposal?" On June 2, 1879, the *Los Angeles Evening Express* published "Bitten by a Tarantula," which told the story of a barefooted farmer in East Los Angeles sickened for three weeks after a tarantula bite.

98. Roadrunners are a native bird species in North and Central America, not Australia. The adult of the Greater Roadrunner species has a bushy crest, long, dark bill and a long, dark tail. The name comes from the bird's habit of racing with moving vehicles and then darting into the brush.

99. A stuffed barn owl donated by the Teegarden/Clark family stands on display at the La Porte County Historical Society Museum in La Porte, Indiana. It is most likely the owl mentioned by Mary Clark. The museum contains a number of family-related items, including a child's China tea set purchased in 1852 by Abraham Teegarden and an 1880 doll formerly belonging to Elsie Clark.

100. On, March 8, 1877, the *Los Angeles Evening Express* printed a story advising of the unprofitable nature of sheep raising in Orange due to population increase, which crowded out the herds. A cherry-plum tree (*Prunus cerasifera*) is a species of plum that flowers very early in the spring.

101. The name Ivan appears in the original typescript and perhaps was Ivan Anderson, son of Joseph W. Anderson (1838–1915) and his wife, Sarah, the mother of "gentle spirit." Ivan was born in 1873, according to the 1880 Census, which would make him a rather mischievous child in Mary Clark's time. Ivan's father operated a store in Orange and cultivated a prominent political standing.

102. The "little doctor" may have been C.B. Andrus, who while not a medical doctor did operate the first drugstore in Orange, known as Andrus & Parker, as early as 1875. According to Phil Brigandi, in personal communication to the editor (2011), Andrus was suffering from tuberculosis and came to California for health reasons. The climate did not cure him, and he died in 1877. Andrus's partner, Millard F. Parker, kept the store for a time. After passing through several owners, Keller Watson purchased it in 1899 and founded the present Orange landmark, Watson's Drug Store.

103. Worsted is a type of cloth made from this yarn, originally manufactured in England.

104. In the 1880 Census, several Johnsons are listed in Orange, but the most likely would be Edward and Imogene Johnson, both born in New England. Of key interest are their children, two daughters named Anne and Josephene, born in Illinois. According to Brigandi, in personal communication to the editor (2011), the phrase "on the gravel land" refers to the area across the Santiago Creek, easterly of Orange. "The gravel" area reached from the creek bed generally along Chapman Avenue to Esplanade. The area further east of Esplanade, where El Modena was later founded, was called "up on the mesa."

CHAPTER 7

105. Helena Modjeska (1840–1909), also known as Madame Modjeska, was a Polish actress famous throughout Europe and America. She immigrated to the United States in 1876 and settled near Anaheim. She eventually built a home called Arden in the Santa Ana Mountains, living there from 1888 to 1906; see Meadows, *Historic Place Names*, 22. Mary Clark's daughter testified in the *Marjory Clark Barker letter* that her mother was a friend of Modjeska but did not clarify the connection further.

106. Terry E. Stephenson, *Shadows of Old Saddleback* (Rasmussen Press: 1974), 28. Stephenson noted, "By common consent, on May Day, everyone who was able to travel took his family to the Picnic Grounds" in what is today Irvine Park. "The Orange picnic ground in Santiago Canyon" praised the *Anaheim Gazette*, May 5, 1877, "is one of the finest natural parks, we venture to say, in the State." The paper also noted, "Orange was almost deserted on May Day." Similar events occurred throughout Southern California, but most community holidays ended in modern times. Mary Clark's reference to Yorba creates a problem, as that community was north of the Santa Ana River, quite distant from the normal picnic routes. Stephenson also notes that there were two paths, with some attempting the steep hillsides that eventually became the Chapman Avenue route to Irvine Park, but that many more took "the long way around by what was known as the old road" along Santiago Creek. Mary could not be speaking of El Modena, as that community did not exist until 1886 and only later assumed a Latino character. Meadows mentions a Mexican-American neighborhood called El Perripe, north of Chapman Avenue in El Modena, but this place likely post-dated Mary Clark's time. Otherwise, she may recall

passing a small homestead or temporary camp. In the editor's opinion, she confused the May Day picnic outings with another excursion, such as the camping trip to the San Bernardino Mountains, during which travel followed the Santa Ana River, passing several Latino places including Peralta; see Meadows, p. 110, for "Peralta."

107. The games recalled by Mary Clark reflect traditional childhood outdoor ring, line or dance play often accompanied with rhyme singing. See William Wells Newell, *Games and Songs of American Children* (New York: Harper & Brothers, 1884).

108. Millinery is defined as women's apparel for the head. During the Victorian era, establishments called millinery shops offered fashionable and often ostentatious hat wear.

CHAPTER 8

109. Charles Scribner's Sons of New York published the children's periodical *St. Nicholas Magazine* from 1873 until the 1940s. The magazine saw contributions from various noted authors of the day, including Louisa May Alcott and Mark Twain, and printed submissions from young readers as well. Another illustrated children's magazine, *Wide Awake*, first produced in 1874 by D. Lothrop Publishing Company of Boston, Massachusetts, will be mentioned later by Mary Clark as among her children's reading materials.

110. The July 17, 1886 *Orange Tribune* took notice of one such pet, reporting, "Mrs. Clark brought a beautiful little Shetland pony home with her from her recent trip to San Francisco. The children evidently consider it a prize of the first magnitude."

111. Also *Tecoma jasminoides*, a climbing shrub or vine with funnel-shaped yellow or orange flowers native to Australia; commonly called a Bower Vine.

112. The spelling "Gipsies," a variant of Gypsies, consistently appears in the original typescript. Also known as Roma or the Romani people, the term "Gypsy" may originate from an English idea that they came from Egypt. The Roma were present in America since colonial times, but larger numbers arrived after 1860. The March 21, 1878 Los Angeles *Daily Star* observed the Roma near Orange: "There is said to be quite a flutter among the lads and lassies of Anaheim, owing to the presence of a company of Gipsies there. Fortune telling is the order of the day." On July

11, 1881, the *Los Angeles Evening Express* reported a group to be camped near Los Angeles.

113. While the oyster story remains undated, the Clarks certainly did travel to Los Angeles together. For example, the May 3, 1879 Los Angeles *Daily Star* included "A.B. Clark and wife, Orange" in a list of those registered at the Pico House, then one of the premier hotels in downtown Los Angeles, which remains standing today. At that time, Mary was about seven months pregnant with her daughter Kate.

114. In "Santa Ana," the November 3, 1876 issue of the *Los Angeles Evening Express* described the town, located south of Orange, as including a school, three hotels, four saloons, a local newspaper and numerous and varied businesses.

115. "Trabuco" is the usual spelling of this rugged Santa Ana Mountain canyon located in south Orange County. In *Orange County Place Names* (page 100), Brigandi advises that early American settlers often spelled it "Trabuca." Jim Sleeper, in his *A Boys' Book of Bear Stories (Not for Boys)* (Trabuco Canyon: California Classics, 1976), retells stories of the Trabuco and mentions trout "being stocked in some of the higher canyons."

116. Abner Bailey (1784–1866) appears by name in the original typescript, a rare family member not given a fictitious name. Born in Wolcott, Connecticut, he was the father of Candace Roberts Bailey, the mother of Albert Clark. Bailey's wife was named Catharine Roberts. Abner settled in La Porte by 1845 and was elected to a judgeship; see *History of La Porte County, Indiana* (Chicago: Chas. C. Chapman & Co., 1880), 552, and an unpublished manuscript in the editor's possession by Catharine Candace Bailey, *Roberts Family Record*, October 1917.

117. The November 11, 1878 *Daily Alta California* listed Teegarden among "the through-bound first-class passengers" leaving Omaha on November 10 "to arrive in San Francisco November 14" on his way to Los Angeles. According to entries in the *Teegarden Ledger/Diary*, he returned to La Porte on February 23, 1879, after more than three months in California.

CHAPTER 9

118. Citrus insect pests did originate from Australia and are discussed in Friis, *Orange County*, 83–84. Albert Clark boasted of some success against them, as described in the article "The Red Scale–It Can be Killed" in the September 2, 1882 issue of the *Riverside Press and Horticulturalist*.

Clark's trees received "a through spraying with whale oil soap and water mixed in the proportion of one pound of soap to one gallon of water. He did the work most thoroughly, and a careful examination afterwards failed to find a single live scale on the trees treated. He has a furnace in which the compounds are heated. He has a force pump, throwing two streams of liquid, and three men can thoroughly drench forty trees per day and do it in a manner to reach every insect on the trees." A report of whale oil soap used as insecticide previously appeared in the *Los Angeles Evening Express* on July 27, 1877. Clark may have improved this technique, but he did not originate it. Toxic chemical fumigation of trees placed under tents eventually became the standard method of pest suppression, although biological controls found use as well; see Sackman, *Orange Empire*, 77, 141–42.

119. The June 16, 1882 *Santa Ana Semi-Weekly Standard* observed, "B.M. Lelong, the noted insect-pest destroyer and educator, A.B. Clark and wife, J.W. Anderson and Lawrence Nordhoff, of Orange, go today upon a fishing excursion to Bear Creek, in Bear Valley, some thirty miles above San Bernardino. If intelligence and geniality is any inducement for trout to bite at, this party ought to return well laden with fish." Lawrence Nordhoff wrote of the trip in the July 7, 1882 *Semi-Weekly Standard* in an article titled "Orange to Bear Valley." The group spent eleven days near the boulder-strewn mountain mouth of the Santa Ana River, where bear tracks were seen near the camp and the fishermen reportedly caught over ninety trout. The journey out was by way of Riverside and Mill Creek Canyon, and the return was via San Bernardino. Nordhoff also noted elderly tribal women lamenting at an Indian burial.

120. Colton developed as a train depot about halfway between Riverside and San Bernardino with the arrival of the Southern Pacific Railroad in 1875.

121. Crosse & Blackwell, an English specialty-food brand, began when Edmund Crosse and Thomas Blackwell purchased an older business in 1830 and applied their own name to the company. The brand's popularity in Southern California received notice from the Los Angeles British Vice-Consul, who reported to London: "I find that the jams of Messrs. Crosse and Blackwell are extensively sold here" despite the low cost of local produce; see *British Parliamentary Papers, Volume 32, Embassy and Consular Commercial Reports, 1887-88* (Shannon: Irish University Press, 1971), 557.

122. A Mother Hubbard dress is a long, wide, loose-fitting gown with long sleeves and a high neck. The garment developed during Victorian times

to cover as much skin as possible and was associated with missionary work among aboriginal peoples.

123. William C. Sturtevant, ed., *The Handbook of North American Indians, Volume 8, California* (Washington, D.C.: Smithsonian Institution, 1978), 570–87. This handbook provides maps indicating that Mary Clark's route of travel ran along the border of two tribes, the Serrano and the Cahuilla. The Serrano conducted a ceremony a month after a death that involved a night of singing and dancing. Both tribes performed an annual mourning ceremony that probably included food preparation and consumption. Mary's reference to a bone whistle may have some significance, and her memory of a kettle cooking and tribal members riding nearby may suggest a grieving family gathering for a meal. A Victorian white woman could easily recall this as strange and incomprehensible.

124. Visitors seeking outdoor recreation have long been drawn to Laguna Beach. For example, the March 24, 1877 issue of the *Anaheim Gazette* told of many people from Orange there, and as Gardner recalls, "it was the custom for some families to take a few weeks at the beach or in the mountains every summer." Illustrating the past abundance of coastal wildlife, the January 9, 1879 Los Angeles *Daily Star* observed that the ocean "in the neighborhood of Wilmington [Harbor] is white with wild geese. The numbers are so great that the line extends for three miles along the coast. There are millions of them."

125. At one time, the Irvine Ranch encompassed 185 square miles in central Orange County and was one of the largest landholdings in Southern California. Consolidating several Spanish and Mexican ranchos during the 1860s, James Irvine (1827–1886) created a grazing, farming and land development enterprise that has partially survived to the present day. *Ramona* (which would be the correct spelling) is an American novel published in 1884 by Helen Hunt Jackson (1830–1885). Jackson intended the book to be a kind of *Uncle Tom's Cabin* on behalf of Native Americans. Mary Clark's comments reflect the book's more common reception, which emphasized the overly romantic imagery of the California mission and rancho era.

CHAPTER 10

126. A citrus fair display of Yale Grove fruit brought the following comment from the March 6, 1880 *Pacific Rural Press*: "Each orange, and they are first-class seedlings, is separately wrapped in neat envelopes of tissue paper

labeled with the full direction of the producer and guaranteed genuine. These fancy packages bring from $1 to $2 a box more than those of the same quality put up in the ordinary manner." The more ordinary manner of shipping was the subject of a series of tips for better delivery by a San Francisco commission house in the *Los Angeles Evening Express*, February 8 1879. The agents admonished ranchers to ship in regulation-size boxes of at least 8x19x22 inches, to nail the boxes securely and not to haphazardly dump oranges into the boxes. The article advised, "We are obtaining for oranges in boxes of 200 to 250, $8 to $12.50" per box. Albert Clark described in some detail his financial balance sheet in a letter to Abraham Teegarden dated April 29, 1882. Albert reported the sale of 1,422 boxes of oranges from a six-acre portion of the Yale Grove netting a profit of $303.45 per acre, with gross revenue totaling $3019.85; see also Clark, "Albert Barnes Clark," 24. In this same letter, he complained that the San Francisco market was "quite unreliable in the hands of commission men."

127. The completion of Orange's first elementary school building appeared in the *Anaheim Gazette* on August 3, 1872. Located at Lemon Street and Sycamore Avenue, this original building was replaced around 1882 with a larger structure. Fire destroyed this schoolhouse in 1886, and a third was completed in 1887 at the same site; see Brigandi, *A New Creation*, 18. As Mary Clark indicates, this was "a new public school building," and given the ages of the two eldest daughters, Elsie and Marjory, the 1882 school probably served her children.

128. A snowstorm, very rare in normally sunny Southern California, reported by the *Anaheim Gazette* on January 21, 1882, caused Orange's irrigation ditches to be choked by snow and left a two-foot snowfall in the foothill mining community of Silverado. The January 14 and January 21, 1882 issues of the *Riverside Press and Horticulturalist* told of snow eight inches deep in Riverside and light snowfall in Los Angeles.

129. Most of the writers and books mentioned by Mary Clark may be better identified. Juliana Horatia Ewing (1841–1885), an English writer, artist and editor of children's magazines wrote *Jackanapes* in 1884 and *The Story of a Short Life* a year later. William Thackeray (1811–1863) was a British novelist and satirist who authored *Vanity Fair* in 1847. He wrote *The Rose and The Ring* as fantasy fiction in 1854. The book revolved around four young royal cousins—Princesses Angelica and Rosalba and Princes Giglio and Bulbo—with Countess Gruffanuff being Angelica's governess. Kate Greenaway (1846–1901) illustrated and wrote English children's books, including *Under the Window: Pictures and Rhymes for Children* in 1879. Jacob

Abbott (1803–1879) was an American author of children's books who penned *Beechnut: A Franconia Story* in 1850. *Hans Brinker, or the Silver Skates: A Story of Life in Holland*, is a well-known novel published in 1865 by Mary Mapes Dodge (1831–1905), a writer and editor of American children's literature. Louisa May Alcott (1832–1888), an American novelist best known for *Little Women* (1868), was an abolitionist, Civil War nurse and women's vote campaigner.

130. The Presbyterian Church organized in Orange during 1874 and built a church at East Maple Avenue and North Orange Street in 1881. The site remains the congregation's home to the present time; see Brigandi, *A New Creation*, 18, and the *Orange Star*, January 30, 1917.

CHAPTER 11

131. The March 6, 1880 *Anaheim Gazette* reported a rainsquall that occurred on March 3, 1880, the night of the raid, that "amounted to eighteen hundredths" of an inch.

132. The typescript contained an unidentified newspaper clipping taped to the page. It read: "Wednesday evening last, about nine o'clock, six masked men entered the store of Mr. Crowder, at Orange, where some eight or ten persons were. The robbers tied the crowd and then went through their pockets and the store, taking some three or four hundred dollars in money and goods, and then quietly decamped. Mrs. Crowder, who was present all the time, released the crowd as soon as the raiders left. Conflicting details reach us of the affair. Officers are on the trail." Several contemporary newspapers document the raid. The March 6, 1880 *Anaheim Gazette*, with the headline "Reign of Vasquez Revived," listed Crowder, Clark and six other men being tied-up, with Mrs. Crowder confined to a chair but not bound and having spunkily retained "the true woman's privilege of having the last word." The bandits rifled the store at leisure for three quarters of an hour and took $276.15 in cash. Clark lost forty cents. Leaving the scene, the thieves gave Mrs. Crowder fifteen minutes to release the men, and afterwards, "there was no trace to be found of the bandits and no sound could be heard. It is presumed that their horses were in readiness and that they rode off in the direction of Santiago Canyon." "The citizens of Orange," the *Gazette* concluded, "are much excited" fearing another raid "upon their stores or houses." The March 5, 1880 *Los Angeles Evening Express* described the episode in "Daring

Robbery at Orange," adding that the bandits, with plausible irritation, "snapped a pistol in Mrs. Crowder's face, informing her if she made the least noise they would blow her brains out." Those seeking the general location of the bandit raid should go to the north side of the Plaza Square at the intersection with Glassell Street.

133. The Los Angeles County sheriff was William R. Rowland. Rowland organized the successful capture of the notorious outlaw Tiburcio Vasquez in 1874. He brought in several of the Orange bandits for justice. For example, the October 16, 1880 *Anaheim Gazette* reported the capture of Ramon Reina in Bakersfield. Two gang members saw prison time, Angel Corona and Ramon Reina, with others escaping to Mexico, gunned down or turning state's evidence. A search in the California State Archives for photographs of the two convicts proved unsuccessful due to loss of their prison mug shots. Reina was released in 1885 and Corona in 1886. Both were twenty-three-year-old former cowboys (*vaqueros*) when they entered prison; see California State Archives, San Quentin Prison Registers, 1867–1882, Roll 2, MF 1:9(11). Although described as Mexicans, one of the gang, named Stoner, was likely at least part Anglo-American, while Corona was native Californian.

134. This bandit raid appears in several later chronicles. The event figures briefly in Gardner's "Community of Orange," in which she recounts recollections of her father, Henri Gardner, who was among the victims. Two Orange newspaper articles retell the story. Alice Armor conveys much the same story as Mary Clark and the contemporary press, varying only in a few details in "Early History of Orange is Recalled," *Orange Daily News*, October–November, 1918. A second newsprint account would be Mary's abbreviated Orange history appearing in the 1917 *Orange Star* article (Appendix A).

135. In *Historic Place Names* (page 120), Meadows lists "Robbers Cave" as a sandstone cliff depression in Fremont Canyon, near Santiago Canyon. This landmark, he states, had no historical significance other than appearing on local maps from the 1920s. Meadows mentions another site, "Robbers Roost," which held folkloric links with desperadoes, located above Santiago Canyon along the ridge easterly of Villa Park in Anaheim Hills. Jim Sleeper, in his *Orange County Almanac of Historical Oddities* (Trabuco Canyon: Ocusa Press, 1974), 96, mourns the destruction of the "Roost" by modern subdivision development. The reference to the 1880 history was to the previously cited *History of Los Angeles County*, with the Orange raid noted on page 87.

CHAPTER 12

136. SAVI Minutes, June 18, 1880, previewed the trip, noting Albert Clark's directorship resignation "on account of an intended protracted absence." The excursion lasted about four months, the family arriving in Indiana about July 1, 1880, at which time the La Porte *Herald* noted, "Albert B. Clark, wife and children, of California, are visiting Dr. Teegarden." The family's return appeared in the October 14, 1880 issue of the *Los Angeles Evening Express*. They must have been among the first to disembark at the new Orange train depot just under construction; see the *Express,* September 27, 1880. The superintendent left in charge of Yale Grove can be identified from handwritings on the reverse of the previously cited Carlton Watkins photographs, which state, "Mr. Clayton had charge of the A.B. Clark ranch during the family's visit East." William H.H. Clayton surfaces in the 1880 Census as a single man from Pennsylvania born in 1840, and he may have been one of the victims in the bandit raid.

137. This refers to Elcy Tracy Treat, the children's great-grandmother and Mary's previously indicated "aged grandmother." Born in 1787 in Saratoga County, New York, Elcy married Samuel Treat in 1808. She passed away in December 1880 at age ninety-four, only a few months after Mary's return to Orange. Samuel Treat, from East Hartford, Connecticut, came to La Porte by 1836. Both rest in Pine Lake Cemetery, not far from Mary's grave; see La Porte *Herald-Chronicle*, December 30, 1880, and Daniels, *A Twentieth-Century History*, 415. Elcy's highboy was likely an item of antique furniture, being a tall, ornate chest of drawers used to keep wardrobe at a time when closets were rare. The floral species in Elcy's garden include many originally from Britain and the European continent, such as bachelor's buttons (*Centaurea cyanus*) or double buttercups (*Ranunculus acris*), while others, such as pennyroyal (*Mentha pulegium*) and horehound (*Marrubium vulgare*), have medicinal uses. Elcy's garden, a botanical showcase of herbal and picturesque flowers, clearly held a warm memory for Mary.

138. The limited information from Mary Clark, as well as the renaming by Kate Clark's typescript, prevents additional identification of the various family members in La Porte County, Indiana. One exception, "great Aunt Caroline," could be Caroline Treat McClure (1824–1899), Mary Clark's aunt and her mother's sister.

139. Flora Bailey Munday (1846–1918), also known as Nonie, received the fictitious name of Fanny in the original typescript. She was the first wife

of John William Munday and the daughter of Volney W. Bailey (1819–1871) and Phoebe Bailey (1823–1893). Volney was the son of Abner Bailey and a younger brother of Candace Bailey Clark, Albert Clark's mother. Under the name of Nonie, Flora is buried in Pine Lake Cemetery near her parents. John William Munday (1844–1924) was the "literary man." Munday, under the pen name of Charles Sumner Seeley, wrote *The Spanish Galleon: A Search for Sunken Treasure in the Caribbean Sea* (Chicago: A.C. McClurg & Company, 1891) and *The Lost Canyon of the Toltecs: An Account of Strange Adventures in Central America* (Chicago: A.C. McClurg & Company, 1893), books which remain in print to the present today. He served as an officer in an Indiana regiment during the Civil War and was later a Chicago lawyer. Mary Clark briefly notes his involvement in her Yale Grove home design (but does not name him) in Chapter 2, "The First Christmas," and in the 1917 *Orange Star* article (Appendix A). Handwriting on the back of the Yale Grove ranch house diagram, in the editor's possession, discloses, "Original drawing of house at Yale Grove by John W. Munday."

CHAPTER 13

140. For an additional description of early Orange housekeeping, see Gardner, "The Community of Orange," 167.

141. The July 25 and August 20, 1882 issues of the *Los Angeles Times* reported Mary Clark and her three children as staying at the Santa Monica Hotel. The reference to Long Beach probably does not refer to the present city of Long Beach. The original typescript identifies the two children of Mary C. Orme (1838–1923) by name. A letter in the editor's possession written by Mary Clark to Mary C. Orme of Los Angeles, dated May 8, 1914, refers to both Alida and Hal. Mary Clark's letter stated that Elsie lovingly recalled Alida "as one of the inspirations of her childhood." Mary Clark's daughter Marjory recalled Mary Orme in the *Marjory Clark Barker letter*: "Mrs. ORME—honored wife of naval officer. Foothills road house full of world treasurers—great shells re-echoing cadence of seven seas."

142. Donald Clark was born on December 4, 1882.

143. The November 6, 1882 issue of the Sacramento *Daily Record Union* records "Dr. A. Teegarden, Laporte, Indiana" among rail passengers to California. The *Teegarden Diary/Ledger* entry for January 13, 1883, read, "Returned from California, expense of travel, extra gifts, etc., $350.00."

Abraham revived his medical skills during the two months with Mary and her family assisting with Albert's care and at the birth of her son, Donald.

144. Albert Clark died on April 24, 1883. He was forty years and eight months old.

CHAPTER 14

145. Robert Browning (1812–1889), an English poet and playwright renowned for "The Pied Piper of Hamelin," wrote the "The Flight of the Duchess" in 1845. The "New Hampshire Grandmother" was Harriet Crosby Clark, who married Amzi Clark in 1849. According to the 1850 Census for La Porte, Harriet was born in Massachusetts.

146. Tustin began in 1870 and grew slowly southeasterly of Orange; see Juanita Lovret, *Tustin as it Once Was* (Charleston: The History Press, 2011).

147. Although Elsie disbelieved in 1884, she stilled trusted enough to pen Santa a letter in December 1883. The letter was published in *St. Nicholas Magazine* 11, March 1884:

> *Dear St. Nicholas: I want to tell you about my home in Southern California. I am ten years old and have lived nearly all my life in an orange grove. Our home is the Yale Orange Grove. Besides oranges, we have lemons, limes, grapes, figs, melons, bananas, pears, nectarines, peaches, apricots, pomegranates, plums, and other things. This afternoon, we had a hard rain, and last night and this morning, we saw snow on the mountains. Once we had a little snow here. One night we went to a concert, and our cats followed us all the way; and when we got to the concert, one of them went home and the other stayed and went into the concert. She got into a man's coat-pocket, and he scared her out, and she stayed down town awhile. After that, I took her home, and then she got sick and died. I think the concert killed her. Your little friend, Elsie Clark.*

148. The Mission San Juan Capistrano, founded in 1776, contains an existing small church built in 1782 and known as Father Serra's Chapel. The earthquake occurred on December 8, 1812, the "Feast Day of the Immaculate Conception," or "La Purísima," collapsing the main church and causing forty deaths. The padre away ministering during Mary Clark's visit was Father Jose Mut, who served the community from 1866 to 1886. The *Marjory Clark Barker letter* adds that Mary "was often

visitor friend of Padres, knew families and Spanish vestments." A variety of works describe the mission and town, including Pamela Hallan's *Dos Cientos Anos en San Juan Capistrano* (Irvine, CA: Lehmann Publishing, 1975).

149. Edwin A. Honey (1854–1938), indeed a beekeeper and a teamster, came to Orange in 1876 and operated a stagecoach service to the Southern Pacific Railroad depot in West Orange until 1887. He was humorously caricatured as "Candee" in the community play *The Plaza* in May 1887; see Phil Brigandi, ed., *The Plaza: A Local Drama in Five Acts* (Orange: Wrangler Press, 1982). William Thomas Brown is noted in Samuel Armor's *History of Orange County, California* (Los Angeles: Historic Record Company, 1921) as having served as the Southern Pacific Railroad agent from 1877 to 1881 at Santa Ana. As the Bradley Family came in 1885 after Brown's departure, this reference may be misplaced in time.

150. Here Mary Clark tells of her sister Myra Bell Teegarden, who received the fictitious name of Isabel in the original typescript, and her family. Myra married a La Porte lawyer named John Henry Bradley (1852–1900), who received the fictitious name of Uncle Henry in the original typescript. The couple had a son, Henry Teegarden Bradley (1882–1955), genially nicknamed "Cousin Buzz" by Donald Clark. Lura Treat Bradley (1880–1964) was their daughter. The October 12, 1885 *Daily Alta California* listed "J.H. Bradley, w & 2c, Ind." as arriving in San Francisco, fixing the year 1885 to this part of Mary's chronicle; see also Vogt, *Descendants*, 82–83.

CHAPTER 15

151. Handwritten names in the Wawona Hotel register dated from November 1, 1884, confirm Mary Clark's trip to Yosemite; see Catalog No. YOSE14392, Hotel Register, Mariposa Big Tree Station, Yosemite Museum, National Park Service, Yosemite, California. Mary's party included Elsie and Marjory Clark, as well as "Miss Rose Clark, New York City." On November 7, 1884, "F.A. Clark" appears in the register, showing Fred Clark's return from Yosemite Valley, followed on November 8 by Mary, her children and Rose Clark. Of interest for a story later in this chapter, a "Lt. Col. J. Mactear, Scotland" appears on November 7 and November 10. The place referred to as Mariposa Big Trees encompassed several names, including Big Tree Station, Clark's Ranch (for Galen Clark) or Wawona. The Mariposa Grove contains a stand of sequoia trees. Yosemite Valley, as well as the grove, constituted the original

Congressional land grant of 1864 to the State of California. In 1906, the grove and valley returned to federal jurisdiction and became part of the much larger national park established in 1890.

152. This was known as the Upper Hotel or Hutchings' House, within which a room that enclosed a cedar tree was added in 1866. This room became known as the "Big Tree Room"; see Shirley Sargent, *Pioneers in Petticoats: Yosemite's Early Women, 1856–1900* (Los Angeles: Trans-Anglo Books, 1966), 34. The hotel was torn down by 1940. The editor located the cedar tree in 1983 and again in 2012 and observed marks on its trunk showing the old hotel's former roofline. The prevalence of English tourists in Yosemite received comment in the May 2, 1885 *Mariposa Gazette*, in which the editor noted that "the visitors to the Valley are principally English and Eastern people."

153. Glacier Point rises over three thousand feet above the valley floor. Note that the age of each child would be about one year older in 1884 than the ages given by Mary Clark. Galen Clark (1814–1910) explored the Sierra Nevada and participated in the effort to preserve Yosemite Valley and the Mariposa Grove in 1864. He served on the state commission administering the park and soon became known as the "Guardian of Yosemite." He was not related to Mary or to her husband, Albert.

154. This adventure played out at the Wawona Hotel. The hotel was constructed in the 1870s, and the name Wawona appeared by 1883. The hotel reflects classic Victorian resort architecture and includes prominent outdoor verandas around the main building. The "Colonel of the British Army" was Lieutenant Colonel Mactear, previously mentioned, an officer with the Highland Light Infantry; see the *Monthly Army List, December, 1882* and *March, 1884* (London: John Murray), 640.

Chapter 16

155. The quotation is from Robert Browning's poem "Flight of the Duchess." Who was the Duchess? She does not appear to be a Teegarden relative, and her identity remains elusive.

156. Mary Clark covers a substantial number of matters in this paragraph, with the time period very likely occurring in 1886. The reference to Rose Clark's drawing of Marjory Clark is not likely the work mentioned earlier entitled, "Hester," as Marjory was said to have searched for her portrait without success, according to an e-mail from Barbara Clark dated January 4, 1998, in the editor's possession. The two families of

cousins were Teegardens, one being the family of "dear cousin" Susan Louisa Teegarden (1839–1890), who married nurseryman William Smith (1823–1877) of Marysville, California. Susan was the daughter of Eli Teegarden, brother of Mary's father, Abraham; see Vogt, *Descendants*, 75–76. All the children of this family received fictitious names in the original typescript but have been correctly identified herein. The second family was that of Francis Josephine Teegarden (1848–1900), who lived in Cloverdale, California, with three children. Francis was married to John Henry Bowman (1830–1882), a merchant and landowner, and was another daughter of Eli Teegarden; see Vogt, *Descendants*, 77. The Geysers and the Petrified Forest were then popular tourist areas. The Geysers is a geothermal area about seventy miles north of San Francisco that developed in the 1850s as a spa hotel accommodating a large number of celebrity guests. The hotel was torn down in 1980. The Petrified Forest in California, not to be confused with the more famous Arizona national park, has attracted tourists since the 1870s and is about fifty miles north of San Francisco.

157. Here Mary Clark recalls the real-estate bubble of the 1880s. In Orange, the Palmyra Hotel served as one of the most prominent structures built during this time, located near the southeast corner of Palmyra Avenue and Glassell Street. Constructed in 1887 by C.Z. Culver, the luxurious wood-frame edifice reached two and a half stories in height, not including an observation tower; see *Orange Tribune*, July 28, 1887. The hotel never lived up to expectations and went through numerous owners after the "boom" before eventually being purchased by James Nunn in 1906. The building was torn down in 1970. Mary almost certainly aimed the "flight to Mexico" critique at C.Z. Culver.

158. The comment about the "boom" passing over seems somewhat premature, given that this conversation probably occurred in the spring of 1887, at which time the boom was reaching its apex. Certainly, a cooling down quickly ensued, with the bubble bursting by 1888.

159. Mary Clark departed Orange by July 3, 1887. The two children mentioned "near the shores of Lake Michigan" were Mary's first grandchildren, Wallace Norton Barker (1897–?) and Margery Barker (1901–1980), the son and daughter of Marjory Clark and her husband, Norton Barker. Alfred Lord Tennyson's poem "The Brook" includes the repeated stanza, "For men may come and men may go, but I go on forever." Tennyson (1809–1892) was famous for the poem "Charge of the Light Brigade." The last poem at the end of the paragraph was from

"A Forest Hymn" by William Cullen Bryant (1794–1878), an American romantic poet noted for the well-known ode "Thanatopsis." Arbutuses are small trees or shrubs with red flaking bark and red berries; wintergreen is another term for evergreen plants.

CHAPTER 17

160. These children were Donald, Duncan, Albert, Suzanne, David and Stuart; see excerpt from 1938 *Orange Daily News* article in Appendix A for a complete listing of Mary Clark's California grandchildren. The "giant eucalyptus tree" appears in *Orange, Cal., Illustrated* (pages 45–46) within a sketch of the Yale Grove. A 1910 photograph of this tree contains a handwritten note on the reverse: "*Eucalyptus globulus*, 'Blue Gum,' planted 1873 by D.C. Haywood, circumference near base 29 feet, 6 inches, height about 140 feet." Sometime in the 1920s, the tree fell to the ground but fortunately caused no harm.

161. Formed in 1892, the Eastman Kodak Company simplified amateur photography with improved cameras and film-developing methods, causing "Kodak" to become a common name, much like "Xerox" came to be associated with copy machines. Some of these black-and-white photo albums still exist throughout the extended Clark family. Kate continued to help Donald and Celia Clark for many years. She took their children on memorable trips around Southern California—to San Clemente in particular.

APPENDIX A

162. The Woman's Club of Orange organized in 1915. The group's current clubhouse on South Center Street was completed in 1924, well after Mary Clark's presentation. Her talk probably took place in a second-story room located in the Kogler-Franzen Building on North Glassell Street, then a brand-new brick commercial building. Mrs. Ray Billingsly of Villa Park is the likely meeting coordinator for the Woman's Club. She and her daughter, Hester, were club members, as indicated by Phil Brigandi in personal communication (2011) to the editor. Mrs. J.E. Parker, or Mary McDonald Parker (1859–1947), married Joshua Everett Parker (1853–1940) in 1896. Joshua came to Orange with his family in 1873. Mrs. D.C.

Pixley, or Florence Boring Pixley (1855–1938), came to Orange with her husband in 1882. Her husband, DeWitt C. Pixley (1857–1937) became one of the foremost business leaders in early Orange; see the Parker and Pixley biographical files at the Orange Public Library History Center, Orange, California. The *Orange Star* served the community between 1916 and 1921. The *Star* proceeded through a chain of earlier newspapers starting in 1889. According to Brigandi's *Brief History of Orange* (pages 63–67), the *Orange Daily News* was a competing newspaper operating from 1908 to 1968.

163. The "architect friend" was John William Munday, who possessed many talents but made his living as an attorney; see note on Munday in Chapter 12, "Glimpses of the Old Home." The ranch house and orange grove were removed in 1976.

164. In Chapter 1, "The Journey," Mary Clark indicates that the first stop was in San Francisco, followed by Vallejo.

165. The "Hygiene Home" is discussed further in Chapter 1, "The Journey." The Ehlen & Grote Building still exists as a two-story brick commercial building fronting on both South Glassell Street and the Plaza Square in historic downtown Orange. Constructed in 1908, it served as the department store of Peter W. Ehlen (1863–1950) and Henry Grote (1842–1920), both prominent Orange businessmen.

166. A review of the 1880 Census, as well as personal communication from Brigandi (2011) to the editor, found nearly all the names and families Mary Clark listed in Orange prior to 1880 and certainly qualifying to be pioneers. The exceptions were the Harrow family, of which no record seems to exist; Walter L. Witherbee, who conducted business in Orange and came and went over time; and George C. Hager, who probably had not settled in Orange when the census was taken. Of interest among the enumerated pioneers would be P.D. Young, or Philanda D. Young (1816–1898), who served as the Presbyterian pastor, and Dr. James N. Truesdell and his wife Helen, who managed the Yale Grove for Mary in the 1890s.

167. The two stores faced on or near the Plaza Square. Joseph W. Anderson kept a store from 1873 until about 1881, when he sold out to Jesse H. Arnold. Anderson appears in the August 9, 1873 *Anaheim Gazette*, while Robert L. Crowder's store is first reported in the April 17, 1875 issue of the paper.

168. Orange's first Chinatown existed near the Presbyterian Church at North Orange Street and East Maple Avenue; see Brigandi, *Brief History of Orange*, 24–25. Marjory Clark recalled the family's ranch help in the

Marjory Clark Barker letter: "Mexican labor in grove, Chinese in house. Untrained, long black hair braided in queue." The queue, a lengthy ponytail, was an imposition of old imperial China. After the 1912 Chinese republican revolution, it quickly disappeared.

169. See reference to the Willows in Chapter 2.

170. See also Chapter 11, "Raid of the Bandits." Details vary somewhat between Mary's accounts in the *Star* and in *Pioneer Ranch Life*. The March 6, 1880 *Anaheim Gazette* listed Crowder and his wife, Marian, Clark, Gardner, Mosbaugh and Rusk, Julian Hunt, Frank W. Gibbs and an individual named Cleighton as the robbery victims. Cleighton may be a misspelling of William H.H. Clayton. Contemporary newspapers do not mention Colman Travis among the victims.

171. This would have been the Christmas of 1916.

172. Most of the children of Donald and Celia Clark passed away by the time of this publication: Donald Teegarden (1912–1990), Duncan (1912–1998), Albert (1914–2003), Suzanne (1915–2011), David (1916–1995), Stuart (1917–2005), Robert (1918–1997), John Neil (1920–), George (1921–2007), Oliver Joseph (1923–2010) and Celia Rosamond (1924–). Only Neil and Rosamond remained through 2012. However, the progress of time extends additional generations across California and throughout the world.

Appendix B

173. The La Porte *Daily Herald* represented a long line of *Herald* newspapers in La Porte. In 1924, the *Daily Herald* and the La Porte *Argus*, a competing newspaper, merged to form the community newspaper of today, known as the La Porte *Herald Argus*. The La Porte County Historical Society formed in 1906. The individuals mentioned in this paragraph provide links to Teegarden's life story; they are briefly sketched as follows: Robert White (1817–1909), about ninety years old at this meeting, farmed 287 acres and owned land in Scipio Township near La Porte earlier in his life. Dr. George M. Dakin (1827–1911) practiced, like Teegarden, the Eclectic school of medicine and arrived in La Porte in 1862. John W. Ridgeway (1824–1909), also spelled Ridgway, came to La Porte in 1837 and owned land in Scipio Township. William Niles (1835–1926) was born in La Porte, practiced law and pursued a banking business. Biographical sources are the *Combined Atlases of La Porte County, Indiana* (Evansville: Whipporwill

Publications, 1989); *History of La Porte County, Indiana* (Chicago: Chas. C. Chapman & Co., 1880); Jasper Packard, *History of La Porte County, Indiana* (La Porte: S.E. Taylor and Company, 1876); Daniels, *A Twentieth-Century History*; the Pine Lake Cemetery in La Porte; and the La Porte County Historical Society.

174. Columbiana County, organized in 1802, abuts Ohio's eastern border with Pennsylvania, with the Ohio River on the south.

175. William Teegarden (1775–1856), born in Greene County, Pennsylvania, joined the pioneer movement westward in 1804. Susannah Rafelty (1780–1849), sometimes spelled Rofelty, was the New Jersey–born daughter of Matthias and Sara Rafelty. See Vogt, *Descendants*, 51–52.

176. The brothers of Abraham Teegarden surviving infancy, starting with the eldest, included Uriah (1798–1880), William (1803–1884), Aaron (1808–1874), Eli (1809–1884), Matthias (1817–1896), Albert (1823–1854). His sisters surviving infancy were Elizabeth (1799–1887), Rachel (1806–?), Sarah (1811–?), Mary Ann (1815–1895) and Barbara Ann (1820–1907). See Vogt, *Descendants*, 52.

177. This was over one hundred years ago. It is unknown whether or not the home stands in 2012.

178. Vogt, *Descendants*. Four of the boys became doctors—Eli in California, Aaron in Ohio, Abraham in Indiana and Matthias in Wisconsin. Albert became a schoolteacher in Ohio.

179. While Mary Clark refers to Indiana as a "wilderness," the state achieved statehood in 1816 and counted 343,000 persons in 1830, rising to 685,000 by 1840. The 2010 Census found about 6.5 million people in Indiana. In Illinois, Fort Dearborn, founded in 1803, saw Chicago grow up around it.

180. Ague is an old medical term referring to an illness involving recurring sharp chills, fever and sweating, sometimes associated with malaria.

181. Le Roy Armstrong (1854–1927) is cited in Chapter 2. This 1902 novel describes pioneering Indiana settlers and incorporates subjects such as building navigable canals, outlaw raids, home life and the impact of cholera. As Mary Clark mentions this author twice in relation to her father, the book probably roused strong emotions in her. The editor, after reading this work, sensed parallels to events witnessed by Mary. For example, the novel's canal project in Indiana resembles the development of the SAVI in California.

182. Joseph Orr (1794–1878) served as an Indiana Militia general during the 1832 Black Hawk Indian War. Orr settled near La Porte around 1833 and came to operate an agri-business of over six hundred acres. The *Combined*

Atlases of La Porte County (pages 9–11), describes him as a retired farmer who had "always been a devoted friend to horticulture and even a lover of floriculture."

183. Scipio Township is a division of La Porte County just southwesterly of the city of La Porte. Several farms with the Crane name existed in the township; see *Combined Atlases of La Porte County*.

184. Salt-rising (or salt-risen) bread uses a bacterium to leaven bread with other microbes, as opposed to more conventional yeast. It is thought that salt suppresses yeast growth and permits flavors from the bacteria to predominate over the more typical yeast flavors. This bread seemingly received wide use in Scotland and Ireland.

185. One of the ledgers kept by Dr. Teegarden, the previously cited *Teegarden Ledger/Diary*, survives in the editor's possession. Within this ledger, a handwritten recipe for one of his "bitters," a medicinal syrup or beverage, appears on January 18, 1875. The formula called for boiling various plant barks, snakeroot and pansy segments in water, afterward adding molasses and "one quart good whiskey." Unfortunately, the intended ailment remains unclear, but "two table spoonfuls three times a day" composed the suggested dosage.

186. This is most likely John Ruskin (1819–1900), a British poet, author and artist.

INDEX

INDEX

INDEX

ABOUT THE EDITOR

A native Californian, Paul F. Clark grew up in Orange and witnessed that community's conversion from rural citrus groves to urban housing tracks. He is the great-grandson of Mary Teegarden Clark. Graduating with degrees in history from California State University, Fullerton, Paul served as president of the Orange Community Historical Society, where he coordinated the successful National Register of Historic Places nomination for the Orange Plaza Historic District in 1982. He went on to work for the Riverside County Planning Department for nearly thirty years, supervising the department's field office near Palm Springs before retiring in 2009. Refocusing on history topics, his articles appear in several Southern California journals. Residing in Palm Desert, California, he serves his city as an architectural review commissioner but also remains engaged with his hometown of Orange, where family and many friends continue to reside.

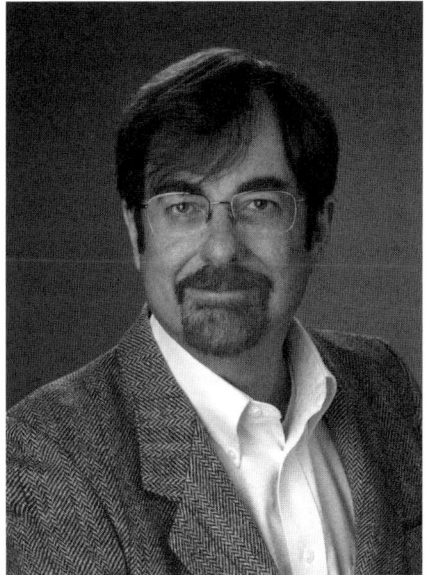